The Michelin Men

The

Michelin Men

Driving an Empire

Herbert R. Lottman

I.B. TAURIS

LONDON · NEW YORK

Published in 2003 by I.B.Tauris & Co Ltd
6 Salem Road, London W2 4BU
175 Fifth Avenue, New York NY 10010
www.ibtauris.com

In the United States and Canada distributed by Palgrave Macmillan
a division of St. Martin's Press
175 Fifth Avenue, New York NY 10010

ISBN 1 86064 896 7

A full CIP record for this book is available from the British Library

Typeset in Garamond by Dexter Haven Associates Ltd, London
Printed and bound in Great Britain by MPG Books Ltd, Bodmin

CONTENTS

ILLUSTRATIONS

ACKNOWLEDGEMENTS

Perhaps it was a good thing after all that the author had to write about Michelin without the help of Michelin. One is always uncomfortable with the notion of publishing an *authorized* history, a book which calls for the co-operation of the subject, for readers can wonder whether they are reading a less objective book because of the authorization and the co-operation.

Be assured. Michelin in Clermont-Ferrand answered no questions. Even the date of birth of the second Edouard Michelin, who was soon to succeed his father as head of the family enterprise, was not obtainable from the company. ('He was born on the thirteenth of August 1963,' an always helpful outside source told me, 'and the family called him Dou-Dou'.)

It made the job more interesting.

But the author received considerable help all the same, and this is the place to acknowledge it: first of all, from Michelin's own Services du Tourisme in Paris, Captain Antoine Champeaux of the Ecole Nationale du Patrimoinem, Elisabeth Dravet of the Bibliothèque Municipale et Interuniversitaire in Clermont-Ferrand, Jacques Salles and Professor Goulven Guilcher, connoisseurs of travel guides, and Anne-Sophie Simonet of *La Montagne* in Clermont-Ferrand.

Thanks also to André Bellerose, of the Librairie Le Temps des Cerises in Clermont, André Chanut, of Librairie Arverne in the same city, Alain Jemain of *L'Usine Nouvelle*, Jacques Wolgensinger, biographer of André Citroën, Anne Boggan, Etty Hoffmann, Professor Emeritus James M. Laux, Chandrasiri Rajakaruna, and Prof. John F. Sweets of the University of Kansas.

Thanks also to the district archives (Archives Départementales) of the Puy-de-Dôme (and to its documentalist Patrick Cochet), the reference librarians of the Paris stock exchange control commission (Commission des Opérations de Bourse), Christine F. Reed, director of the Milltown (New Jersey) Public Library, the reference librarians and documentalists of the Fondation Nationale des Sciences Politiques (and Nicole Richard), and Jérome Lacharmoise of Keystone-*L'Illustration*.

1

A LITTLE
RED BOOK

In the spring of 1900 – in time for the Paris World's Fair that would draw visitors from all France and much of Europe that summer – a motorist waiting to be served at a petrol station or mechanic's workshop would have had to notice the pile of little books in flexible and impertinent red covers stamped *Guide Michelin*, given away without charge.[1] Impertinent is an appropriate word for a guidebook conceived for automobilists when they were still rare birds (you could walk or drive behind horses a considerable distance before coming upon a horseless carriage). Taking no precautions, the makers of the little red book – measuring some three-and-three-quarter inches by five-and-three-quarter inches – announced at the start that this first effort would usher in a 100-year cycle: 'This work appears at the same time as the century; it will last as long. Automobilism has just been born; it will develop year after year and tyres along with it, for tyres are the essential organ without which automobiles cannot run.' Another bit of boldness. For while motorcars would change in every imaginable way as the years went by, who could have predicted that the single constant would be their rubber appendages?

The extravagance of the Michelin wager continues to astonish. This 400-page travel guide for users of a mode of transportation then only in its infancy represented considerable investment, both financial and creative. True, France was then world leader in automobile use, production and export, with some 5600 owners already registered (as well as 619 builders and 3939 petrol stations – some in garages, others in grocery stores).[2]

These early automobiles were hand-tooled, of course, produced – slowly and expensively – by a considerable number of small companies, only a few of which are still familiar names, like Peugeot, Panhard, Blériot, Renault. Some car-makers, Peugeot among them, were then better known as bicycle manufacturers, and the new Michelin guide, as if hedging its bets, announced that it was also designed for cyclists. In publishing this first little red book, the house of Michelin had the benefit of no predecessor from which to copy. Traditional guide-books, like those of Hachette in France and Baedeker in Germany, were designed for travellers by rail, who at their destination might hire horse-drawn coaches to reach smaller localities. The compilers of the new Michelin were covering new ground, but they knew they still had a long way to go.

> The present edition will obviously be found to be imperfect, but the work will improve from year to year; it will become perfect all the sooner if drivers will reply more precisely and in greater numbers to the questionnaire… Without them we can do nothing; with them we can do everything.

Then followed an uncompromising pledge:

> We promise to strike from this book without pity all hotels reported to us as having poor food, inadequate rooms or toilets, deficient service; all gas stations lacking sufficient supplies; Michelin tyre dealers who give cause for complaint. On the other hand, we shall add to our listings hotels and dealers appreciated by our readers…

They were writing the rules for the Michelin guides of their generation and the next, and the next after that – rules their successors are still following.

Michelin – meaning one particular Michelin, the engineer André Michelin, who handled sales and promotion in Paris while his younger brother Edouard made the tyres down in Auvergne – seemed quite pleased with what he had achieved in the diminutive volume that fitted easily into any adult hand. He was aware of the shortcomings of his creation; it had been put together in haste, to be ready for the great Paris World's Fair (the first since 1889), whose grounds spread across the heart of new Paris. But if he had not been able to do every-thing he wanted in this prototype guide, André Michelin promised to do better in the following year, by which time he would be able to include small maps of all significant urban centres in France. Curious readers of the new guide-books discovered other elements of what in retrospect can be called the new automobile culture. Motorists would always be in a hurry; they required easy-to-read symbols, and Michelin supplied them. Later the format of the *Guide Michelin* would change (to become larger, more like other books on one's shelf), but the colour of the jacket remained the same, and so did the spirit (ever more detail, greater precision, uncompromising judgments evidenced by frequent revisions and excisions).

The famous Michelin stars, awarded for fine food, were still many years away. In this 1900 debut volume, stars were used only to indicate class or cost of hotel accommodation, a convention already familiar from established guides conceived for users of trains and other existing means of transportation. There was a symbol indicating garage facilities for hotel guests (in principle free of charge), another to indicate the availability of a pit to allow one's chauffeur to get under the chassis for a repair job.

The punctilious editor of the *Guide Michelin* had even devised a symbol for each kind of motor fuel the hotel might stock, even indicated (by another symbol) whether it disposed of a darkroom in which the traveller could develop photographs made along the way. But only in the following year, the writer apologized, would the guide be ready to say whether a hotel toilet had a flush, and if bath or shower were available.

Nearly everything else that counts for a tourist was to be found in what might be called the 'ur-guide', the listing of every village or town one would wish to visit or be obliged to drive through along the way, with vital statistics such as the number of inhabitants, the distance to Paris and significant nearby cities, amenities such as railway, post, telegraph and telephone offices, hotels, garages, shops and workshops likely to be useful to a pioneer motorist.

The Michelin guide would continue to be given away for many years to come, and obviously a free guide published by the Michelin tyre company was going to give the reader considerable information about its products, couched as instructions for use of tyres in general – getting them on and off the wheels (no easy job in those years), repairing them (this section, liberally enhanced with diagrams, filled

20 pages of the first edition). A separate section described equipment available for cyclists.

That was the point, of course. All they wanted to do, then and later, was to sell the tyres they manufactured, and which they knew were the world's finest. This meant getting people into the habit of utilizing vehicles equipped with tyres, making it less hazardous, more enjoyable, to drive more and further. And that called for better roads and roadsigns, and eventually numbered routes with maps that used these numbers. Anything that could get more people to join the automobile age was good for Michelin. Before motorists knew that they were a new class, the red guides provided them with compelling reasons to try out their cars and wear out their tyres, such as a good restaurant for lunch, a pleasant hotel in the evening. Later, the restaurant or the hotel could become the reason for the journey, and Michelin stars spelled that out – two signifying 'worth a detour', three 'worth a journey'.

'The fox knows many things, but the hedgehog knows only one great thing,' goes an ancient proverb. Edouard and André Michelin knew only how to make tyres – but knew how to make them indispensable.

2

PREHISTORY

Often enough, new entrepreneurs have come to heavy industry by trial and error; this is one way to make sense of the prehistory of Michelin, and of the partners who preceded the Michelins and paved the way for their success – Aristide Barbier and Edouard Daubrée. The Daubrées, to begin with them, had created their fortune in trade – notably the sugar trade, which collapsed during the Napoleonic Wars with the crippling blockade against French shipping. But sugar was in their blood, one might say, and Edouard Daubrée – until then a career soldier – was next seen operating a sugar refinery on the banks of the Seine in Paris, while his widowed mother ran a boarding school whose pupils included young English girls of good family. Then, when Edouard was ready to open a proper sugar mill (not simply to refine imported sugar cane, as he had been doing, but to create it from locally grown beets), he chose a site in far-off Auvergne, on the Allier river less than ten miles south and east of Clermont-Ferrand – capital of the province destined to become the capital of the Michelin dynasty. And apparently, help could be obtained from the government, for ever since Napoleon learned what a British blockade could do to vital imports from the colonies, there had been official support for domestic production of beet sugar.

*　　　　　　　*　　　　　　　*

We can put a date on the opening of the Daubrée enterprise: 1830. Some two years later, Edouard Daubrée, who was then 31 years old, was joined by Aristide Barbier, just a year his senior.

Daubrée did not migrate alone to the remote Auvergne. He was accompanied by his 21-year-old, pert, pretty and quite pregnant wife, Elizabeth, née Pugh-Barker, who had been a pupil at his mother's boarding school. After what must have been a risky courtship – for a young man was not supposed to mingle with the young ladies, not even if the young man was the son of the institution's headmistress – Edouard made it all right by accompanying Elizabeth to London for a proper marriage in her family circle, the ceremony taking place at traditional Saint Marylebone Church. The scene switches to a mill by a stream, where their first-born, Ernest, would have been just learning to walk when the elements turned the benign stream wild. For legend – it is still legend, as industrial history was still being created by word of mouth – places a fortuitous flood here, quite early in the history of the sugar works – a dramatic rise in the water level of the Allier sufficiently destructive to do away with house, plantations, refinery.

But the pioneers could begin all over again, and in more secure circumstances, thanks to the arrival of Aristide Barbier, a distant cousin but a close friend from childhood.[1] This is the Aristide Barbier who now made his appearance in Auvergne, with daughters Emilie and Adèle (who will become one of the important people in this book). He seems to have arrived with a little capital and considerable experience. The partners agreed that it was time to try other things – to produce goods that people needed right there in Auvergne. They began with their mastery of refining, and turned out light machinery needed in the region's sugar mills, and agricultural implements such as pumps.

Here a novelist would be free to imagine how the partners came to rubber, rubber which at the time was largely the natural product – a substance hardened from the latex oozing out of tropical forest rubber trees – but never easy to transform into something useful. It was certainly not an obvious choice for a factory so far away from the raw material of those tropical forests, a rugged cross-country trek from those ocean ports at which it might be landed. But if we accept the legend, the right woman was in the right place to help these partners, who were so ready to try anything. One can reconstruct the dialogue between Elizabeth and her husband: 'Edouard, do you remember what

I told you about my uncle Charles and his rubber works? When I was a child he would fashion little bouncing balls for me to play with; all the children adored them. They'd be so easy to make – I'm sure I'd remember how – if we could just get some rubber.'

Whatever else she brought to the marriage as dowry, Elizabeth Daubrée apparently was the niece – at any rate she had grown up in the shadow – of Charles Macintosh, the Scot who made rubber work for him at a time (1823) when inventors and entrepreneurs were looking for ways to manipulate the strange substance, and then to find practical uses for it. A little later, the miraculous process known as vulcanization – essentially the application of heat and sulphur to transform crude rubber into something at once stronger and more pliable – created an industry.

A decade and a half before this process was tried and proved successful, Macintosh had begun to strip off slices of crude rubber – hardened latex – to dissolve it in low-boiling naphtha, encasing it between layers of fabric to produce waterproof clothing material. By 1824 he was running a company bearing his name to make and sell his patented rainwear. Still later, his genial creation would be known universally as the 'mackintosh'.

To let André Michelin tell the story, at this difficult time in the fortunes of the partners, Daubrée's wife saved the day. Perhaps her husband smiled when she offered her suggestion, but he did go out to order a stock of latex. Soon everybody was smiling, for the bouncing rubber balls turned out to be a commercial success.[2] (In the official Michelin version of the story, Elizabeth's intention was only to give them away to neighbourhood children.)[3] The thing to remember is that rubber did come to Clermont-Ferrand through the young partners at the origin of the Michelin empire; let it be Elizabeth's gift. Michelin's official historian describes Elizabeth as 'shop stewardess' of the nascent factory; for some years thereafter she would direct a team of women workers in the cutting of strips of Brazilian rubber utilized in making the balls.

The Michelin archives preserve a letter written by Barbier as early as 1833, in which he enumerates possible uses of rubber; one of them was 'to cover wheels of light vehicles'. Quoting this, Michelin's historian shows impartiality by pointing out that British manufacturers also began thinking of tyres early in the rubber age; the famous patent

1. Bibendum – 'Michelin Man' – collecting rubber from a rubber tree, in an early advertisement. *Illustrated London News*, 17 June 1911.

of Robert William Thomson (another Scot) dates from 1845 – by which time vulcanization made it possible to do with rubber what one wished to do.

It was a rough moment in the Industrial Revolution. There was a race to be the first to file a patent, another race to be the first to exploit new and potentially profitable manufacturing processes. In 1839 Charles Goodyear first stumbled upon the vulcanization process that was to make all the difference, yet he had not had the business sense to nail down his patent in time. He even thought he could keep the discovery to himself while he negotiated its sale, letting samples get out of his hands, at which point a clever Englishman, Thomas Hancock, unravelled his secret by sniffing out the sulphur in it – and filed his own patent for vulcanization a year ahead of Goodyear's (in 1843, to be precise). Goodyear fought back, threatening legal action if Europeans violated his rights. French rubber-makers who ignored Goodyear's moral priority were taken to court, their defence led by none other than Aristide Barbier – armed with his legal background – and they won – in France at least; the year was 1854.[4]

Henceforth there seemed no limit to what one could make out of processed latex from *Hevea brasiliensis* plantation trees (and the trees did not even have to grow in Brazil). By 1835, in addition to a broad range of metal goods, chiefly for the use of agriculture and industry, the partners were producing a growing variety of rubber products – including belts and tubes as well as Elizabeth's private line of bouncing balls – at the new site; their descendants the Michelins are still using it, and grandly.[5]

From then on, and for a long time, the little factory on the north side of Clermont-Ferrand was to be a significant factor in what was then still a very small town – in fact two townships imperfectly united, each – Clermont and Montferrand – clustered around its own lava mound a kilometre apart. Sited in a region of extinct volcanoes often veiled in mist, the little city was and remains dominated by the soaring cone of the Puy-de-Dôme, and in the heart of old Clermont, by a unique gothic cathedral all in awesome black – the black of the volvic lava employed in its construction.

At the time of the installation of Barbier & Daubrée, Clermont-Ferrand could hardly have been called a factory town, its industry largely confined to foodstuffs, hat-making and weaving. Of a total population of 28,000 in 1831, some 4000 persons were employed in such light industries, another 2000 in agriculture, including a still-significant winegrowing culture. Rubber was to change all that, converting farmers and wine-makers into factory workers, drawing more labour from rural communities in an ever-growing radius.[6]

3

A MICHELIN IN
THE FAMILY

Adventurers perhaps, but in the end Barbier and Daubrée proved to be sound businessmen. They just happened to be industrialists at the dawn of industry, with a factory that had not been designed (they just let it grow), and some handy sources of energy (like a rushing stream underground).[1] Then, after learning their own jobs, they had to teach others – rural labourers as removed from the discipline of factory work as they themselves had been not very long before that. Doing jobs they were not trained for – and performing them better than average – would be a trait passed on to the first generation of rubber-making Michelins.

Looking at the Barbier–Daubrée achievement from the distance of a century and a half, it does seem as though they were keenly aware of how to make machinery that would allow other factories to work better. And so they devised implements for sugar mills, distilleries, and saw mills, turning out hydraulic presses, steam engines, boilers, pumps for irrigation or fighting fires. And everything anyone could then imagine that could be made from rubber.

Rubber was about to define Clermont-Ferrand. Soon there was a second manufacturer, Jean-Baptiste Torrilhon, a vendor of clothing and miscellaneous household goods. He did so well selling rainwear that he decided to make his own, and the cousins helped him get started. Meanwhile the cousins were discovering any number of uses for rubber now that rubber had been tamed – valves, pipes and springs, even elastic threads and garter belts, toys, of course – those ubiquitous bouncing balls heading the list – but also more intimate articles for hygiene.[2]

At the apex of their own activity – and shortly before they were to pass the company on to the next generation – the partners were advertising themselves thus:

> BARBIER, DAUBRÉE & Co. at Clermont-Ferrand (Puy-de-Dôme).
> Construction of Machines and Iron and Copper Foundry. Finished Rubber Goods. Factories in Clermont and Blanzat; dépôt on Rue du Faubourg-Poissonière in Paris. Six Bronze Medals. Twelve Silver Medals. Ten Gold Medals. Six Repeat Awards of Gold Medals. One Emperor's Prize. 2nd Prize for Steam Engines at National Agricultural Competition of 1860. Two Medals at the London World's Fair of 1862.[3]

The original Barbier–Daubrée combination worked like a charm until the end, but the end always comes. They even died in harmony – Aristide Barbier in 1863 and Edouard Daubrée just a year later, having ensured the succession as best they could – given that Daubrée left two sons and widower Barbier two daughters. Of the Daubrée sons the elder, Ernest, already 34 years old at his father's death, seemed to give the better guarantee that he could handle the succession. But now there was – or could be – a male pretender on the Barbier side.

During the early years of the Clermont-Ferrand adventure Aristide's daughters Emilie and Adèle had lived in Paris, raised by the sister of their long-departed mother. The story goes that when they were of the age to marry, the daughters had access to the best drawing rooms. But it was in Clermont-Ferrand that Aristide eventually found a man for Emilie, who by then was 24 years old. The prospective husband, a recent widower, son of a property lawyer, was himself a lawyer. And it was still further away from Paris – in Luz, a spa in the Pyrenees frequented by Aristide Barbier in his late and prosperous years – that his second daughter Adèle (then a ripe 21) was first seen in the company of a gentleman named Jules Michelin (a dozen years her senior).

Jules Michelin, if technically an employee of the French customs service, was better known to society as an artist; perhaps he had been invited to some of the social events frequented by the Barbier daughters. Why a father anxious to find a suitable male successor as head of a growing and profitable manufacturing company employing some three hundred workers would desire the union of his daughter and a civil servant, an artist to boot, is hard to understand. Indeed, he seemed to be favouring such a union at a time when the succession was wide open in Clermont-Ferrand, since Ernest, elder son of Barbier's partner, was still serving his emperor, while Barbier's second son had dedicated his life to the high seas.

That Jules was an anomaly in his own family is clear enough. His paternal grandfather Louis, a property lawyer, had a mind for business; Louis's second son André-François – he had five sons in all – was a tradesman dealing in silks and ribbons – perhaps not a noble calling but one requiring a certain ambition and a calculating head. Respected by his peers, he was a notable giver to charities, a proud member of the Legion of Honour.

They knew how to do things in those days. That is, André-François knew that to ensure the survival of his business he would have to leave it to just one of his three sons – the eldest; the two others could work for the government. That explains the presence of Jules Michelin in the customs service of the Finance Ministry. There was then nothing demeaning about the civil service. To be employed by the state indicated that one was honourable, opened the way to influential connections and (not incidentally) guaranteed a lifelong income.

Adèle Barbier and Jules Michelin were united in marriage in April 1852. Soon after that Jules resigned from the civil service, reporting for work at the Paris office of the company run by his father-in-law and Edouard Daubrée. But his main contribution to the family company – now his family's too – would be to sire André Jules Aristide Michelin (born to Adèle on 16 January 1853) and Edouard Etienne Michelin (on 23 June 1859).

*   *   *

It was a bad time to be running a factory without firm leadership. France was now fully integrated into the industrial age, which meant business curves with abrupt highs and lows – both kinds difficult to predict or to explain. And then different industries achieved their peaks – or peaked – at different times. After years of relatively unhampered and joyous growth, the Clermont-Ferrand company languished.[4] Ernest leaned more and more heavily on his accountant, the property lawyer Jean-Gilbert Bideau, who was soon helping out with cash as well as counsel. If at the outset Ernest Daubrée had held a little less than half of the shares of the family firm, his equity began to shrink

2. André and Edouard Michelin. *L'Illustration*, 11 March 1911. Reproduced by kind permission of the Mary Evans Picture Library.

even further. Soon he had to make a place for Bideau as managing partner. And then the day came when Bideau and not Ernest sat in the director's chair; by 1868 it was time to print new letterheads reading 'Jean-Gilbert Bideau & Co. – Formerly Barbier & Daubrée'.

Certainly what is known of the life of the Michelins in Paris at this time suggests ignorance of, although possibly not indifference to, the goings-on in Clermont-Ferrand. Jules was an artist, after all, and if Bideau could make the factory hum again, Adèle's share would only gain in value. Alas, he did not make it hum; a good manager perhaps, perhaps even a better accountant, Bideau was not an entrepreneur, not a man at home with machines – and he did not seem to know how to recruit people who were. At the close of the Bideau regime the payroll – once as high as 320 – was down to 30 – and it was no longer being met.[5]

*   *   *

It was time to bring the little factory back into the family, the family back into the factory. By then Jules Michelin, that contented master of etching, had died. (Died in the service of art, one could say; a collector of china, he had gone to Limoges to help establish a porcelain museum there; he succumbed, so reported *Le Temps*, 'to smallpox whose germ he had brought with him from Paris'.)[6] Scrutinizing their ranks, shareholder descendants of the original partners saw only one possible candidate. This had to be the elder son of Jules Michelin and his widow Adèle, daughter of the company's late co-founder Aristide Barbier.

Still a relatively young entrepreneur, André Michelin enjoyed one qualification none of his predecessors in the company had possessed: he was actually a trained engineer, a graduate of Paris's no-nonsense Central School of Arts and Manufacturing. At the age of 30 he opened his own factory in Bagnolet on the outskirts of Paris, to produce metal frames and girders – inspired, one industrial historian noted, by an earlier graduate of the Central School, Gustave Eiffel.[7] Indeed, André seemed nearly as much artist as engineer, a predilection reinforced by his marriage in 1881 to Sophie Wolff, and thus into the astonishing household of Auguste Wolff – the famous piano-maker.

Not surprisingly, when family duty summoned him to Clermont-Ferrand to try to salvage the collapsing heritage of the Barbiers and Daubrées, André Michelin decided, prudently, to hold on to his Paris business all the same.[8]

4

THE BROTHERS MIRACULOUS

The Michelins were artists, but not always in words, although André would later show himself to be as gifted in explaining tyres as his brother Edouard in designing them. But if André ever said anything about his first impressions of Clermont-Ferrand, that utterance has been lost. It happens that in 1886, the very year that André settled in that town (temporarily, as we now know and he did not), Emile Zola published a saga of the artist's life, *The Masterpiece*. Christine, the woman who married Zola's fictional painter Claude Lantier, had come up to Paris from Clermont-Ferrand; she would talk about the atmosphere of the streets André Michelin was just then discovering.

At that time, a smaller Clermont-Ferrand was closer to its country-side than it is now. 'Mountains? Yes, there were mountains on one side, which you would find at the far end of streets,' remembers Zola's heroine. 'While on the other side, down other streets, there were fields as far as you could see…' Of course, Christine must speak of that strange eruption in the landscape called the Puy-de-Dôme, 'quite round, looking like a hump', along with 'sloping lanes and boulevards, a city of black lava sliding down the hill, where heavy rain rushed along like rivers…' A contemporary guide-book is no less expressive than Zola's heroine, placing the town atop 'a mound, on the edge of a vast half circle formed by the volcanic peaks of the Auvergne'.[1]

*   *   *

Today we should say that 33-year-old André Michelin, when he took up quarters in Clermont-Ferrand to see what could be saved of the languishing family business, was overqualified. A constructor of promise, an innovator both in designs and materials, he had already begun to prove himself in the capital of France. What could he gain by trying to rescue a little factory in a dim town that he and his siblings had probably inherited too late? If we listen to legend, what he found on entering the little plant was a stack of bills – and ominous warnings to pay them; a reduced team of workers had stayed on but had not received their wages in months. Banks refused further credit; bankruptcy and a sale of remaining assets by court order were just around the corner.

André did get the machinery running again. And it is likely that after the sophistication of his metalwork plant up north he found the possibilities of Clermont-Ferrand paltry and determined to focus on what the family's white elephant did best and few others understood – making things out of rubber. Perhaps the most successful of the innovations that came in his brief reign was a rubber brake shoe for horse-drawn carriages. (It was christened 'the silent', since it made business sense to use an English word when one wished to suggest industrial progress.) Michelin's advertising – and from what we know of André's subsequent activity we can be sure that he created it – guaranteed users of the new brake a totally noiseless ride: 'Everybody knows the disadvantages of iron brake shoes: the strong smell of heated metal, the irritating screech of iron against iron, which in the end proves exhausting. We had become used to this and hardly pay attention any more, but its absence will be most appreciated.' The Michelin style – direct, often imperative, always logical, addressed as it was to thoughtful users of new machines – was born.[2]

Advertising was also a way to put forward the new company name – now A. Michelin & Cie – thereby associating the family with innovation. The brake shoe was ready for the 1889 World's Fair, during which Gustave Eiffel unveiled his bizarre ironwork tower dominating the exhibition pavilions along the Seine. André made a more modest impression with his humble new product, for which he won another humble bronze medal. Under his management the little company went out for what we now call niche markets, for he was determined to make the most of what his little crew in Clermont-Ferrand could do, such as the belts, pipes, valves and joints, for which rubber seemed the ideal element, not to forget the company's standbys such as Elizabeth Daubrée's bouncing balls.[3]

In the end André himself was the problem. For all his dynamism, his openness to the future, his proven ability to do the most with little, he could not make a success of Clermont-Ferrand from Paris, and Paris was where he preferred to be. But the choice of a successor could not have been odder.

*   *   *

We know from his own testimony that Edouard Michelin, the younger of the brothers by half a dozen years, had (like André) been visiting Clermont-Ferrand regularly since childhood with his Paris family, notably during school holidays. Later, he was to recall one of his return visits when was going on twenty years old. His curiosity had been aroused, as he strolled in the garden alongside the factory, by two workers who were boiling a tree trunk in an iron kettle. He quickly discovered that, unknown to the factory manager, the men were hardening wood from a service tree in order to make their own tools – gearing teeth as it happened. If they had to go out to buy such tools it would cost the factory a lot more. But the manager did not want his workers messing about in the garden area. 'He mustn't hear about this,' one of the men told Edouard, 'because if he gets angry we'll hear about it! You won't sell us out, will you, Mr. Michelin?' The young man listened to their calculations as to how much they were saving.

He would remember that moment, he said later, for here were two men who put the interests of the company ahead of their own. It taught him 'that one can and consequently one should trust good workers. A chief who trusts his good workers and relies on them is supported by them, and the others follow.'[4]

For, however improbable it may seem, Edouard Michelin was tapped for the job of running the family factory. Improbable, because if elder brother André was a trained engineer and an industrialist, Edouard was a student of the arts. Already 27 years old when his elder brother agreed to go to Clermont-Ferrand to see what could be done to save the family business, Edouard seemed a carbon copy of their late father Jules. Like Jules, he was blissfully ignorant of the business world, thus to his potential heritage. He was doing what he wished to

with this life and simply assumed that he'd never need to worry –
others would do that in his place.

André had gone from the Central School of Arts and Manufacturing
to the architecture section of the School of Fine Arts in Paris – and
where do we find Edouard but in the painting section? He was in the
studio of William Bouguereau, a popular and financially successful artist
then, creator of tame, sexless nudity, a safe choice to decorate great
churches and new theatres.

A reproduction survives of one of Edouard Michelin's works.
'Les Pélerins d'Emmaüs' portrays Jesus and two disciples after the
Resurrection – an academic theme *par excellence*, already painted
majestically by Titian, Caravaggio, Veronese and Rembrandt. In
describing the canvas over a century later, a Michelin editor believed
that he found in it several traits of Edouard's character: 'his disdain for
academic traditions, his taste for simplicity, for humble truth'.[5] It still
seems likely that, had he stayed in Paris to paint, we should never have
heard of Edouard Michelin.

The story – passed on to us by Edouard's older brother – is that
when the call came to Edouard to abandon his Montparnasse studio
to join brother André in Clermont-Ferrand, the 63-year-old
Bouguereau shook his head reprovingly. 'Without any doubt he painted like a pig,' grumbled the master, recalling that instant later. 'But he
drew like a Master!'[6]

    *   *   *

Apparently a family council in Paris debated the succession. The most
important decision would of course have to be Edouard's. And he had
a letter of Aunt Emilie in hand, mixing peremptory judgments and
tenderness. 'Do come, all is not lost if you come.' And, 'It's for you
to save what our fathers passed down to us'. One can guess that no
manuscript letter of the sort will ever be found, but something did
happen all the same. Legend has it that it cost the Beaux Arts student
a night of sleep to decide to give up painting for rubber.[7] Summing
up that moment in a humorous reminiscence decades later, his older
brother André, the graduate engineer, wrote: 'Which of the two
brothers saw himself as a rubbermaker? It was the artist!'[8]

Soon Edouard was back in Paris, where he informed Aunt Emilie
that he needed 500,000 francs – nearly 1.4 million of today's euros[9] –

and she asked him to wait until the following day for her reply. When he returned, it was to hear her say that the required sum was at his disposal. She had used the time between her nephew's two visits to make certain that a room would be hers at a convent should the factory investment fail.[10]

We can believe that Edouard's single greatest asset just then – 1886, when he was just 29 years old – was the recent experience of his older brother, who had taken the time to see what was wrong with the family enterprise, and what could make it work. Clearly they were on the right track by sticking to rubber; the point was to be inventive, ahead of the market. That also meant weeding out the non-essential.

'I had to run a factory employing fifty persons,' Edouard later explained, in a talk to his factory engineers. 'Some of the production was good, some poor. The plant didn't have an engineer, only a foreman who was incompetent and only understood a part of the work being done. So the factory ran – as extraordinary as that may sound – only thanks to the workers and their routine.' In his first half hour on the scene he fired three employees and raised the pay of two others.

The younger Michelin himself knew nothing about rubber – making him, in his words, 'absolutely inferior to my fifty employees'. The first step was to learn his job. 'I could learn it only by questioning the workers.' Henceforth it became his personal style. As he remembered it later, he would pose his questions in a tone of friendly conversation – 'How will you proceed here? Why? Couldn't you do it another way?'

At last the time came – he could no longer postpone it – when he had to give an order. After doing so he explained why, and asked for objections: did the worker see any likelihood that he would not be able to do the job that Edouard wished him to do?

'I noticed that even when I knew the problem rather well this friendly talk was extremely useful in getting more details,' he later confessed in a talk to his engineers.[11]

5

A TYRE
IS BORN

Aphotograph survives in which a still-young Edouard Michelin, with dark moustache and hairline already receding, sits with crossed arms on a bench with two of his accountants and the chief clerk. Behind them stand eight more men – some of them clearly just off the factory floor, one specifically identified as production manager. In all, 12 men, including Michelin and his office staff. The caption under the picture, 'Edouard Michelin with his personnel in 1889', led more than one writer to conclude that the factory payroll had been reduced to a dozen men at the moment of Edouard's arrival. The truth, as we know from Edouard's own recollections, is that he found 50 workers on the job when he reported for duty in Clermont-Ferrand. Obviously only shop stewards got the chance to be photographed with the chief.[1]

The corporate name of the family enterprise was legally changed to Michelin & Co. on 28 May 1889. New bylaws confirmed Edouard as the company's sole manager (we would say managing director); he had celebrated his thirtieth birthday only the day before mailing out a formal announcement of the new dispensation. Edouard would receive an annual salary of 7000 francs, expenses included – the equivalent, to the extent that such values can be given an equivalence, would be a modest 20,000 euros. But he was also to get a share of profits, and free housing inside the factory compound, plus heat and lighting; he also had a right to fruit and vegetables growing on the grounds (planted by the workers alongside their company-provided housing).[2]

3. Edouard Michelin (second left, seated) with his personnel, 1899. © Collection Viollet.

The point, just then, was to save what could be saved, to recognize the factory's best cards, and to play them hard.

One day Edouard picked up a company circular that had gone out to educational institutions of the region to sing the praises of bouncing balls – 'still made the same way, of real rubber – something unfortunately quite rare today since many manufacturers do not hesitate to mix unknown materials into the rubber'. (His brother André, the confidently outspoken André, would have written that; it betrays his peremptory style.)

The balls came in varying sizes, available either in solid rubber or hollow, the latter suited for a game called Tambourin (in which a parchment tambourine replaces a racket).

Edouard had copies made of the original circular, and distributed it with a new one which used the new Michelin & Co. letterhead. When the first advertisement was composed two years earlier, he said, there were only 14 customers buying their rubber balls; now there were 120. Readers of the prospectus would have to notice that Michelin also manufactured gas tubes of all kinds and widths, hoses for irrigation, fire pumps and more.[3]

But not tyres – not yet.

They were, however, being made elsewhere. Thus, in Belfast a transplanted Scot veterinary, John Boyd Dunlop, had patented a pneumatic tyre in 1888 – an air-filled rubber tube wrapped in a sheath of rubber and canvas.[4] It went on the market in the very year Edouard took over his family factory. Early versions – glued or otherwise affixed to the wooden rims – held to the wheels with difficulty, and had a dismally short life, but while they lasted they did much to make cycling less rugged, thus a more practical means of getting from here to there. Inventor Dunlop sold his patent – but the company founded to exploit his invention would make use of his name forever after.

Edouard Michelin soon had a couple of those tyres in his workshop. The time is the early spring of 1891 – a warm day, as remembered. The first thing that came into view at the entrance to the factory yard was a farmer's cart drawn by two oxen. It carried a passenger, a local eccentric known as Grand Pierre, famous for riding around the Auvergne countryside atop one of those still-rare contraptions, a velocipede. The two-wheeled vehicle usually came equipped with solid strips of rubber around the wheels. But this time Grand Pierre was using air-filled tyres – objects still rarer than velocipedes. And both tyres had gone flat.

It turned out that the rubber tyres were glued to the wheel rims. To remove them for repairs, the rider was obliged to follow a complicated set of instructions in order to perform a long and arduous job. Instead, Grand Pierre decided to ask for help at the Michelin workshop, knowing that it 'worked in rubber'.

It would have to be a collective effort, and Edouard Michelin was never very far from his workers and their foreman as they tackled the problem. Removing the glued tyres required three hours of resourceful effort, and then after the repairs the tyres were glued back on again – and left to dry overnight. Next day, says the legend (and how could the story of the first tyres touched by Michelin not be the stuff of legend?), when Grand Pierre turned up to collect his velocipede, he exclaimed with some pride: 'Climb aboard, Mister Michelin! It's easy as pie!' Edouard had already tried pedalling such vehicles equipped with solid rubber tyres, not to speak of earlier models with unforgiving iron wheels, and he knew what they did to one on unpaved roads – what it cost in backache. But he let himself be tempted by the experience of riding on brand-new Dunlop tyres cushioned with air.

In a very little while he was back at the plant, the tyres flat again; the repairs had not taken. At once, so he later recalled, two things occurred to him. 'Number one, tyres are the future. Number two, Grand Pierre's tyres are beneath contempt.'

That evening he summoned his chief engineer to announce that tyres were here to stay. 'But we've got to find a way to replace an inner tube in fifteen minutes without calling in a specialist. In other words, invent a removable tyre any fool can install.'

Thus concludes the founding myth of the Michelin dynasty.[5]

Edouard's devoted team lost no time in getting to work on ways and means of installing tyres and removing them from bicycle wheels (and never mind that the principle of air-filled tyres had been invented and patented by others). As soon as they had put together a tyre that could be attached (or detached) in a quarter of an hour with the help of nuts and bolts, they resolved to broadcast the good news in the manner makers of automobiles as well as bicycles and their equipment would be doing from now on: by public demonstration.

The time was May 1891; the Michelin factory began producing removable tyres then – and it never stopped. At first there was no question of selling any, Edouard making it a point of honour not to put removable tyres on the market until they were perfect – a scruple that became a house rule. He got his first patents before making his first sale.[6] (Both the original Michelin patent claim filed on 18 June 1891, and the supplementary one for improvements submitted on 14 August noted – presciently – that the tyres were designed for 'velocipedes and other vehicles'.)[7]

But there was nothing wrong with trying out the newfangled tyres in a bike race, and in September of this *annus mirabilis* the Paris daily *Le Petit Journal* provided the opportunity he was waiting for, organizing the first national competition from Paris to the furthest point in Brittany. 'We've got to win,' decided Edouard Michelin. 'I was about to say that,' brother André echoed, or so he remembered later, also remembering that at this time the Michelin removable tyre required no fewer than 34 bolts to adhere to the rim.[8]

Of course, they should have liked to be readier than they were. The occasion called for both brothers to drop everything else in preparation for what would prove to be a decisive event. They happened not to have a single removable tyre in the shop, so the Clermont-Ferrand crew neglected food and sleep to turn out a few.

The hardest part would be to find and recruit a cyclist to carry their colours; the favourite in the race was already engaged with another sponsor (and of course would ride on air-filled rubber tyres glued to the rim). But then there was an already famous veteran racer from Bayonne, Charles Terront. His trainer told Terront – and the Michelins – that they were crazy. 'You don't change anything at all four days before a race.' The brothers persisted, calling on Terront alone, making sure to have blank legal paper in their briefcase so as to be able to dash off a contract on the spot.

Terront admitted to the visitors that he had been expected to ride on tyres he did not trust, since they tended to slip off the rim. So they asked him to do a road test. The makeshift removables may have looked odd – raising mocking laughter from professionals as Terront glided by – but the tyres held in place, and the other important thing was that they could be detached quickly for repairs.

The Paris–Brest race was scheduled for 6 September 1891, drawing 210 cyclists representing 59 different brands and kinds of tyre. Terront, riding a Humber cycle, maintained his position, trailing only the champion, arriving in Brest nearly an hour behind him. His tyres failed him five times – and Terront was convinced that the punctures were caused by nails strewn across the road – and not accidentally. Repairs were effected by two Michelin men. They travelled by local trains from stop to stop to keep up with their rider – an enterprise requiring considerable planning. Legend has it that at the Saint-Brieuc station a bystander pointed them in the wrong direction, and they discovered he was the trainer of their chief rival.

Way out front on the return stop at Guingamp, the champion decided to take a nap. Terront was kept awake and alert thanks to a large cowbell wielded by his own managers. He swept to victory with an eight-hour lead over the number two, a full day over number three – with 1200 kilometres (some 745 miles) swallowed up at an average speed of 10.5 mph, and no sleep for three days and nights. Terront was a hero, and, in knowing circles, so was Edouard Michelin.[9]

The little tyre shop on the grounds of the Clermont-Ferrand factory had only 12 tyres in stock at the close of the race. The first leaflets announcing the Terront–Michelin victory – printed while their rider had taken a clear lead in Brittany – were being handed out as the new champion entered Paris at the Porte Maillot:

> On the 14th of July Louis XVIth, learning from Lafayette of the fall of the Bastille, cried out: 'But then it is a revolt'. 'No, Sire,' replied the marquess, 'IT'S A REVOLUTION'.
>
> We are certain that the bicycle-riding public will say of our tyre: 'Is it an improvement?' 'No, IT'S A REVOLUTION.'[10]

Just a month later, at a London industrial fair, the Michelins wrote orders for 4000 pairs of removable tyres; back in Paris, a magazine for cyclists reported that the 'Removable' was 'the hit of the show'.[11] By the end of the following year some ten thousand French riders had Michelin tyres bolted to their wheel rims.[12]

For his part, 'on a foggy morning in February 1893', addressing a meeting of the Society of Civil Engineers on the subject of 'Bicycles and the progress that rubber tyres allow them to achieve', André Michelin – seeking to explain precisely what the new Michelin tyres could do on rough and gravelly roads – found the right words: 'A tyre envelopes the obstacle it encounters. We can say that "The tyre drinks the obstacle".' He received a rousing ovation for that. André also pointed out that bikes had become great time-savers. Americans say that time is money: a French philosopher had observed that 'time is life itself'.[13]

Later, with the confidence born of success, André would be more daring still. One detects his pen in a Michelin insert in a Paris daily newspaper in 1907:

> When your wife makes a scene … if you make the mistake of replying her anger grows in direct proportion to the soundness of your position. But if you are smart enough to remain silent, or better if you meet violence with sweetness … the most bitter discussions end in caresses …
>
> Well, the tyre arranges a friendly understanding between wheel and obstacle. It bends but doesn't break. It lets itself be had … [14]

6

OF BIKES, CABS AND MOTORCARS

If it needed to be proved, the Paris–Brest bicycle race showed that the intrepid Michelins would never shy away from a scrap. They had one coming. For while they were sole inventors of easily removable tyres, it happened that these tyres that were so easy to install or take off were filled with compressed air. They were pneumatic, and John Boyd Dunlop, when he perfected that principle, had made sure to patent it. Now the British company that manufactured pneumatics bearing his name intended to see that Dunlop's patent was respected, and not only in the United Kingdom. France was a promising market for Dunlop, just as Britain had been for Michelin's French-made 'silent' brake shoe.

So the Michelins had a legal battle on their hands, and they'd win it. At some point in the litigation the lawyers stumbled upon a choice piece of evidence. Yes, Dunlop discovered and patented his pneumatic tyres in 1888. But no, his were not the first. Unknown even to Dunlop, Robert William Thomson had obtained a patent for 'aerial wheels' all the way back in 1845, describing his invention at the time as air-filled rubber belts permitting 'the wheels ... at every part of their revolution [to] present a cushion of air to the ground, or rail, or track on which they run'.

Further, some of Thomson's aerial wheels were actually produced in his time, tried out on horse-drawn broughams. Although admired and even marvelled at, the Thomson tyres did not catch on (both price and the difficulty of installing them were discouraging factors). And so they disappeared, along with the very memory of their ever having existed, and in due course Thomson's patent expired. But now that the original invention had been brought back into history, Dunlop no longer had a case against Michelin or other French manufacturers of pneumatics. For the Dunlop firm, the belated discovery of the pre-existing Thomson patent was a double blow: it not only lost its protection, but thanks to its enthusiastic promotion of pneumatic tyres, saw competitors sprout up all over.[1]

Henceforth – after the Dunlop suit – nobody would be greater promoters, more ardent defenders, of the late Robert William Thomson than … André and Edouard Michelin. Naturally, every word of praise for Thomson's aerial wheels was a nail hammered into the coffin of Dunlop's pretensions, and a message of reassurance to tyre dealers who may still have been reluctant to stock Michelin tyres for fear of further harassment. As early as 1908 a Michelin 'Monday', one of the promotional articles that appeared regularly in *L'Auto-Vélo*, praised the true inventor (the late Thomson) and the true patent (which of course had expired). 'Like the parliamentary system, pudding, and Shakespeare,' concluded the anonymous writer (probably André Michelin) 'tyres are of British origin'.[2] 'It's not with Dunlop's glued sausage skins,' scornfully remarked another Michelin column – undoubtedly also André Michelin's – 'that the bicycle would have had the resounding success it attained soon afterwards'.[3]

*   *   *

Now the brothers were to fly from victory to victory. Sales in 1891 – the *annus mirabilis* that saw the birth and the ascension of Michelin's removable tyres – reached the equivalent today of some 1.35 million euros; in 1893 the figure would be over four times higher. And the modest Michelin workforce of 62 rose to 182 in 1892, and to 268 in 1894. Thanks to Michelin's technical superiority, France was already the world's number-one tyre-maker before the end of the century, and the number-one exporter.[4]

Technical superiority – and knowing how to talk about it: from the very start of their adventure the Michelins showed that they had learned how to wed new (and superior) product to the right words and signs. A good new tyre tube got the perfect name in 1892 – 'the unpuncturable' – even before it was put on sale. It was shown at a

London salon that autumn, after which the press was informed that it would not actually be ready until January 1893; the Michelins were simply waiting for praise from specialized magazines before making it available.[5]

In the same year – even before tyres became a familiar household word, in the midst of plant expansion in a frantic attempt to keep up with exploding demand – the public relations-oriented Michelins (and one imagines André Michelin as prime mover here) provided an irresistible argument for would-be customers. They reduced their prices, saying that this had been made possible by both the acquisition of improved equipment for the factory and rising sales. In fact, Edouard Michelin had just hired an important asset in the person of an Alsatian chemist, Maximilien Gerber; research and development were going to have a lot to do with keeping Michelin ahead of the pack. Edouard Michelin talked up the notion of manufacturing as a science, and there is firm evidence that both brothers really believed and acted on this principle.[6]

And if they did not like the way bike races were organized, they would mount one of their own. Hence an International Michelin Competition, whose itinerary was quite simply from Paris to Clermont-Ferrand, seat of the kingdom. The basic requirement was also simple: riders had to utilize Michelin tyres. And the sponsors added spice to the race by seeding the roads with nails – thereby allowing a demonstration of how easy it was to change a Michelin tyre. Edouard Michelin, so went the authorized version of the story, stood on the road some six miles before the racers reached Nevers, dropping the nails himself or supervising the sabotage of his diabolic helpers, to make sure that nobody would get through without a flat tyre.[7]

In the unauthorized version of the story, the Michelins somehow got word that the two favourites in the race were secretly going to equip their cycles with Dunlop tyres. By making sure that all the contestants got flats, Michelin would triumph, since loyal contestants would be using its easy-to-remove brand:[8]

> We hope that after this race no one will try to tell us that nails are an insurmountable obstacle for tyres, at least for air-filled Michelins, since 61 of the 73 contestants attained Clermont-Ferrand, and not one of the twelve who failed could blame it on his tyres; all contestants without exception made repairs along the way.[9]

André Michelin could not have written it better, and it is quite possible that he did write it.

*   *   *

The announcement regarding the Clermont-Ferrand rally had not bothered to mention that it was a bicycle race; at that time, before recognition of the potential of the automobile, what other means of locomotion could have been involved?

But it was now that the brothers looked about them for new worlds to conquer. They did not have to look very far. Neither could have gone very far without one of those ubiquitous horse-drawn cabs that took them from home to workplace, or from home or workplace to railway station. Such rides were mighty uncomfortable on uncushioned wheels; how could they not have dreamed of smoother journeys? Precisely at what moment they gave concrete form to their dream is not clear. An official Michelin history places the event in 1894, when Edouard Michelin is said to have convinced a small company to equip its five cabs with Michelin tyres.[10]

There has always been a kind of sibling rivalry. The chief owners and operators of Michelin have always been direct descendants of Edouard and not André; Edouard's tribe writes or approves the company history. Actually, the first tyre-equipped horse carriage surfaced on the paving stones of Paris in February 1896, and it was André Michelin's initiative, designed to serve as a prototype and good example. Since André was the Michelin brother responsible for sales and promotion from his Paris headquarters (which then served both the Michelin tyre company and his personal industrial activity), we can be sure that he and not Edouard made the rounds of the coach companies to find a first customer.

He recalled that moment later (in one of the unsigned Michelin columns that so clearly bear his mark), not forgetting to speak of the days before rubber tyres when 'the slightest drive through Paris was a continuous series of tremors from which one emerged exhausted, deafened, the back and liver torn apart'. He remembered having said (that very year) that 'tyres for automobiles probably have no future, but tyres for horse carriages are quite another thing. Silence, comfort, ease, economy of energy – they have every reason to succeed.'[11]

Thanks to the daily press we can pinpoint the date – correcting the official history – at which horse cabs saw their first pneumatic tyres.

A front-page story in *Le Petit Journal* on 11 February 1896 is the evidence. 'My God yes!' begins the unsigned report. 'There's a horse cab on tyres in Paris, and at the end of the month there'll be 50, and perhaps 300 at the end of the year.' The exaggeration at once reveals the source – André Michelin, of course.

The reporter for *Le Petit Journal* had just taken a ride in the vehicle fitted out with Michelin tyres, and found it an enchantment. In future, he was sure, cab number 6234 of the co-operative called La Nouvelle would not lack customers. 'At last,' concluded the reporter, 'one will be able to chat in a cab!'[12]

In André's own account of events, delivered in a talk to an early convention of automobile enthusiasts, after a year of prospecting he had put only 83 horse-drawn vehicles on Michelin tyres in Paris (out of the total of 8000 circulating); he would have to wait until 1897 to see significant progress, with 300 Michelin-equipped cabs on the streets. Another statistic: by 1903, of 4000 cabs equipped with air-filled rubber tyres in the capital, 2350 preferred Michelins.[13]

* * *

André Michelin's admission that in 1895 he saw no future for automobile tyres deserves an explanation. Horse-drawn vehicles were half as old as time; nobody could have conceived of civilized existence without frequent recourse to them. As intelligent manufacturers the Michelins would have had plenty of time to reflect on how they were equipped, if only during their regular daily cab rides. Bikes were for the nimble, perhaps, but they too were more than sport – they did save time. But automobiles?

If André Michelin really expressed doubts about automobiles, his scepticism was not shared by all of his industrial peers. It was certainly true that automobiles were not for everybody – yet. They remained rich men's toys, requiring the service of full-time chauffeurs doubling as mechanics; unable to stray very far from the vicinity of a reliable repair shop, the nascent motorcar could easily be dismissed by seasoned entrepreneurs on the lookout for realistic investments. As early as 1894 – the year before André expressed his doubts (or later remembered that he had) – he and his brother Edouard had stood before their shareholders, almost all of whom were members of the founding families, to propose a commitment to automobile tyres.[14] 'Now we've begun to make money with bicycle tyres,' Edouard is quoted. 'Instead of distributing enormous profits, let's use them to make a tyre for automobiles.'[15]

For long years the challenge to engineers (and amateurs in their garages) was to perfect a credible motor, one light enough and safe enough, and with a reasonable degree of autonomy, and then to link it to the appropriate carriage. The ancestor of all such machines was the legendary prototype tried out in 1770 by Nicolas Cugnot, driven by steam. In the 1870s an Englishman living in Boston, George Brayton, got cars moving with petrol vapour. Even earlier, in Germany, a self-educated inventor named Nikolaus Otto, who found a backer for his petrol engine and then recruited a mechanical wizard, Gottlieb Daimler, to run his factory, produced a rudimentary but workable engine, and cars were now ready to try the open road.

There were others – notably Karl Benz in Germany, which country motorcar historian James Laux saw at the centre of the new technology. He credits Benz, thanks to a single-cylinder engine adapted to a tricycle, with producing the world's first petrol-driven motorcar in 1886; Gottlieb Daimler, with his assistant Wilhelm Maybach, was not far behind. Apparently inspired by Benz, Charles and Franklin Duryea designed their own petrol engine in Springfield, Massachusetts in 1891, harnessing it to a buggy the following year to produce what may have been the first credible American automobile.

By 1895 – the year in which so much happened at Michelin, or happened elsewhere by their doing – one could say that France was on its way to the consolidation of a true motorcar industry, the very first in the world, with some 350 vehicles already on the road, compared to only about 75 in the runner-up country, Germany. True, the French pioneers looked to the Germans for innovation. René Panhard and Emile Levassor, manufacturing motors under licence from the Germans Daimler and Maybach, came out with a Daimler-powered automobile in 1894, and soon the manufacturer Armand Peugeot was installing Daimler engines in his first automobiles. The United States was not quite there, not yet.[16]

Clearly it was the moment for the Michelins to set their watches to automobile time. But, as André later recalled that germinal instant in motorcar civilization, when Edouard began to look for a means of testing his first automobile tyres, pioneer constructors such as Levassor and Peugeot would not let him bolt his prototype tyres onto their cars even for a simple trial. As for putting Michelin tyres on automobiles to be delivered to customers – certainly not; that would mean an unending series of flats – keeping the precious vehicles out of circulation. No, thank you.[17]

7

PARIS–
BORDEAUX
OR BUST

Competitions as means of testing – above all, as opportunities to parade new equipment – began almost as soon as there were ridable bikes, workable autos, flyable planes. Those first auto races must have been fearful. It was not only a matter of hanging on until the finish line; often the problem was how to get started. On 22 July 1894 *Le Petit Journal* sponsored what is believed to be the first ever automobile race, on an itinerary running from Paris to Rouen; it was billed as a 'contest of horseless carriages'. In all, 102 vehicles were entered in the race but only 21 of them were ready at the starting line. The first prize was shared by two constructors who were to mark their century – Panhard & Levassor and Peugeot.[1] Nobody seemed to think much about tyres just then.

But when a second competition was announced for the following spring, the Michelin brothers were ready. The chief promoter of the rally was the Marquis Albert de Dion, a pioneer in engines and body-work who early in 1895 had founded the Automobile-Club de France. De Dion and fellow organizers mapped out an itinerary from Paris to Bordeaux and back again, a 720-mile race on unpaved roads totally unprepared for, and usually hostile to, the delicate mechanism of the early motorcar.[2] Of course, there was a way to cushion those rickety vehicles from the pits and stones of uncared-for highways, to shield the sensitive bones of their drivers, who were then (if they thought of rubber at all) using solid rubber tyres, a pitifully inadequate protection against the treachery of the open road.

34

The Michelins had the answer, but nobody was going to listen to these wild men, who proposed to have automobiles glide on air, as André Michelin put it. He remembered the sceptical remark of Emile Levassor, the engineer who was one half of the Panhard & Levassor team: 'What the devil do you stuff into your tubes? Cotton? Hay? Cork?' So the brothers had to pump air into a tyre, let it out, pump it in again…to convince Levassor that there was nothing but air in an air-filled Michelin tyre. And even then Levassor was not ready to put the tyres on one of his precious automobiles.

So they decided to bring their own to the race; after all, they did have a metalworks factory, and if anyone cared about the feasibility and the future of motorcar travel, the Michelins certainly did. They tested this and tested that, first trying a tyre on a horse-drawn vehicle; later they would remember, almost with nostalgia, that on the first try the tyre was flattened by a puncture 22 times in 20 miles, with the vehicle doing a maximum of 12 mph. Starting with an existing chassis, they found a way to connect it to a 4 hp motor designed for a boat. In the end they possessed three prototypes, baptizing them Swallow, Spider and Lightning, each equipped with an outsized tool chest, with tiny drawers numbered so as to allow quick retrieval of the right implement. The wheels were protected by the same spindly tyres, 65 millimetres in width, that one might find on a bicycle or a tricycle.

On the way to Paris, the Swallow gave up the ghost at Orléans – a victim of motor failure. The Spider came to grief against a tree near Moulins. As if by a prophecy, Lightning – which they had built on a Peugeot chassis – survived. Yet, to hear the brothers' own loving account of the journey, this car too veered so treacherously from one side of the road to the other that no professional driver was willing to touch it. ('It went to the ditch,' André remembered, 'as a pig to a truffle'.)

And so Lightning, all 2550 lb of it, would not only be the first ever automobile equipped to display Michelin tyres to the world at large, it was going to have Michelins – André and Edouard of course – as drivers. They and their mechanics had managed to manoeuvre it all the way from Clermont-Ferrand to Paris – a route of 235 miles even more hazardous than the one they would confront in the race itself. On Avenue MacMahon, minutes from the meeting point at Place de l'Etoile on the morning of 11 June, they had a first break-down. André later recalled hearing murmurs from the crowd to the

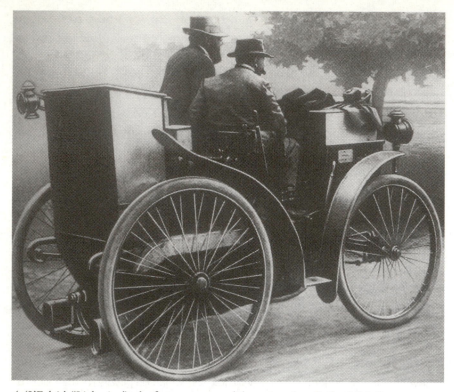

4. 'L'Eclair' ('Lightning'), the first ever automobile equipped to display Michelin tyres to the world at large, driven by the Michelin brothers in the Paris–Bordeaux race. © Boyer-Viollet.

effect: 'It wants to go to Bordeaux and can't even make it to the Arc de Triomphe!'

Then they were off for a race that would prove less than glorious for their colours, although their entry averaged an encouraging 18 mph. 'Each of our tyres was attached to the rim by twenty bolts and blew out, with mathematical regularity, every 90 miles.' The Michelins did their best. In Bordeaux, which they attained after 38 hours of driving, they did not dare take time out for dinner, nibbling on a roasted chicken that smelled of petrol. (That should have warned them.)

On the way back to Paris they lost their second and third gears near Poitiers; during the last 120 miles the motor caught fire, the water pipe clogged, the carburettor disconnected, there was a gas leak. They lost the race famously – they were ninth and last (but most of the other entries had not arrived at all). They had been slow – but comfortable. They proved that automobiles equipped with tyres could run on roads, and stay on course. If they had lost the race, they won the day. 'It was good all the same,' Emile Levassor confided – after coming in first on a vehicle designed by his own company. 'I never thought you could do it, you boast so much.'

Of course, the Michelins were already experts in self-advertising, advertising that was even better than their tyres in those pioneer years. 'If the tyre drinks the obstacle,' one wit remarked – alluding to André Michelin's famous line, 'it chokes on it'.

But from that day onward the Michelins would show themselves to be at least as versatile in talking up as in designing tyres. They intended to find out just what caused flats and how to reduce their occurrence, and indeed the tyres got a little better every day. The plant in Clermont-Ferrand became the archetype of research and development, of field testing. 'In ten years,' Edouard predicted (the day after his not very glorious return from Bordeaux), 'all motor cars will ride on tyres!'

*   *   *

Mark the date: Michelin's first automobile tyres went on sale in February 1896, when the brothers felt that they had a product worthy of their name.[3] By then André Michelin, Engineer of Arts and Manufacturing, utilizing a Paris address, had informed the trade that he had a vehicle equipped with Michelin tyres available for demonstration.[4]

For the actual launching the brothers devised a curious strategy. They appeared – only appeared – to begin modestly, by putting the new tyres on three-wheeled light cars called tricycles, equipped with petrol engines. Then they contracted to buy the total production – over a six-month period – of two of the most promising constructors of these relatively inexpensive vehicles, Albert de Dion and Léon Bollée. Further, they targeted young men, affluent young men of course, who were likely to be ready to try something new and adventurous, and thereby drag their elders into the automobile age.

From the earliest days the Michelins used economy as a sales pitch. Their tyres were not only comfortable and less hard on the fragile vehicles then those being produced, but they would save fuel every time. In August 1896 the firm of De Dion & Bouton lent Michelin one of its larger steam-driven cars for a comparative test of solid rubber wheels and Michelin pneumatics. On the route from Clermont to Issoire, equipped with solid tyres, the vehicle consumed 85 gallons of water and 86 lb of coke, running at an average speed of 17 mph; with air-filled tyres the consumption was 61 gallons of water and 60.5 lb of coke, running at 20 mph.[5] Later, de Dion was to say, with a touch of hyperbole: 'We build the locomotive and Michelin provides the rails'.[6]

In these early days of automobile tyres, the charts show no immediate explosion of sales, but rather a moderate improvement of turnover from year to year (the explosion would come only at the end of the decade and of the century). The factory payroll rose from 315 in 1896 to 520 the next year, and to 684 the year after that.

By 1897 the brothers felt the need to recapitalize, raising the company's value in late March of that year from 900,000 francs to 1.6 million. Most of the new money came from within the extended family – heirs of the Daubrées, Adèle (mother of André and Edouard) and her sister Emilie. Adèle was to die the following year.

Then, and for a long, long time to come, the overwhelming majority of Michelin stock – voting stock, certainly – stayed within the family, thanks both to the family's desire and to carefully drafted company bylaws – no matter how much this might limit expansion. (When a new family name appeared on the list of shareholders it was usually thanks to a marriage.) All the same, there were exceptional circumstances. In 1897, at a general assembly of stockholders – a family gathering, in other words – Edouard proposed that 300 precious shares, then representing 7.5 percent of total capital, be offered for sale to influential automobile and bicycle manufacturers.[7] Obviously, more than money was involved here, for the new shareholders were certain to be eager to hear about anything and everything Michelin might produce.

Edouard showed family solidarity, and the desire to maintain a closed circle, in another way. His elder brother had married Sophie Wolff in 1881, when André was 28 years old. On Wolff's death six years later, his widow and her unmarried daughters moved into André's Paris home on Boulevard Pereire – which also served as the company's Paris embassy, meeting place of leaders of the nascent auto industry and influential journalists. Then in 1894 Edouard proposed marriage to Sophie Wolff's sister Marie-Thérèse; presumably a dozen or more years of seeing the Wolffs in the intimacy of their joint home made it seem safe to do so.

Later, after the death of his wife Sophie in 1918, André proposed to and won the hand of Sophie's sister Jeanne (who had been a child of seven when he had married her eldest sister).[8]

8

BIBENDUM

By making better tyres – more resistant, capable of supporting ever heavier vehicles, with sturdier chassis and more powerful engines – Edouard Michelin was doing as much for the development and acceptability of automobile travel as he was for the future of Michelin. On his side, André, from his ample and growing Paris headquarters, was making Michelin tyres known to the world, certainly to the world that mattered to his company: pioneers of the new industry, makers and carriers of public opinion.

There is no way of knowing how much money went into promotion – the notion of an advertising budget certainly did not exist then – but the surviving evidence (posters, handbills, paid publicity in the press) clearly shows that André spared neither effort nor money in the service of the cause. The labours and ingenuity of either brother alone would probably have been insufficient; together they changed the history of transportation.

And they seemed to do these things with energy to spare. André Michelin, in the month of his forty-fourth birthday, took the wheel of a De Dion & Bouton motorcar powered by steam – a vehicle weighing 5720 lb – to win the exalting La Turbie lap in a rally that followed the Mediterranean coast from Marseille to Nice, on a road climbing 1640 feet above sea level, its summit marked by the Trophy of the Alps monument dedicated to the Roman emperor, Augustus.[1]

And, while automobiles were still new, offering more promise than performance, there was something newer still just over the horizon –

manned flight. So of course we find André Michelin, as early as July 1896, rising into the sky with the balloon of the Touring-Club de France, and loving it. Soon enough – in October 1898 – André was to become one of the founding members of the French Aéro-Club. At the beginning of the twentieth century, before there were any credible heavier-than-air flying machines to speak of, he was honorary president of the Aviation Committee, dedicated to experimental aircraft. There is no reason to believe that at this early stage André saw aviation uniquely in terms of its business potential.[2]

And here is Edouard, in the more down-to-earth, less exhilarating environment of the factory in Clermont-Ferrand, yet using his flair to encourage invention, then rushing to patent the most practical solutions, and to find ways to put them on the market. In the half dozen years leading up to La Turbie, an industrial historian discovered, Michelin had filed over fifty patent claims, either for specific manufacturing processes or for improved materials.

Meanwhile, home in Clermont-Ferrand, Edouard was producing tyres not only for bikes, motorcars and horse-driven vehicles, but also for baby carriages and even for wheelchairs. Michelin & Co. had become the exclusive supplier of some of the leading car-makers of the time – Bollée, De Dion & Bouton, Peugeot, Panhard & Levassor among them.[3] Between 1894 and 1898, Michelin more than doubled its annual turnover, while its labourforce increased from 268 to 698.[4]

And while his brother was inventing new ways to talk about what Edouard was doing, Edouard was applying his own energies to the elaboration of a worker's paradise – one of the first. The alliance between capital and labour hammered out in the earliest years of his reign became a model of what a manufacturer could and might do for its labourforce. That included at least symbolic worker participation in the company's gains, company-supplied housing, medical facilities including doctors, clinics and sanatoriums (this long before the era of government health benefits), counselling by social workers and legal experts, company-endowed schools, sports facilities and vacation camps, company stores – even company-endowed churches.

Later, such involvement in the lives of workers would be dismissed as paternalism, a system designed not to create a worker's but an owner's paradise. It would be seen by trade unions as a means to keep unions out of the plants. And it was certainly true that the intricate rules devised for bonuses helped to stabilize the workforce, making it costly to leave a Michelin job of one's own volition. It was also the case that company-run health and social services, as well as on-site housing, contributed to the transformation of untrained rural labourers into model factory workers, keeping them reasonably comfortable and healthy, giving the men gardens to tend and their wives kitchens.

In the Michelin system, the company – personified in Edouard Michelin, the 'patron' – chose workers and office staff deemed worthy of shares, and determined the number of shares each deserved. 'This will be a model factory,' promised the first participation handbook in 1898, 'on the day that all workers become partners in the company and worthy of being so'. It was a way to hold on to one's best, and best-behaved, workers. To hold in the literal sense, for their bonuses were blocked until retirement or a given number of years after departure from the firm – voluntary or not – and then only if during that period the worker had not taken a job with a competing rubber company.[5]

Michelin workers, recruited as they were from remote villages of the rural Auvergne, were hardly likely to be confused with their brothers of the industrial north – descendants of the Communards, ancestors of the Communists, Socialists and Trotskyists, or anarchists of our time. From the earliest days the firm enjoyed a climate of relative serenity, and this right up to the mid-1930s and the Popular Front. If Edouard Michelin kept labour agitation far away from his door, the coddling of the most docile from the earliest days had much to do with that.

At the end of what was surely a landmark year for the Michelins, 1898, a writer for an elegantly printed weekly magazine published for makers and drivers of automobiles paid a call to Edouard Michelin, thereby providing one of the rare glimpses of the patron at work. There he was, 'the father of the tyre', on the factory grounds in Clermont-Ferrand, supervising the putting up of 'an enormous hangar which will cover the large courtyard known to drivers who have had tyres repaired here, and in which they may have admired four century-old elms'.

It was the writer's first visit to the plant in five years – and what a transformation! The great old trees were gone, replaced by sheds. The factory surface had been tripled, and was now to be doubled again – tangible evidence of the rapid development of the bicycle and motor-car industries. Michelin was about to float a bond issue. The visitor allowed himself an opinion (and one can guess that this was the reason he had been invited down to Clermont-Ferrand): investing in a firm that could produce 900 kilometres of tubes in a year could not be bad.[6]

The year 1898 was also the official birthday of Bibendum – that jolly fat man composed of a stack of tyres that has been the symbol of Michelin for a century. Although the matter of paternity has been disputed – which one of the Michelins conceived him, or was he simply the brainchild of an illustrator? – it is more than likely that both inspiration and execution were André Michelin's. (André even looked a bit like Bibendum, with his protruding belly – unlike his 'frugal' brother; he, after all, lived the grand life in Paris while Edouard patrolled the factory floor.)[7]

In a credible version of the birth of Bibendum, we have both brothers at the Michelin stand at the International and Colonial Fair in Lyon in 1894. The local Michelin man responsible for the stand had decorated it with stacks of tyres. André – or was it Edouard – could have remarked, standing before one of the stacks, 'If we added spectacles, a cigar, and two arms we'd have a funny character'.

Some time later, the illustrator Marius Rossillon, who signed his work O'Galop (in the eve of a long and successful career), showed André Michelin a poster he had done for a Munich brewery, but which had been turned down. The central figure was a stout man holding up a beer mug as he says 'Nunc est bibendum' – now is the time to drink, a phrase from an ode by Horace on the occasion of the defeat of Mark Antony by Octavian (who was to become the first Roman emperor, Augustus).

André had been talking for years about how Michelin tyres swallowed obstacles. Why not use O'Galop's poster, replacing the corpulent beer drinker with a stack of tyres?

The redrawn poster was ready in April 1898. Then a racing driver who happened not to know Latin saw André Michelin drive by and shouted, 'That's Bibendum – long live Bibendum!' From a slogan Bibendum became a personage – standing both for the fat tyre man and (to hear André Michelin tell it) for André himself.[8]

The poster worked. Bibendum began to appear everywhere. Sometimes André signed his newspaper columns with the name. The factory in Clermont-Ferrand was growing, seemingly doing everything right, and the same was happening at Michelin's Paris headquarters, which under André Michelin functioned with the energy of a well-oiled ministry of propaganda.

*   *   *

In the last decade of the nineteenth century, advertising was coming of age both in Europe and the United States, and by the time André Michelin began experimenting with new ways to throw the spotlight on the family company, there was already enough to say about earlier promotional campaigns to make it possible to compile a history of advertising.[9] Yet, in the annals of advertising (on either side of the Atlantic), there cannot be many other brand identifications that have lasted over a century. The little man made of stacked tyres seems as alive and alert as ever on recent Michelin promotional materials, posters, maps and guides. Bibendum stayed young because new generations of artists kept him so.

And those lively, easy-to-remember slogans – products of André's good-humoured imagination: Michelin drinks (or swallows) the obstacle, nunc est bibendum. Alongside them, the early slogans of that other international brand, Coca-Cola, a soft drink invented in 1886, seem pale: 'Delicious and refreshing' (1904), 'Coca-Cola Revives and Sustains' (1905), 'The Great National Temperance Drink' (1906).[10]

9

1900

In the bustle of André Michelin's domain on Boulevard Pereire – which served at once as Paris headquarters of the family firm and warehouse for tyre sales and repairs – the little red book published in the spring of 1900 may have seemed a minor affair. It was certainly dwarfed by the polychrome posters, the leaflets and the bold advertisements in newspapers and magazines. Soon there would also be picture postcards – then a fashionable way to show off one's product, or even one's factory; this new medium was much utilized by the Michelins in the early years. Alongside all these things, how much attention would be given to a little red book you could hold in the palm of one hand (or lose on a shelf)?

*   *   *

It had another peculiarity, this first *Guide Michelin*. It would only be picked up, could only be used by that small minority called motorists (and of course by cyclists). A poster might appear on a building wall, or inside a garage, an advertisement would be seen by thousands, even tens of thousands if the right newspaper printed it. In contrast, the Michelin guide was inconspicuous, disconcertingly so.

Yet somehow it found its readers. It helped that the little volume was given away for nothing. (It was free for the first 20 years of its existence, free – so runs the official legend – until the day André Michelin discovered that one of his dealers was using copies of the *Guide Michelin* as wedges under the legs of a table.)[1] The 1900 edition was easy to

44

handle (or to use as a wedge!), and for several years it would appear in the same format, fitting easily into a vest pocket.

And then André Michelin's candid appeal for help in correcting and perfecting the guides must have struck the right chord. Readers then and later were asked to confirm the exactitude of the guide-book's information; for example:

> a) I paid so much per person and by day; this price does not conform to that indicated in your guide by *, **, or ***.
>
> b) I was or was not satisfied in a certain hotel, where I paid so much a day. Give helpful details here.
>
> (Inform us especially of the presence of bed-bugs if you found any.)

André Michelin, who (we remember) went from engineering school to the map department of the Interior Ministry, would have been anxious to see less official-looking maps in the hands of his customers, maps more appropriate for leisure travel. At the time (as one discovers in the back pages of the *Guide Michelin* 1900) the best maps he could suggest were the official ones, notably that of the French Army (known as the General Staff map) on the scale of 1:80,000, requiring 274 sheets to cover France, and one he himself had worked on after leaving engineering school – the 1:100,000 map of the Interior Ministry, comprising no fewer than 587 sheets.

The first *Guide Michelin*, compared to those immediately following, was rudimentary; originality would come later. Already Baedeker and other guide-books were employing stars (asterisks in fact) to indicate recommended hotels or sights, while the first Michelins used them only to indicate price range. But maestro André Michelin demonstrated that he really meant what he said about making his guide-book better and better each year. As he had promised in 1900, the 1901 edition contained a new feature: 'Roads tedious and picturesque'. It also included a warning: don't search this guide-book for information about 'natural, artistic, or archaeological sights' – for many guide-books provided that sort of information. Regal Monsieur Michelin, obviously not wearing his Bibendum good-fellow smile, insisted, 'We wish to put in the Michelin Guide only that which can interest the driver, and which he cannot find elsewhere'.

This second edition contained a detachable questionnaire addressed to hotels and garages asking for details concerning their establishments, and in August 1901 André issued an appeal via the press for help in making the next edition better still: you are out on the road at night with a breakdown, regretting that your *Guide Michelin* does not mention a nearby hotel; you'll turn your vehicle over to a mechanic who will damage rather than fix it, while you, Madame, will 'introduce the marvels of your delicate body into a bed that the guide, poorly informed, has recommended and – horrors! – will jump out of it covered by those little brown beans as disagreeably smelly as canni-balistic'. So, Monsieur or Madame, it's in your interest that the guide be as accurate and complete as it can be. For if Michelin had to work only with its own resources it would take several years to produce 'an accurate and perfect guidebook'.

André Michelin's call for help was an early example of a form of publicity he may have invented – containing a question or announcing a competition, engaging the reader's participation, at the same time reminding them of the name and fame of Michelin. Each such message took the guise of a newspaper article, published in the same place and style as the news of the day (with nothing to indicate that it was paid advertising). For such messages André chose either the general or the specialized press.

André Michelin was not only an inventive, resourceful and cheeky publicist, he was also a defender of the faith. He never forgot that Michelin as it grew was contending with two formidable competitors, Dunlop in England and Continental in Germany, both of which were present on the French market. There was then no law against com-parative or even negative advertising. And in attacking his commercial adversaries, publicist André was well aware that he could make use of French patriotism against hereditary enemies – notably against Germans. So the eighteenth Michelin 'Monday', early in July 1901, revealed that several customers had written to question Michelin's par-ticipation in a Paris–Berlin automobile rally (Michelin had sponsored some of its prizes): 'Our excuse is simple: We arrived in Berlin as victors'. Each automobile as it turned up at the finish line was saluted by its national anthem, rendered by a German military band, hence La Marseillaise was played a dozen times. French victories in competition were going to lead to sales of French products in Germany.[2]

But a fortnight later André Michelin was charging the enemy once more. Michelin had written to the president of the German Automobile

Club, he reported in another Monday column, to complain that the Continental Tyre Company had interfered with the normal operations of Michelin, Panhard and Mors (predecessor of Citroën) during the Paris–Berlin rally, and had assigned more workers to each of the German vehicles than the rules allowed – besides carrying out acts of sabotage against French automobiles.[3]

The war with the English, which had begun years earlier in the courts when Dunlop claimed its patent rights on air-filled tyres, now continued in the market place. Dunlop could sell its tyres in France but Michelin could not penetrate the British market – and yet only Michelin made tyres suitable for heavier vehicles.

The pressure on Dunlop actually came from British car owners, via their automobile club, which warned that Dunlop's interference with the importation of Michelin tyres was slowing the development of British automobile use, and in the end Dunlop ceded. A British company – actually a Dunlop franchiser – would be allowed to import and sell Michelin tyres at prices comparable to those of Dunlop. It should be no surprise that the battle, with its victorious outcome, was reported in André Michelin's 'Mondays'.[4]

Keeping readers waiting became one of André Michelin's favourite tricks. A delay in publication of the 1902 guide provided another opportunity. Requests kept coming in for the previous year's guide, but all 52,800 copies had been given away, André told readers of his 'Monday' in mid-March. When the guide-book did appear – in the first half of May – readers found that it contained a large (24 inch square) detachable map of France. The 600-page volume itself now had a solid binding, which at the same time was 'more carefully conceived and more elegant'.[5]

The new Michelin contained over 100 small city maps. Good roads, difficult or arduous roads and pleasant or boring itineraries were clearly indicated. Another new feature was a list of surgeons available in the event of an accident. The guide-book also indicated bicycle paths and roads with shoulders and surfacing, as well as distances between towns. By now the remote, relatively peaceful Boulevard Pereire had a factory of sorts inside the head of André Michelin. One of his 'Mondays' in *L'Auto-Vélo*, addressed to garages and innkeepers, listed an impressive catalogue of advertising posters available for the asking, one of them ('The Michelin Tyre Drinks the Obstacle') measuring three-and-a-half by four-and-a-half feet designed for outdoor display, the others (20 by 13.5 inches) for indoor posting; automobilists and collectors could obtain them by mail for a modest sum.[6]

Indeed, André had found a way to have readers pay for advertising. Since the Michelin 'Mondays' contained useful tips for drivers, some readers had expressed the wish to receive them directly. Henceforth, subscriptions to the Monday edition of *L'Auto-Vélo* would be available at a reduced price...[7]

All the same, André knew when not to smile. At the beginning of December 1902 he made it known that Michelin would not be showing at the Bicycle and Automobile Show. Michelin had put considerable effort into that event in recent years, famously with that amusing merry-go-round allowing a comparison of the comfort of air-filled tyres to the bumpy rides without them. Only the previous year it employed a young lady dressed in a typical Auvergne costume as a demonstrator of tyre repairs. There would have been more surprises this year – had the exhibition management been more co-operative.

But Michelin had not only been refused the position it had had in the previous year, it was assigned to the basement, in the section for dealers in accessories. 'Bibendum's majesty deserves finer surroundings,' snapped André Michelin (who assured visitors to the show that they'd find Michelin men there all the same, based on the *Auto-Vélo* stand).[8]

> *   *   *

And then at last came the 1903 edition, 'waited for so impatiently by drivers and tourists'. It appeared only in June, because of the enormous quantity of information that had to be included. This time 60,500 copies were published. 'The success of our Guide exceeded our expectations,' began the unsigned preface, 'and one can say without exaggeration that one finds it nowadays in the hands of all drivers, and all over France'. The new volume showed the attention to detail which would make every successive edition a joy to hold and behold. The first section of the small book – André was still using the pocket-sized format – presented cities and towns significant enough to deserve a map, each map bearing conventional symbols to indicate the location of hotels, Michelin tyre suppliers, repair services, petrol stations and electrical stations (to charge batteries). And then post, telegraph and telephone offices, principal sights, tram lines. In smaller towns – 'the only ones about which one might have doubts' – symbols indicated the presence of doctors and pharmacies. Sights worth seeing were indicated – except when there were too many of them, in which case the guide-book simply said, 'numerous curiosities'. (A star – actually a printer's asterisk – singled out those most worthy of attention.)

Hotels also received stars – but only to indicate price range. A detachable questionnaire addressed to hotelkeepers asked whether they had 'modern toilets', defined as 'those equipped with a flush and a moveable seat, its walls decorated with tiles, maintained in strict cleanliness and always supplied with toilet paper'. Also: 'Do you have a darkroom for developing photographs?'

Much of the contents of this 672-page book sang the praises of Michelin products, but who could blame the brothers for wanting to get some of their own back? The products included the 'silent' brake shoe, and a new gadget called the renfort, which facilitated repairs of inner tubes. Note too that this edition contained advertising for automobiles, garages, and hotels. But the brothers showed remarkable restraint, for some of the hotels that advertised were not recommended in the accompanying text.

The Michelin guide was so good, it had to be copied. The guilty party was Michelin's arch-rival Continental, whose tyres were made in the land of the hereditary enemy, Germany. Already, publicist André had been agitated by Continental's claim to be a French company manufacturing tyres in France; the only thing Continental did at its Clichy headquarters, he said, was to receive shipments from Hanover.

But now they had been caught with their fingers in the jampot. For here, like a rabbit pulled out of a hat, was the first *Guide-Itinéraires Continental*, dated 1904, which seemed the mirror image of the *Guide Michelin*. 'Offered free to tourists driving an automobile,' the jacket announced. Little attempt had been made to disguise the similarities with Michelin – starting with the table of contents, which began with information about the company's tyres, and the use of asterisks to denote the price range for room and board (although Continental added a quality rating, grading hotels A, B or C depending on facilities). The chief difference was in the format – the Continental volume organ-ized by itineraries, which (in part because of repetition, since the same towns necessarily appeared in different itineraries) required a book of 1192 pages.

Each year Continental's guide-book became more like Michelin's. And the Michelins eventually took their case to court. The Continental editors had been blatant in their utilization of the famous original, and the evidence of plagiarism was conclusive. But then again how could the Michelins have lost against the Germans, in France?[9]

10

COMING
OF AGE

Michelin's boycott of the Bicycle and Automobile Show in December 1902 can be attributed to André Michelin's easily ruffled temper. It was also a sign of the Michelin company's strength. The brothers could afford to be absent from an event now so central to their industry precisely because (as André himself pointed out) they were present everywhere; they were the future.[1]

It is indeed remarkable, in those days before the coming of age of the automobile, that so many of its protagonists realized that they were witnesses to seminal change. 'Never have the turnstiles of the Grand Palais seen a busier two weeks; never have so many crowned heads, presidents and ministers demanded their right to an official tour of the stands,' the correspondent of the influential weekly *L'Illustration* told readers as the event drew to a close.

> From this first evidence we must draw the proper conclusion concerning the enormous prosperity of an industry born in France, the attraction that its manifestations hold for all classes of society despite the deep changes it will bring to our habits and the desire it inspires – still latent for the moment – to be one's own chauffeur. Our native intelligence has in the past five or six years undergone a significant transformation which likens it to American native intelligence.[2]

Boycott or no, Michelin was to share in the prosperity of 'this industry born in France'. Taxation records indicate that 5386 automobiles were produced in that country in 1901, of which 4427 were for private use, and there would be 9207 more in 1902 (7358 private); the figures for

the four following years were 12,984 (9922), 17,107 (12,519), 21,543
(15,011), 26,262 (17,358) – this last in 1906, when some 23,000
automobiles were manufactured in the United States.[3] That same year,
Michelin factory turnover soared to the equivalent of some 120 million
euros. By then the company had 3400 workers on the payroll (jump-
ing to 4000 the following year).[4]

As ever, the Michelins ran a tight ship. The company remained
a partnership, with liability limited to actual shares held. Then, as
now, there was only one boss, answering to the somewhat modest title
'manager'. As manager, or first among equals, Edouard kept 12 percent
of profits, the remainder being distributed among the other shareholders. Until it became obligatory, no publicity was given to the
company's balance sheet. It helped, in keeping secrets, that the firm
made little or no appeal to outside sources of financing. As long as the
size of the company allowed, and until its needs for fresh capital
became imperious, current operations and expansion were financed
out of profits.

It also helped that managerial jobs, to the extent possible, stayed
within the family. In the course of time, the sons of André and Edouard
would also find their places – suitably lofty places – in the family firm.[5]

One student of the family compared the Michelin dynasty to that
of the Rothschilds: 'The same allegiance of each member to the tribe,
the same allegiance of all to one'.[6]

At times the Michelin system proved cumbersome. Discretion
concerning family affairs obviously extended to factory operations;
surely no company has done as much to protect itself. This unwillingness to communicate to press and public, coupled with the well-known
secrecy clauses in employment contracts, perpetuated a climate of
mystery from generation to generation. And this climate was generally
blamed, especially by those on the outside, for rendering the company
even more vulnerable to rumours and negative criticism.[7] It is true
that from the outset Michelin did have avid and combative competitors.
In the early years its prosperity depended on being first with an improvement, such as better resistance, surer adherence to the road, easier
handling... Half a century after launching its first credible tyres,
Michelin would again catch the world by surprise with a totally new
concept for what had long since been taken as a commonplace object
– the radial tyre (the 'X'). A student of the Michelin saga saw it,

simply, as mystique. He noted the attention paid at Michelin to the architecture of the tyre, the way it was designed having far more to do with performance than the materials employed or their weight.[8] The perfect tyre came from the research department, from patient trial and error, testing on the track. And that of course is where a little secrecy helps.

*   *   *

But if architecture was Edouard's job down in Clermont-Ferrand, it was for André the engineer to make those tyres sing. He would do it with his souvenir postcards and other drum-beating, but most of all through those newspaper columns which he composed with evident pleasure, even when the dryness of the subject might have discouraged another writer.

Side by side with his technical explanations André offered drama, such as his commentary on the infamous Paris–Madrid automobile rally of 24 May 1903 – a competition interrupted by decree of the Interior Ministry at the end of the first day (the Paris–Bordeaux lap) because of the number of accidents causing death and serious injury due to excessive speed and inadequate policing of the route. One of the dead was Marcel Renault, brother of Louis Renault and co-founder of the legendary automobile company. Louis had also participated in the race, like his brother driving a light Renault car.[9]

In his column André Michelin chose to stress the fact that the race's victor, 'at the ferocious speed of 66 mph', had been riding on Michelins (as had the victors in earlier Paris–Berlin and Paris–Vienna races).

Indeed, of the first ten vehicles to reach Bordeaux, eight were equipped with Michelins. And precisely because Michelin was the hands-down winner, André felt that he could raise a delicate issue. Racing drivers should be choosing the tyre most likely to guarantee success; instead, they often chose second-best because rival tyre-makers paid contestants to use them. Clearly, money was being used to falsify the lessons that a race like Paris–Madrid could provide.[10]

That autumn the Automobile Show offered another opportunity for engineer André to display his word engineering – on the Michelin stand first of all. But if he found his own Michelin stand impressive, he pointed out that it is not what you say about your tyres, but what others say that counts, and in that year over 1400 wheels on display

5. M. Gavriel wins at Bordeaux on Michelin tyres in the Paris–Madrid race, 1903. Reproduced by kind permission of the Mary Evans Picture Library.

were equipped with Michelins (the runner-up had only 400); 68 car-makers showed only Michelin tyres.[11]

* * *

Then, in an angry column in 1904, engineer André cited examples of bicycle races in which nails had been deliberately placed along the route. Now for the first time the same thing had happened at an automobile rally, the Bastogne Circuit, an itinerary across the Belgian Ardennes. Here sharp pieces of flint as well as large nails had been strewn along the route. Two months after the race everybody still remembered the 'epidemic of nails,' as one eyewitness called it, but they forgot the cause – a deliberate attempt to hurt Michelin. André urged that automobile clubs organize their own patrols, prepared to haul saboteurs into police stations.[12]

When he was happy, André did not hesitate to tell the world that too. At the end of 1904 he placed a large advertisement in the automobile press: O'Galop's Bibendum smokes a fat cigar as he stands proudly astride the continents – the United States beneath his right foot, Western Europe beneath the left – holding (or juggling with) the trophies he had won that year; Michelin tyres had indeed equipped winners of all the important races – including the Rothschild Cup, the Gordon Bennett Cup, the Italian Cup, the Vanderbilt Cup ... 'Le Cup Trust,' announced the headline.[13]

* * *

Still, his masterpiece was the *Guide Michelin*. Each new edition was a *tour de force*, requiring painstaking checking, updating, and the introduction of new features. If man does not live by bread alone, drivers cannot live on open roads either; they need a roof over their heads at night and precise indications of where to go in the event of a breakdown. 'Fortunately,' engineer André boasted (after publication of the fourth edition in 1903), 'these days there isn't a driver around who would want to travel without having a Michelin Guide handy'.[14]

The fifth edition of the guide, published at the beginning of June 1904, once again placed information about tyres up front; one quickly learned where they could be obtained, how much they cost. Of course the main section of the volume was an alphabetical listing of cities and towns possessing at least one good hotel, repair shop, or simply a petrol station. For the hundred or so most significant towns, listed separately, maps showed where to find essential facilities.

André's presentation of the new edition in the press was modest; he begged for 'everybody's collaboration, for no matter how much care has gone into preparation of this work, there is so much data in it that errors and omissions are always possible'.[15]

That year André Michelin tried something new. He went back to press with the 1904 edition, but this time ordered better quality paper, an elegant binding, and extra-wide margins leaving ample room along-side the text. One or more copies of the wide-margin edition went to hotels mentioned in the guide, accompanied by an invitation to motorists to use the wide margins for corrections, observations and criticism. Hotelkeepers had agreed to place the special edition where it could be seen (and if it could not be seen, users were invited to demand it). There was also a warning: in order to avoid false or ill-intentioned corrections, Michelin would take notice only of those which were followed by a signature and address.

One hotelkeeper, who happened to be the director of the Grand Hotel in Vichy, was delighted by Michelin's initiative. 'As for me, I'm a great admirer of your Guide,' he explained, 'although repelled by any other kind of promotion, for the hotel gets its name from the way it looks and is run. So I'll be happy to take on your new edition, and even have a special stand made, placed where everybody can see it.'[16]

Thanks to André Michelin, the tyres manufactured with loving care by his younger brother in remote, rude Clermont-Ferrand were now used everywhere, the name Michelin on the tongue of every auto-mobile owner, not to forget the designers and the manufacturers. And when Edouard came forward with a truly new product, the publicity machine kept well oiled by André was ready to run with it.

The product was the flat-tread tyre, billed as skidproof. Until then, tyres – Michelin's and everybody else's – were round and smooth where they touched the ground. The new tyre, whose tread consisted of a strip of leather reinforced with tiny steel rivets, promised to give the motorist more control. And while the name was not everything, the new tyre got one to be remembered, 'la semelle' (literally, shoe sole). 'Everybody wants the SEMELLE MICHELIN' – so boasted one of André Michelin's advertisements in 1905.

To prove it, he reproduced a telegram received from Michelin's office in Frankfurt, Germany. Their Berlin dealer had just telephoned, requesting urgent delivery of a set of tyres for Kaiser Wilhelm II, then residing at his Renaissance lake castle at Glücksburg.[17]

Somehow André Michelin, usually prompt to tweak the nose of his detested German rival Continental, did not bother this time.

11

FRIEND OF
THE PEOPLE

Not all the news could be good. Rapid development called for equally rapid expansion of the labourforce, leaving less time for Edouard Michelin to handpick the surest workers, those most likely to accept the Michelin management style with docility. For the Patron, now a ripe 45 years of age, there were going to be fewer opportunities for face-to-face dialogue with individual factory hands. Henceforth he was obliged to delegate most contacts with personnel to a buffer force of supervisors and shop stewards.

Yet for a long time to come Edouard took full advantage of the make-up of his labourforce, drawn for the most part from the Auvergne's rural hinterland, one-time farmhands willing to accept lower-than-average wages (after all, they began as unskilled migrants, and learned by doing). And although profit-sharing was already a Michelin principle, the company had only begun to introduce the system of health and social benefits that were to make it a casebook study of paternalism, against which militant workers would eventually revolt.

Yet there were minor outbursts even at the beginning. The first came as early as November 1904, when personnel in a strategic department – tyre stamping – staged a work stoppage to protest new pay rules. For they now risked a fine for every tyre found to be unusable – something that depended on circumstances they could not control. They also demanded a rise in the hourly wage in view of their 'extenuating work, which consists of manipulating and opening scalding moulds weighing 250 and even 350 kilograms from which emerge insupportable odours capable of suffocating the sturdiest of workmen...'.

Michelin management in response pointed out that bonuses were awarded for difficult jobs. But the protesters called for a fixed hourly wage 'appropriate to the heavy task demanded of them'. The revolt fizzled out after a meeting with Edouard Michelin himself, followed by the dismissal of seven alleged anarchists.[1]

By chance, the infinite minority of Michelin militants had now found a voice outside the tight confines of the factory grounds. Clermont had given birth to one of France's most original political journalists, the independent Socialist Alexandre Varenne, then 34 years old, who in autumn 1904 was to launch a local labour weekly *L'Ami du Peuple* ('friend of the people'). Later, following the First World War, he would publish a regional daily newspaper no less independent, *La Montagne* ('the mountain'), which not only survived its founder but continues to serve Clermont-Ferrand and its region today.

Varenne and Michelin seemed to have been created for each other – one the fighter for just causes, the other experimenting with ways and means to create a modern industrial empire. In another place, perhaps, nascent labour unrest in a modern factory might have gone unreported. But now *L'Ami du Peuple* was there, establishing a link between the most socially conscious of Auvergnats.

At the start of their lifelong feud Varenne chose to deal with Patron Michelin in a series of reports on 'Our Industrial Penal Colonies'. Thus, in late November 1904 he reported the firing of three Michelin workers who had joined the rubber-workers' union. They had been denounced by one of the company's spies, the reporter declared. More recently still, a husband and wife who both worked for Michelin were fired; when the husband asked why he was told, 'Mr. Michelin made use of his right to hire or to fire whomever he wishes'. In fact, the husband was a member of the union and had attended the meeting of local rubber-workers (with some 300 other members) only a few days earlier.

The same issue published what Varenne's reporter called a masterpiece, the contract that new Michelin employees were expected to sign:

> Between Mr. Edouard-Etienne Michelin, manufacturer, acting in the name
> and as manager of the limited shareholding partnership Michelin & Co,

whose seat is at Place des Carmes-Déchaux, Clermont-Ferrand, on one side, and X, on the other, the following has been decided:

1. Mr. X undertakes to give all his time and activity to the company; he recognizes and declares that before entering the House of Michelin & Co he never worked with rubber and knows nothing about how it is made. He also understands that the disclosure of the manufacturing processes of Michelin & Co, of their mix of substances, their appliances, tools or machines…would be of a nature to cause them considerable harm.

2. In consequence, he undertakes to remain silent with everyone about everything he sees or learns during his tenure in the factory, to take or to carry off no notes or documents concerning the industrial or commercial operations of Michelin & Co and to give no information about these matters to anyone during or after his stay in the factory.

3. He undertakes, in addition, in the event he resigns from Michelin & Co, to accept either in France or abroad in the three years following his departure, whether he has left of his own accord or the company ceases to employ him, and no matter how long he worked here, any collaboration either by working or imparting advice or investing capital, in any establishment performing all or some of the operations or work now carried out by Michelin or that it will undertake in future, or in an establishment making machines for the purpose of carrying out such work or operations.

In the next clause, the worker agrees that since he has committed all his time and labour to Michelin, any inventions or improvements that he contributes belong to the company. In the three years following his departure, the worker must not file a patent connected with the rubber industry or based on what he learned as an employee, or concerning articles that would compete with those made by Michelin. And should Mr. X violate any of these rules, he must pay Michelin a minimum of 2000 francs, and lose his gains from profit-sharing. Furthermore, Michelin would then be able to claim ownership of patents taken out by the employee.

The new employee would receive an hourly wage, plus a profit-sharing bonus based on dividends paid to Michelin shareholders.

'With this contract,' concluded *L'Ami du Peuple*, 'the profit-sharers of the Michelin factory are less free than the blacks of central Africa who harvest the rubber'.[2]

Varenne's paper pursued the offensive the following week, reporting the uncovering and dismissal of more union members. 'Mr. Michelin is an excellent marksman; all his shots strike home,' said the reporter with irony. 'It even happens, as in one of his recent hunts, that the same shot kills a number of victims.' *L'Ami du Peuple* characterized Michelin as a feudal lord who 'would feel he'd lost a day if he didn't fire a union member or a worker thought to be one'.

An incident is described in which another couple was fired, the man because he was a member of the union although night work at the plant had prevented him from attending a union meeting, his wife because she had attended the meeting although not a member of the union. They had been denounced by a company spy – a fellow union member who had been at the meeting. 'And this is certainly only the beginning, since faced with dismissal many people of good conscience can turn to the shameful job of spying.'

A week after publishing the Michelin contract for new employees, Varenne's paper reproduced what it said were company regulations, in effect the rules governing profit-sharing, which also explained how an employee could lose rights and money. For the worker's share was to be considered a 'donation' from management, provided that the employee not go to work for a competitor within three years of leaving Michelin. 'If the profit-sharer violates this stipulation the donation will be cancelled and all sums will revert to the company.' To make sure the stipulation was respected, Michelin would hold on to the retirement fund during the three years following the worker's separation from the company, and release it only if the employee did not violate the rules.

If those eligible for profit-sharing were handpicked by management, it was because they were the best workers, declared Article 6 of the rules. Further,

> The title of profit-sharer implying serious qualities in those who have obtained it, no profit-sharer can be discharged except by decision of Mr Michelin and following discussion with him. In case of a reduction in personnel, profit-sharers will be the last to go. Profit-sharers being part of the company, they can always be received in private by Mr Michelin to inform him of what they judge useful in the interests of the company.[3]

Without a doubt, Edouard Michelin saw himself in the avant-garde of managers, he who had conceived the ideal marriage of capital and labour, and a system that would work to the benefit of both employer and employees. Clearly, his chief concerns were the protection of company secrets – this at a time when Michelin was ahead in creativity and knew it had to keep that lead or fall by the wayside – and maintenance of a stable workforce. Undoubtedly he would have read the attacks in Alexandre Varenne's crusading weekly with astonishment.

Soon after that, *L'Ami du Peuple* published a letter attributed to a group of former Michelin workers, written to encourage Varenne's weekly to pursue its campaign. 'It will be easy for you to prove that the Michelin company, which until now was believed to be a model factory, is only a den of injustice and maliciousness, and where all the principles of humanity are transgressed, not to forget the law.'[4]

It remained for Alexandre Varenne himself to take up his pen on New Year's Day 1905, with an angry editorial summing up his case against Edouard Michelin. 'In the Michelin factory...the Chief thinks that he can abolish the laws guaranteeing freedom of the citizenry as well as those laws that give workers freedom to organize,' he began. 'Then he should stop trying to fool us. If he is ferocious, let him be it frankly. If he wants to be absolute master, let him not disguise his authoritarianism as philanthropy.'[5]

Edouard Michelin, whose motivations for sharing in the company's prosperity surely contained a mix of genuine social consciousness and a need for industrial peace, was only at the beginning of a programme of assistance to his personnel, in the factory and at home. He would continue to believe that he had found the right way to run a modern enterprise, and this as long as he lived.

And as long as he lived, he would be harassed, both inside the factory and out, by doubters who believed that a company should not own that much of its workers, even if it gave them the peace and security they could not find anywhere else.

12

EXPORTING THE MICHELIN WAY

So much of the Michelin story defies belief. The rapidity with which this company hidden among the volcanic hills of remote central France became an international brand, for example. The answer, of course, was peerless product. In the first decade of the twentieth century, Michelin tyres were already being exported to the homeland of Dunlop, the homeland of Continental, the homeland of Pirelli – traditional rivals all. Michelin's sales in Britain were important enough to justify the establishment of the Michelin Tyre Company there in 1905, taking over from an existing sales organization and depot (by then Britain possessed 74,000 motor vehicles). In Germany Michelin distribution was the responsibility of the Deutsche Michelin-Pneumatik Aktiengesellschaft in Frankfurt-am-Main. It seemed to make sense to manufacture Michelin tyres in Italy rather than export them from France, so a proper tyre-making plant was built in Turin, not far from the still young and growing Fiat Company, whose automobiles it would equip.[1]

And where the tyres went, there went André Michelin's wizardry. An early poster for British Michelin, drawn by O'Galop, shows 'Sir Bibendum' equipped with knight's helmet and shield, above the slogan, 'My strength is as the strength of ten, Because my *rubber*'s pure. Tennyson.'[2] Often the same poster could serve in different markets, as in 1905, when a Panhard & Levassor motorcar equipped by Michelin whipped from Paris to Calais and back – some 370 miles – in six hours and 50 minutes, thereby beating what was then

6. 'Rail vanquished by Michelin tyres'. Advertisement in *Le Rire*, 11 November 1905. Reproduced by kind permission of the Mary Evans Picture Library.

the world's fastest railway train. And providing Michelin with an unbeatable subject: 'The Rail Vanquished by Michelin Tyres,' so British Michelin's poster had it, showing racers in an open motorcar swerving round a bend in the road, with a chugging locomotive in the background.[3]

Another early poster, placing a Michelin tyre at the summit of a mountain as competing tyres roll back down the slope ('Michelin on Top', a reference to automobile racing victories in 1905), utilized American English – 'tire' rather than the British 'tyre' – with American and French flags waving in the breeze at the peak. It clearly indicated Michelin's incipient sales efforts in the United States.[4]

*   *   *

The time came for guide-books to become attuned to export strategy. But while André Michelin's advertising leaped over oceans, the first foreign counterpart of the *Guide Michelin* was to follow surface roads travelled by French motorists. So in 1904 there was a first *Guide pour la Belgique*, only incidentally including Belgium's larger neighbour, the Netherlands, with Luxembourg, Alsace-Lorraine (German since the Franco–Prussian War of 1870–71) and even the Rhine river valley. In 1905 the 800-page *Guide Michelin* for France annexed French Algeria and French-protected Tunisia. The announced print run of 60,000 copies continued to be distributed free of charge.[5]

By now, André Michelin's system for collecting and checking data for use in the French guide-book had become routine, and his taste for precision, wedded to his experience in cartography, guaranteed that fact would rule over fancy. He had learned, in constructing his French guide-book, how to make use of Michelin's travelling salesmen, as well as regional and local tyre distributors and dealers. For these first guide-books to neighbouring countries he would have to begin the same way. He could enlist salesmen who also crossed frontiers, and, increasingly, staffs of foreign Michelin companies and local dealers, not to forget foreign map and survey services.

Thus, in July 1908 a guide-book was launched for Switzerland, another country sharing a border with France; it included an atlas and 16 city maps. By 1907 Algeria and Tunisia were given a volume of their own. Then in 1908, Algeria, Tunisia, Egypt and Corsica were united in the *Guide Méditerranée*.

Another innovation in 1908 was an English edition of the guide for France; in fact only the introductory sections on Michelin tyres and 'How to Use the Guide' had been 'Englished'.[6] In 1910 the indefatigable team on Boulevard Pereire had added guide-books for Spain and Portugal (in one volume) and Germany (this last a German-language edition including Switzerland).[7]

Automobile racing was also bursting through national fences. In 1905, Michelin tyres equipped the winner of a Brescia competition, in 1906 the Targa Florio and the Coupe d'Or de Milan.[8] But Michelin's promotional resources obviously worked best when the event was French, and in 1905 the Coupe Gordon-Bennett seemed the answer to a prayer. The trophy had been established five years earlier by American press lord James Gordon Bennett, son of the founder of the *New York Herald*, who built up the circulation of his newspapers by financing news-making events such as the African expedition of Henry M. Stanley (to find explorer David Livingstone, discoverer of Victoria Falls).

7. The Gordon Bennett race, 1905. Circuit Michelin, descent and bends in the Bois de Bourg-Lastic, Auvergne. Courtesy of the Archives Départementales du Puy-de-Dôme.

In 1904 the Coupe Gordon-Bennett had been routed through Germany's Taunus mountains. Now the Michelins were going to bring it to their very own turf – the Auvergne. Here was an opportunity to call attention to the beauties of their province, but also to build up suspense – by echoing fears that the route chosen was dangerous. 'It is certain that by its very nature the itinerary is difficult,' conceded André Michelin in one of his Monday columns. 'On this route some 85 miles long there are nearly symmetrical passes each 3300 feet high, and another point is as low as 1400 feet; the difference in altitudes is sufficient to confirm the existence of rather steep climbs and descents.' But if the Circuit d'Auvergne is rough, 'it's all the more interesting'.[9]

It certainly turned out to be an interesting race for Michelin. The first four automobiles to cross the finish line were equipped with Michelin tyres – an indisputable if expected success, celebrated in O'Galop drawings of a triumphant Bibendum; in one of them he is seated outside a tavern, holding a bottle marked 'Obstacle', as two stunned and emaciated comic figures – representing rival makes of tyre – sprawl collapsed on the ground.[10]

André was quick to draw the 'lessons' of the Auvergne circuit. In past races the practice had been to choose itineraries that were not too difficult, with as many straight lines as possible to permit good average speeds – but that told you nothing about the value of the tyres, for just about any brand could get one of its cars through the race without the need to change tyres along the way. 'That was the error,' wrote André the Monday following the victory. For when the Michelin people had suggested the Auvergne it was clear that no tyre – not even a tyre made by Michelin – would make it to the end. 'The soil of the Auvergne is a grate.'

That was precisely the point: 'We wanted such an itinerary precisely to be able to compare the resistance of different tyres'. André concluded with the judgment of car-maker Henri Brasier: 'One doesn't have to say that Michelin is the best, but admit that it's always the least bad'.

'We never wished for more praise than this,' commented André, whatever he may really have been thinking.[11]

Racing did what it was vaunted for doing: it motivated, inspired innovation. Under new rules, racing drivers had to do their own repairs, with no assistance from their support teams. That did a lot for the Michelin innovation of 1906, removable rims – baptized the 'Miracle Rim'.[12]

But one did not have to take Michelin's word for the advance represented by the new equipment. In a feature article in *L'Illustration*, which summed up lessons learned during the French Automobile Club's grand prize competition in June 1906, the writer spelled it out: 'Among vehicles more or less equal, driven by chauffeurs of similar qualifications, the winners owed their victory in large part to a recent improvement, not in tyres themselves, but in the mounting of tyres'. Thanks to the innovation, it now took three minutes to change a tyre – rather than a quarter of an hour. Readers were shown a cross-section of a wheel with the new Michelin rim, and a photograph of the winning driver changing one (to which a Michelin tyre was attached, of course).[13]

By the time the Salon de l'Automobile opened its doors that December, so a writer on the new automobile culture wrote in *L'Illustration*, every automobile had to be equipped with detachable rims.[14] Truly a triumph for Clermont-Ferrand.

That autumn the feisty journalist-statesman Georges Clemenceau, who was to mark his time in politics and in war, received his first appointment as prime minister. Leaving a conference room to confront the press, he announced with confidence: 'My cabinet has been formed. Like the well-known tyre, I drink the obstacle!'[15]

*   *   *

8. Winner of the French Automobile Club's grand prix competition of June 1906, illustrating Michelin's revolutionary 'Miracle Rim'. From *L'Illustration*, 7 July 1906. Reproduced by kind permission of the Mary Evans Picture Library.

It is no surprise that Michelin saw itself at the centre of the automobile age. Never content to let others speak for him, André Michelin now created the company's most impressive advertisement to date, a large-format illustrated booklet called *L'Automobile et le pneumatique en 1905*, at once a panegyric to travel by road, and an insistent reminder that the way to go was with Michelin.[16] 'All the vehicles shown in this booklet are mounted on Michelin tyres,' we learn – as if it could have been any other way. That included military vehicles, baby carriages, bicycles, delivery trucks and buses, as well as automobiles transporting King Edward VII of Britain, Kaiser Wilhelm II of Germany (in a Fiat equipped with Michelin Semelle tyres), Léopold II, King of the Belgians, the Russian czar Nicolas II, Spain's King Alphonse XIII, the queens of Italy and of Holland and more.

The celebratory volume would not be complete without a page or two about Michelin guide-books. In 1905, 60,300 copies of the French guide had been distributed free of charge. Using a comparison that would be repeated often, André calculated that so many books, each about an inch thick, if piled up would equal five Eiffel Towers – one atop the other. A drawing depicted Bibendum holding a measuring rod in one hand, and the pile of Eiffel Towers in the other.

Published in 1906, ostensibly to commemorate the year 1905, the booklet announced something new for 1907 – a freshening up of Michelin guide-books, with new maps in colour on a scale of 1:1,000,000, so that each page would show a section extending about 100 by 100 miles. These were among the first products of André Michelin's own cartography department, a departure from the classic Interior Ministry maps on which Michelin guide-books had depended until then.

In André's new maps, wide roads would be marked with a double line whether they were local or national highways, the point being to let drivers know what to expect. There were more and better suggested itineraries and revised indications of distances between destinations.

Henceforth the tourist information department of which André was so proud was thrown open to the public, equipped to deal with questions concerning itineraries, distributing pamphlets produced by local tourist offices and regional automobile clubs.

Soon Michelin could propose a whole gamut of tourist maps, distributed both in Clermont-Ferrand and at the Boulevard Pereire. The

1:1,000,000 four-colour map of France, launched as part of the *Guide France*, could be purchased in four sheets. More important, a new series of maps of France in 47 sheets on a more readable 1:200,000 scale was in progress; the first, on the Clermont-Ferrand region was being given away free. Maps of the Marseille-Nice region and the surroundings of Paris were on the press, with five more in preparation, and a leather case to contain them could be purchased separately.[17]

A visitor to the Paris Automobile Show in December 1907 was surprised to find no tyres at all at the Michelin stand – only some of the new accessories, such as a small air pump for quick repairs. 'Michelin, which always knows how to strike the imagination of the public,' noted a reporter for the austere professional journal of the rubber industry, 'had placed an enormous Bibendum on its ground-floor stand at the Grand Palais. A pump inflated it irregularly, producing amusing gestures that drew storms of laughter.'[18]

*   *   *

Not all the news was good. Automobile driving remained a sport, and the sport of an elite, and it was inevitable that the point would come when that sporting elite, feeling itself adequately equipped, would shop less often. France was now exporting half of its motorcar production, but meeting a formidable competitor in that industrial giant across the seas. In 1907, when France entered into a momentary economic slow-down, there were an estimated 143,200 registered automobiles in the United States, 63,500 in the United Kingdom and 40,000 in France (re-presenting, respectively 608, 640, and 981 inhabitants per automobile).[19]

Still, perhaps the best tyres you could get for your car, French, British or American, were Michelins, and soon enough Americans would be able to buy them from the company's own factory in Milltown, New Jersey. Michelin set up a company there in March 1907, with a capital of three million dollars and a factory manager imported from Clermont-Ferrand; the plan was to turn out 1500 tyres a day.[20]

Edouard himself crossed the ocean for the event. He sponsored a dinner at the swish Café Beaux Arts in New York to announce his intentions. 'We came to the United States,' he began, in stiff English but a no-nonsense business language his select audience would certainly comprehend, 'because notwithstanding the fact that we have to pay an enormous duty, we sell here a large quantity of tyres'.

'What is the reason of the vogue of the Michelin tyres?' he asked.

My opinion is that American roads are very trying for the tyres. We have always set our minds to make the best possible tyre or 'the least worse' and have always noticed that the harder the strain on tyres was, the more the Michelin tyres were appreciated.

Our French and American factories will compete, good-naturedly, and this competition will be very useful to the progress of tyres. I am rather at a loss to say which one will overcome the other in popularity, but I think the French ingenuity and American brains will prove a great success.[21]

Now begins one of the most fascinating of all the true stories in the Michelin saga. It is the story of how a stubbornly provincial manufacturer from the Auvergne became so convinced that America signified the future that it attempted to transplant Michelin methods, Michelin people and even the Michelin way of life to a small town on the other side of the Atlantic Ocean.

There was sufficient reason to select this particular small town, Milltown, in the smallish state of New Jersey; Milltown, with a population dominated by hard-working German immigrants, was already a factory town and rubber happened to be its most important product. Until then, the biggest company in the field had been the Meyer Rubber Company, founded in the 1840s by Christopher Meyer on the Lawrence Brook, which crosses the town from east to west, and which made everything from shoes to pontoon bridges and boats; in its best days it had employed some 600 persons. Meyer ceded its place to an India Rubber Company, which was replaced by an International Rubber Company – the corporate name at the time Michelin arrived in town. The French company took over the existing plant, expanded the main factory and added new buildings.

To run the Michelin Tyre Company Edouard Michelin had dispatched Jules Hauvette, one of the six children of his sister Marie; a local man, one Harry R.B. Meyers, was taken on as industrial manager. The new company made tyres and tubes the Michelin way, including low-pressure balloon tyres after the company introduced them in France in 1923. But while all Michelin factories, wherever they were, turned out an identical product, Milltown was to innovate with the first Michelin Universal Tread, similar to the company's racing tyre (the tread consisted of a series of Ms whose outer surfaces were flat).[22] There was also considerable testing activity on factory grounds, and townspeople were impressed by the ubiquitous company cars that covered the whole state of New Jersey (and one would guess, went considerably beyond it).

In the best years Michelin employed some 2000 workers – male and female. Many of them were local people, of course, but in its fashion Michelin also shipped over reliable foremen from Clermont-Ferrand – their families too. So Milltown itself became a little French, and as soon streets were opened and paved they were given the names of celebrated Frenchmen; soon there was a church called Our Lady of Lourdes.[23] Just ten years after its incorporation, a report on Michelin's American operations noted that the factory grounds then comprised 22 separate buildings covering 'many acres' of surface – all the more impressive in an accompanying photograph showing the sprawling plant and its own waterfront reflection.

With expansion, Michelin imported another tradition – company housing, beginning with 50 bungalows and eventually managing over 200 such units. Each cedar-shingled and slate-roofed bungalow contained four rooms, equipped with modern comforts, and were rented to workers 'practically at cost'.[24] It was a company town in the 'best' sense of the word, so a local historian heard from old-timers who remembered the Michelin years, its paternal influence extending from social and sports activities to religion. The French influence was there all right, but it was also a very American factory town. Already in 1917 the Michelin Athletic Association possessed its own grounds, including a quarter-mile track, a baseball diamond, soccer field, tennis courts, and a grandstand seating 1500. By then Michelin had organized a gun club (also known as a trap shooting department) and quickly won members, who competed with other such clubs in the county.[25]

But Bibendum was omnipresent. The roly-poly man of tyres appeared on company cheques and stationery, even on the heads of thumbtacks; there were Bibendum balloons for parades, three-foot replicas for window displays. Apparently the best-remembered Bibendum was the one painted on the side of the Community House to advertise the Michelin cafeteria. 'It was,' the historian recorded, 'a picture of the tyre man with a chef's hat on, pot and spoon in hand, cooking at a stove'.[26]

Still, the real competition in what was now and forever the world's biggest market was coming from American-made tyres, made the

American and not the Auvergnat way. Edouard Michelin's ingenuity confronted an advanced technological civilization and the phenomenon of mass production. He would have to learn to live with, eventually to copy, the American way. It would take a number of decades, a failure and a second try before his successors learned how to do that.

13

ROOM AT
THE TOP

As if the Michelins did not have enough on their hands making tyres that could sip, swallow or quaff obstacles along the surface roads of Europe and America – in no time at all they were up in the air.

André Michelin had long believed in the practicality of flight, as a novice ballooner a dozen years earlier, later an ardent advocate of heavier-than-air craft. It was as if his preoccupation with lowly tyres turned his thoughts upward. That the interests of the family rubber company might be furthered by the proliferation of aerostats with rubber envelopes, and aircraft making use of rubber in fuselages, as well as tyres would have been a consideration – but it still took vision to begin when the Michelins began.[1]

Just to get a manned aircraft into the air and to keep it there was an achievement then. A true pioneer, pilot Henri Farman, had broken the previous world record with a flight of one kilometre on 13 January 1908. On 6 March the Michelin brothers stepped in, with a letter to the Aéro-Club de France offering to sponsor the next great adventures in the sky. 'Wishing to contribute to the development of aviation,' the letter began, 'this new industry which – like so many others – was born in France, we are happy to offer a Cup and a Special Prize for heavier-than-air flying machines'.

The cup itself was conceived to be an *objet d'art* worth at least 10,000 francs, with a 15,000-franc cash prize (some 44,000 present-day euros), which the brothers would contribute each year for the next

10 years. The winning pilot would have to fly a distance – on a course determined by the French Aéro-Club or a foreign club affiliated to it – at least double that of the winner of the previous year's prize.

In any year without a victor, the 15,000 francs would be added to the following year's award. As for the cup, it would pass from hand to hand, remaining the property of the winner in the tenth year.

The second challenge required somewhat more explanation. Even the Michelins in their letter qualified it as a 'Special Prize (eventually)'. Between then and 1 January 1918 – that was ten years away – the winning pilot, in a two-seater aircraft with a passenger, would have to follow a very particular route. Taking off from any point in the Paris region, he would circle the Arc de Triomphe, then fly south to circle the cathedral of Clermont-Ferrand before landing on the summit of the Puy-de-Dôme (at an altitude of 4800 feet). The flying time between the Arc de Triomphe and the Puy-de-Dôme was not to exceed six hours. (On the ground, according to the 1908 *Guide Michelin*, the distance between Paris and Clermont-Ferrand was some 235 miles.)

Obviously the cash prize of 100,000 francs – over 292,000 euros today – seemed well out of reach.[2]

*   *   *

It was as if the Puy-de-Dôme summit were a form of exorcism for the brothers, who could never, in Clermont-Ferrand – whether at home, in the office or the factory – escape its ascendancy. For the rest of the world, the very idea of proposing a flight to the distant Auvergne seemed a bit mad. At this distance we can only know how that world reacted from surviving press clippings. At least one daily newspaper chose to take the whole thing lightly. 'In establishing this trial, our great national rubberman seems to be a straight-faced wag,' wrote an editorialist in *L'Aurore*, clearly hostile to the proposal. 'This first demonstration of his humour should get him elected unanimously to the honorary presidency of the deadpan fraternity…'[3]

L'Illustration, which had watched the progress of the Michelins with benevolence until now, was more severe. 'I persist in thinking,' wrote Henri Levedan (novelist, dramatist, French Academician),

> that heroes deserve protection from their own and their neighbour's heroism. If tomorrow an American billionaire had the silly idea of offering a prize of two million for the aviator who flew over the poles or rose to 30,000 feet,

I maintain that he'd be committing a stupid and criminal act...In other words, our aviators must not become gladiators.[4]

Then there were the things that were said and not written. 'Jokers! They're announcing a prize they'll never have to pay out. It'll take fifty years to achieve that kind of exploit!'[5]

It was to reply to the sceptics – sceptics including customers who wrote to say that the Michelins could better spend their time figuring out how to make tyres that would not burst or collapse so often – that André took up his pen to publish another of the columns only he knew how to write. If the Michelins were committing a total of 260,000 francs to prizes, he said, it was so that customers would eventually save money on their tyres.

Let him explain. Aeroplane motors were already considerably lighter than the engines built for automobiles. Michelin had been saying for years that weight had more effect on the life of a tyre than speed. In his writings engineer André had been crusading for a reduction in the weight of the chassis and every other component of the automobile. In time and thanks to experimental aircraft, manufacturers would also be getting lighter motors. 'We said from the outset [concluded André Michelin], that we invited pilots to circle the Arc de Triomphe and then fly 235 miles to alight delicately on the Puy-de-Dôme like a butterfly on a flower, so that one day we'd be able to reduce our TYRE bills by 50%.'[6] But the cards were dealt now, bets placed. The year 1908 would see a succession of broken records – Farman again, doubling his achievement with two kilometres flown on 21 March, then challenger Léon Delagrange with 3.9 kilometres, and Farman with 19 kilometres. On 5 September Wilbur Wright, the already famous American pilot – brother of Orville, who accomplished the very first mechanical flight in North Carolina five years earlier – kept his craft in the air over a distance of 22 kilometres, overtaken two days later by Delagrange with 24.7 kilometres.

Wright, who was in France to build and demonstrate a prototype of the plane he and his brother had invented, with the hopes of selling French patent rights to a group of investors, tried again for the Michelin Cup, and moved ahead with 66.6 kilometres, officially clocked on 21 September, and 99 kilometres on 19 December. Then, on the last day of the year, within the deadline for the first Michelin Cup, Wilbur flew another 124.7 kilometres – about 78 miles – of which 123.2

kilometres counted for the prize.[7] That night André Michelin called at the daily *Les Sports* to hear the latest news, and to leave a message to be conveyed to Wright. 'We are at once proud and happy to see a name that one day will be inscribed in the history of humanity, inscribed on the Michelin Cup.'

In truth, commented the editor of *Les Sports*, Wright certainly flew a total of 150 kilometres on that record-smashing flight. And that represented nearly half the distance to the Puy-de-Dôme. So that other Michelin prize was not so far-fetched after all.[8]

The sculptor selected to design the coupe took as his model a Farman aeroplane; that obviously would not go for Wilbur Wright. He would get his cheque from the hands of André Michelin at a lunch at the Aéro-Club on 12 January 1909, but he'd have to wait a while longer for a more appropriate trophy.[9]

*   *   *

A busy year for the man who made words, not tyres (André Michelin). But preparations for the new guide – in its attractive elongated format – had not been neglected. The editor began calling for information from motorists at the end of February, which was more or less when he would have been giving final touches to the prize announcement. The French, he reminded French readers, used not to travel in France; they thought of their country as the most beautiful in the world but let foreigners take the trouble to verify the fact. Instead, they'd make expensive trips to classic and sunnier lands.

The automobile had changed all that, but road travel did require initiative on the traveller's part, and Michelin was there to help. 'If automobiles revived travel by road, the Michelin Guide has been, for all who use it, the systematic discovery of every region of France.'[10]

It was ready to be handed out (still free of charge) in April 1908, with 532 pages of text and 67 pages of maps. There were a few surprises. For one thing, one continued to find advertisements for car and bicycle manufacturers, equipment suppliers, baggage vendors and publishers of books and magazines – but hotel adverts were out. Calling it a radical move, André explained that the intention had been 'to demonstrate clearly that we wish to remain impartial and that our only purpose is to inform tourists with precision and sincerity...'. Henceforth, hotels were to be graded – not just by price, but 'according to level of comfort, from the sumptuous palace to the good village inn'. Now for the first time the guide introduced those reassuring little doll-house symbols that we continue to measure with care in each new edition of the guide because they tell us about level of comfort. Thus, a house with five gables signified a first class hotel – in other words, a 'palace'. Four gables stood for 'great comfort', three for 'comfort without luxury'. A two-gabled house served a warning, for it meant 'comfortable in part', while a single gable was nothing more than a 'fifth-class hotel'.

Moreover, a great number of hotels listed in the guide had agreed to indicate prices for each meal and for rooms, prices representing 'a formal engagement to holders of the Michelin Guide', an engagement Michelin was able to obtain thanks to the publicity value of the guide-book to hotelkeepers.

> Our purpose is to help tourists avoid all those discussions which too often spoil a trip. Nothing is worse than uncertainty about the bill one will have to pay. Thanks to the Michelin Guide tourists and drivers will not have to travel in ignorance or as strangers. The Michelin Guide is experience in your pocket. In a handy format, it's your budget established before you leave, the road to take, assurance of a good place to stay. It is being certain.[11]

And for those who were still unconvinced, André published a some-what risqué tale of a wedding night – not consummated because the titled young couple lacked the *Guide Michelin* and after a breakdown took shelter in a hotel whose bedbugs kept them otherwise occupied all the night long.[12]

Taking up the 1908 red-bound *Guide Michelin* for France, travellers could almost feel that they have seen it before, so much does it resemble the volume we use now, 90 years later. A full three pages of small print are devoted to explaining the symbols, many of which would need no explaining to us today. For in those pioneer years of automobile travel everything had to be learned, and there was a legion of new drivers each year eager to soak up the knowledge Michelin could impart. What were national highways, where did they go, how were they marked? What were the laws governing driving, in France and abroad?

All that was missing, now, was a listing of restaurants not in hotels, but neither Michelin nor France was ready for that. The 60,000 copies printed, in any case, were gone before midsummer.[13]

Now the Michelin tourist office on Boulevard Pereire, embryo of today's Service du Tourisme, attained cruising speed. Almost from the start – when it opened there was only a single clerk behind the counter – it was able to handle 'hundreds' of requests in the year (eventually it would employ a staff of over a hundred). Visitors to the office needed only to indicate the kind of trip desired and the time available; Michelin did the rest, and without charge. Early in 1910 in a Monday column, André Michelin described the bureau's 'vast well-lighted lounge, with upholstered chairs'. The public would find 'a complete collection of guidebooks to all countries, detailed maps, three-dimensional photographs to let them see the route they will travel' – an uncanny anticipation of the audiovisual, electronic world Michelin offers today.

But Michelin's best contribution to early-twentieth-century tourism was surely the information obtainable over the counter, tailored to the needs of individual inquirers: 'This is the shortest route, or at least the one that will get you there fastest; it's not necessarily the most direct, but if I suggest it to you it's because the surfacing is better, obstacles less frequent, curves easier to manage'. Or: 'This is the road to avoid; it's monotonous, boring, full of potholes, poorly surfaced, with too many railway crossings...'. Finally: 'Here is the round-about way to take if you have the time, if you like good food and want to try local specialties and regional wines...'[14]

That year, the tenth edition of the guide was bigger than ever – 650 pages – but held 'ten times more information than its size,' boasted André. Printed – according to the certification on the title page – in 76,000 copies, it covered 175 more towns than the previous volume, contained 70 new town plans, adding 25 suggested itineraries (for regions not focused on until then, such as Normandy, Brittany and the Loire Valley castles).

Again, God was in the details. Thanks to readers' corrections and the co-operation of highway authorities, all distances had been verified. Town plans had been simplified. For smaller towns and villages, a new category of hotel had been introduced, represented by a glass and a fork, symbols 'eloquent in their clarity'. All maps had been checked once again, and symbols calling attention to monuments were easier to read. The large map of France at the end of the volume now called attention to the larger mountain chains, the main valleys and best-known provinces.[15]

It was a year-round business promoting Michelin's image and its wares. As soon as the 1909 guide was launched André had a new poster contest underway. 'We were the first to do illustrated posters,' André reminded readers of his Monday column. 'Unforgettable Bibendum has become a national hero.'

This time the subject proposed for the poster was the most recent invention of the Clermont-Ferrand plant: dual wheels and tyres for small trucks and buses, which served both to reduce the load on individual tyres – and to keep vehicles on the road in case of a flat.

'The subject lends itself to fantasy,' André assured would-be contestants. For tyres helped cars beat railway trains, tyres drank down obstacles and had but one enemy: weight. André used his space to appeal not only to poster artists but to all illustrators, for 'each year we publish a heap of notices, prospectuses and treatises that allow opportunities for illustrating texts, adding sketches or frontispieces'. Even the poster contest was open to amateurs; Michelin would be happy to launch new talent, thus creating 'a universal reputation overnight. We have dealers and other outlets all over the world.'[16]

One can imagine that concocting these schemes, then presenting them to faithful readers of the Monday column (who may have been wondering what else the witty columnist had up his sleeve), must have been among the more pleasant of André Michelin's tasks. A sound business could clearly support a dose of fantasy.

*   *   *

On 23 September 1909, the French dirigible *République* crashed. The accident was attributed to a tear in the lining of its gas-bag. Engineer Michelin quickly fired off a letter to the French war minister, warning of the danger of using the inadequate cloth which Germany's Continental was selling to the French (he even claimed that Continental was making stronger material for Germany's own dirigibles).[17]

As published in the press, the letter did not specifically mention arch-rival Continental, but did reveal that Michelin had been asked by the French government more than once to consider furnishing covering materials for dirigibles. After testing existing gas-bags and finding them inadequate, Michelin had developed its own, representing a significant advance over materials manufactured abroad. Yet Michelin had no intention of going through all the bureaucratic procedures necessary in order to sell its process. The brothers preferred to give the government the secret patent free of charge.

There was a condition: that the material be manufactured, in secret, by a French company – a genuine French company, not a foreign one only pretending to be French.[18]

Clearly, Bibendum was no longer going to stay on the ground. 'Having conquered the earth, he must now … extend his domain to the skies,' engineer Michelin revealed candidly in another Monday column, this to explain the presence of Bibendum at an air motor show held at the Grand Palais in October 1909. 'From autos to airplanes there is only a step.' The range of Michelin offerings included materials for wing construction and extension cords – not excluding 'pneumatic wheels to facilitate taking off and alighting gently on the ground'. He concluded: 'Having offered magnificent trophies to pilots, Bibendum would have accomplished only half his task if he had not also furnished the means to win these trophies'. Indeed, one of the salon's attractions was the monoplane of the young French pilot-adventurer Hubert Latham, most recently famous for having fallen into the sea in an attempt to be the first to fly across the English Channel. (That was on 15 July; on 25 July Louis Blériot made it all the way.) Oh yes, the wings of Latham's monoplane – in rubberized canvas – were signed 'Michelin'.[19]

14

AT HOME

In 1909 – see the *Guide Michelin* for that year – the population of Clermont-Ferrand numbered 41,113. (Michelin was particularly generous with its homely home town, taking three-and-a-half pages to describe the little city and nearby sights; Cherbourg was as big a city but got a little less than a page.) Those 41,113 inhabitants included children and old people and the handicapped, so the Michelin factory payroll for that year, numbering 4000-plus, represented well over a tenth of the active population.

Clermont-Ferrand was Michelin's town – as the biggest employer by far, the most conspicuous presence. The factory grounds were shaded black on the guide-book map; everything else was in light grey. That was because Michelin wanted visitors. 'It will be a pleasure for us to receive customers passing through, to listen to their comments and complaints, to remove or mount tyres, etc.' One guesses that there were not many bodies separating those visitors with serious observations or complaints from the Patron himself, now a mature 50 years old. He would want to know everything.

He would also want to control everything. Already from the beginning of the century the factory sponsored its own dispensary, and in 1905 created a structured health service for workers and their families. Michelin paid all costs, which was later attributed to the Patron's unwillingness to accept worker contributions, which might result in sharing management of the service with personnel.[1]

Legend has it that it was after hearing a description of the slum

conditions in which workers lived in old Clermont that Edouard
Michelin decided to embark on a programme of company housing.[2]
In fact, the law now encouraged the building of inexpensive housing
financed by private or public funds, designed for rental (or eventually
for sale) to wage-earners lacking adequate shelter.[3]

Michelin's first solution was collective: three-storey structures built
alongside the factory, each containing 35 apartments, presumably to
get the most deserving, the least privileged, under roofs as quickly as
possible. Soon after that, some single-family units were put up, although
by then the programme had been redesigned (if only for reasons of
cost) to focus on two and four-family houses.

The first lodgings that can be considered prototypes for those that
followed were built in 1911, consisting of 50 living units. There would
be 200 more before the outbreak of war in 1914.[4]

'The dwelling is designed for the housewife, for she lives in it more
than the worker does,' so a between-the-wars Michelin brochure on
social benefits explained the philosophy underlying the architecture.
'The rooms will be large enough but not too large; it is important
to avoid exhausting cleaning. There will be tap water, electricity, a gas
oven, a laundry room. An adjacent garden will supply the family with
vegetables.'[5]

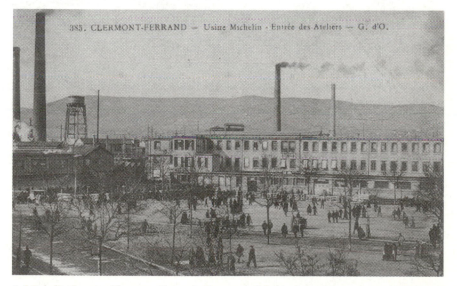

9. Michelin factory, Clermont-Ferrand. Courtesy of the Archives Départementales du Puy-
de-Dôme.

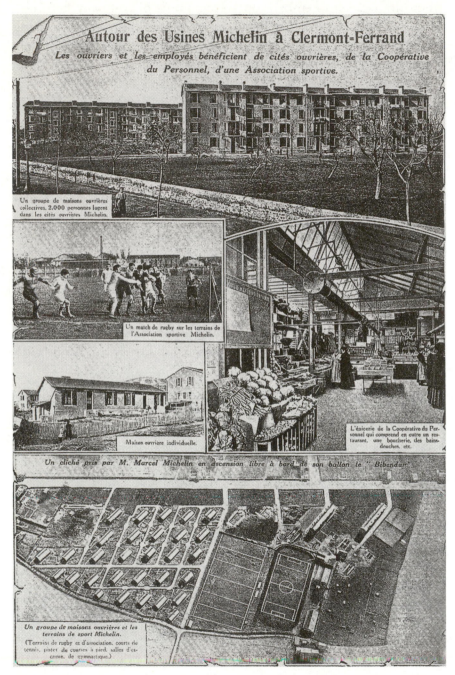

Autour des Usines Michelin à Clermont-Ferrand

Les ouvriers et les employés bénéficient de cités ouvrières, de la Coopérative du Personnel, d'une Association sportive.

Un groupe de maisons ouvrières collectives. 2.000 personnes logent dans les cités ouvrières Michelin.

Un match de rugby sur les terrains de l'Association sportive Michelin.

Maison ouvrière individuelle.

L'épicerie de la Coopérative du Personnel qui comprend en outre un restaurant, une boucherie, des bains-douches, etc.

Un cliché pris par M. Marcel Michelin en ascension libre à bord de son ballon le "Bibendum".

Un groupe de maisons ouvrières et les terrains de sport Michelin.

(Terrains de rugby et d'association, courts de tennis, pistes de courses à pied, salles d'escrime, de gymnastique.)

10. Michelin looks after its personnel. *La Petite Illustration*, 12 July 1913. Courtesy of the author.

It was all planned, and all in the interests of users, for their hygiene as well as their convenience, and that from the earliest beginnings. Indeed, principles of hygiene were elevated to doctrine, with careful designing of rooms according to use (for example, high ceilings for kitchens); separate rooms for parents and their children – not always an obvious arrangement then; adequate separation of families in the same dwelling unit; ready access to schools, stores and churches – but not cafés – but no public spaces either.[6]

In all, from the very first parcel cleared for building until 1980, Michelin put up or sponsored nearly 8000 family housing units located on available land near the spreading factory grounds. Housing that would hardly qualify as luxurious, it stressed simple comfort, optimal hygiene – and the moral laws the chief hoped to inspire (women in the kitchen, men spending their idle hours in the vegetable garden). Later there would be separate housing tracts for office staff and their families. These were designed with less garden space, on the assumption that their occupants were not of rural origin and therefore would not do as much digging and raking.[7] In all, between 30,000 and 50,000 men, women and children lived under Michelin roofs at one time or another.

With expansion, the company required an increasing number of reliable workers, and continued to recruit most of them from rustic raw material. Once it trained such people, it had to find ways to hold on to them – which meant keeping them happy and keeping them healthy. For this the Michelin system of paternalism has been called pragmatic; a group of social investigators was forced to conclude that far from being deplorable, Michelin-style paternalism helped bring a rural population into the industrial age, for the benefit both of the labourforce and of those who employed it.[8]

Once Michelin had found the right workers, had trained and housed them, the company saw to it – through an increasingly comprehensive programme of social benefits and amenities – that the beneficiaries need not look elsewhere for salvation. One team of social investigators summed it up as 'the confinement of the wage earner in a closed universe by the breeding of a proletariat and the selection of the best specimens'. For in Michelin City, as it was sometimes called, the company could expect to harvest the best of the next generation too. 'When a child finishes his compulsory schooling the company knows his parents (tenants), the head of the family (the worker), the outcome of his studies thanks to the grades and comments of his teachers from elementary school onward,' so the researchers explained. 'The company can then decide whether or not to ask his parents to enter the Michelin technical school, usually called the Mission.'[9]

Early on, Michelin extended its involvement in the daily lives of its charges by facilitating the purchase of essentials, beginning with items the factory had on hand in the normal course of operations – firewood for example, later, coal for heating, then such common-place foods as potatoes. When company stores were outlawed in 1910 Michelin opened a co-operative offering basic foods (even wine), as well as coal – eventually adding a restaurant for personnel and temporary housing for single workers. Soon there were branches in outlying housing projects, with a constantly increasing variety of goods on offer.

Critics pointed out that Michelin's was a co-operative in name only. Edouard Michelin held nearly all of the shares, at least in the early years, although the Michelin stores did operate strictly in the interest of its users – the rank and file of the factory and administration.[10]

By the end of the Second World War the Coopérative du Personnel included 10 grocery and butcher outlets, alongside the original Carmes plant and head offices, plus three clothing stores and separate sales units for shoes, furniture, hardware, table services. The co-operative restaurant for personnel and their families, connected to the main store, was open weekdays for breakfast, lunch and dinner.[11]

*   *   *

Michelin benevolence came from the top; Michelin was not ready to show a friendly face to those who claimed to speak for its personnel. In 1909, the very year that ground was being cleared for the first model community, Michelin also did some aggressive union-busting. Once again rubber-workers – at Michelin, but also at Bergougnan, then Michelin's chief competitor in Clermont-Ferrand – felt themselves strong enough (and presumably dissatisfied enough) to join the rubber-workers union, which, according to Alexandre Varenne's crusading weekly, 'has lately been receiving a great number of new memberships, and a certain tyre that drinks obstacles won't swallow up the trade union of the workers who manufacture it'.

The crusaders spoke too quickly. In May and June, both Michelin and Bergougnan fired personnel identified as union members – 86 at

Michelin alone. The total number of unionized rubber-workers in the city, which had reached 196 earlier in the year, dropped to 30.[12]

Paradoxically, it was now, at the beginning of the century's second decade, that Michelin increased the wage, becoming competitive and more than decent for its time – an affirmation that came not from Michelin but from its socially conscious critics. With further expansion Michelin needed better workers, and more of them, calling for recruitment in a wider radius; that meant matching existing wage scales not only in Clermont-Ferrand but well beyond. The next concern was improved productivity of the workforce, and this required healthy workers as well as contented ones. Decent housing was now more necessary than ever.[13]

Of course, Michelin's expansion reflected the persistent optimism of the time, not yet darkened by impending war. Up in Paris, Edouard's brother continued to prospect for customers through extravagant promotions. André's new *Guide Michelin* for 1910 was once again bigger and better: 'Readers who are careless or hurried could be overwhelmed by the abundance of material,' he explained, as if he had to apologize for that. Not to worry, a special chapter had been included to assure 'the intelligent use' of the guide-book.[14]

Previous editions had contained questionnaires to be completed by repair shops and hotels; for the 1910 volume, ingenious André was going to let rank-and-file travellers have an opportunity to speak up (and thereby to feel closer to their favourite guide-book, and to its sponsor). The editor begged respondents for their 'sincere' opinions. How did they use the guide? 'Do you prefer, for travel from one town to the next, a description of the route or a map?' 'Do you consult our suggestions for the use and care of tyres?' 'What information do you look for most often … and seems the most useful to you?' (Room was left at the bottom for the user's name, address and signature.)[15]

By now – after the previous year's test launching – the company's own maps (on the 1:200,000 scale) began to roll off the presses. The first, covering the Riviera from Marseille to Cannes, was helpfully put on sale 'in this dreary season' – the winter of 1909–10 that is. It was followed by a map of the environs of Paris, still the most travelled area of all for French motorists. Introducing the new series – when finished it would total 47 sheets, each covering a surface 57 miles from east to west, 47 from north to south – André was quick to point out that, rather than basing the new maps on existing models, Michelin had chosen to design totally new maps. ('Bibendum is often imitated, he never imitates.') Another innovation was to change the way everybody everywhere read maps: the unfolding accordion was introduced. 'Everyone who has struggled with a spread map waving like a flag in the wind will appreciate the pleasure felt by a driver or cyclist who can follow a route comfortably from the steering wheel or handle bar.'

The new maps were printed in four colours to allow the maximum number of details, including the width of each road, whether it was paved or not and the quality of the surfacing. Another welcome innovation was the inclusion of road numbers for both national and district roads, numbers which attentive drivers would find on milestones and directional signs, 'allowing them to know where they are at all times'. All this on a map, and yet 'it costs only a franc'[16] – each, he might usefully have added.

15

ANDRE'S
AIR WAR

The year 1911 was to be another good one for André Michelin (and for Edouard too). For what had seemed a mad and even cruel challenge – landing a light plane on the summit of omnipresent Puy-de-Dôme – proved to be both feasible and, under the right conditions, safe.

But not for everyone.

In April of the previous year, French airman Louis Paulhan had taken a London *Daily Mail* prize for a successful flight from London to Manchester – 186 miles in all, or a considerable part of the distance separating Paris from Clermont-Ferrand. In an earlier rally in Los Angeles, Paulhan had soared to an altitude of 4990 feet, which was higher than the highest point of the Puy-de-Dôme. Now it seemed to make sense to try for the so-called Special Prize established by those Michelin hotheads when neither aircraft nor airmen were ready for it.

One pilot who aimed at Clermont-Ferrand in September 1910 racked up a total of 260 miles – because he lost his way in fog and storms – but was eventually forced to land at Volvic, ten miles short of his goal. Then the famous brothers – Léon in the pilot's seat, Robert as the passenger, required under terms of the contest – took off from Issy-les-Moulineaux just south of Paris in a spanking new Blériot monoplane, with what was then an impressive 100 hp engine. Thirty minutes later, flying at a height of some 165 feet near Boissy-Saint-Léger, the plane suddenly took a nose-dive, seriously injuring both men.

Apparently the extinct volcano, the highest of the Auvergne chain of *puys* (a local term for the region's rounded peaks) was not quite ready to receive guests.[1] 'Mr. Michelin had indeed insisted that contestants touch the soil at a place he chose himself, despite protests,' recalled an aviation specialist in a somewhat disapproving tone. 'This place, located on the mountain top, and whose dimensions are quite inadequate, could be selected as a landing field only by sacrificing the aircraft, and probably the pilot as well.'[2]

Then the right man arrived, in the person of Eugène Renaux, like many of his predecessors a cyclist, motorcyclist and automobilist before he learned to fly during the summer of 1910, picking up a number of prizes in his first competitions; at the age of 34, he was – in this new world where nearly everyone seemed a beginner – a seasoned flyer.

Yet when Renaux took off for the Auvergne shortly after nine o'clock one morning (from a small field south of Versailles in the Bièvre valley) he had had little experience of flying over open country. He went about it – so observers would soon be reporting – with the method that had characterized his career, practising glider landings – even taking the train down to Clermont-Ferrand to inspect the landing site.

It had been on 7 March three years earlier that the Michelin brothers had announced the Puy-de-Dôme prize, and it was on a 7 March that Renaux flew off (with Albert Senoucque, the obligatory

11. Eugene Renaux arrives at the summit of the Puy-de-Dôme to take the Michelin Special Prize, 7 March 1911. Courtesy of the Archives Départementales du Puy-de-Dôme.

passenger, himself a scientist) to try his luck. Under the rules, the time limit for the flight was six hours; after a single fuel stop at Nevers he landed on the controversial piece of volcanic rock five hours, ten minutes and 46 seconds later.

It seemed as if all of Clermont-Ferrand had turned out to watch the little plane touch down, although because of fog only those who had actually climbed toward the summit were able to see the landing. The others caught up with the heroes on their drive into town, with what a reporter called a 'delirium of applause and hoorahs'. 'And so,' began another chronicler, 'three years sufficed to accomplish a pro-gramme for which the donors had allowed ten and which everybody else expected would take thirty or forty'.[3]

The event deserved and got the front page of *L'Illustration* – which was then selling over 100,000 copies weekly (and seemed to be read by everybody before being added to the pile on coffee tables). In a small insert, a photograph showed the biplane circling the weather station at the highest point of the hill, after which Renaux set it down in a narrow corridor bordered by canvas strips.[4] (Henceforth, all of France would be able to follow the flight from take-off to touchdown in picture postcards.)

Clearly it was more than a local event, this absurd dream born of too much staring (by the Michelin brothers) at that strange mound out of the window: 'The date of March 7, 1911 will count as one of the most important in the annals of French aviation,' so affirmed the Paris daily *La République Française*.[5]

On the evening of the Renaux landing a banquet was hastily con-vened at Clermont's Hôtel Terminus (rated in that year's *Guide Michelin* by a house with three gables, signifying 'comfortable' and not much more, but it was the best that Clermont could offer). André Michelin (of course) was the main speaker. 'When my son Marcel phoned at 2.23 p.m. from the weather station to report that Renaux and his companion had just landed in a remarkable manner,' he began, 'I cried out in relief, joy, and pride. A cry of pride because I am proud to see my country rank so high in this new industry that will revolutionize the world, don't doubt that for a minute.' A strong statement and a curious one for a man committed to that other revolution still far from finished, the automobile age that Michelin helped make, and that would largely make Michelin.

Engineer-publicist Michelin could have stopped there, but he went on to draw some political lessons from the feat – lessons that took on meaning in the context of the perceived military threat from across the Rhine, in a time of colonial rivalry and power alliances presaging a European war.

> If the War Minister were with us this evening I'd tell him: 'Instead of playing politics a man of your value should be making history. For that, I beg you, Mr Minister, go to the rostrum and tell parliament that there is a new empire to conquer, the empire of the skies. Ask for a budget for aviation equal to that voted for construction of one of those enormous battleships…'

He was saying these things when the First World War, in which aviation was to play a timid and hardly conclusive role, was still a long three years into the future, but the words that followed indicated clearly that he was talking about war: 'Which nation will dare to attack us that day it realizes that at the first alert 5000 aircraft flown by 5000 bold men are ready to fly over enemy armies?'[6] Words worth remembering, for if André was yet to spell out his doctrine of airpower, it is clear that as early as March 1911 he was convinced that aeroplanes could be utilized not only to observe and defend – but also to carry the offensive to the enemy's heartland. Few of his peers were ready to advocate such things even after the Great War of 1914–18, and into the 1930s, and those who did on the eve of the Second World War were deemed not serious. On the other hand, many French military and political leaders now remembered, as prophets never did understand, what airpower signified (or if they did, they never told anyone else).

Henceforth, the coming air war – a war that would not actually take place in his lifetime – was never very far from the preoccupations of André Michelin. By the month of August it had taken the shape of what was surely the most curious aviation prize offered in its time.

Once again, it took the form of a letter signed by both Michelin brothers, addressed to the president of the Aéro-Club de France. 'There is much discussion,' the incendiary document began, 'as to whether military aircraft are simply reconnaissance planes or can be transformed quickly into frightful instruments of war'.

> Can they put bridges out of commission, railway junctions, cut a nation's military preparations in half, destroy a fortress, blow up a battleship?…Can they do even more: destroy arsenals, supply centres, munitions depots, and thus render useless enemy cannon and rifles?

They wished to put these questions to the test, to 'demonstrate the power of airplanes with facts': 'We hope that once we have proved this, public opinion and the government won't hesitate to accept the need to order aircraft from French industry, not some dozens of planes but five or six thousand, which won't really cost more than a battleship'.

They would back their conviction with more cash, to endow a Michelin Air Target Competition. The first prize would go to the aviator who before 15 August of the following year could – in a single attack – place the largest number of projectiles in a circle with a 33-foot radius. The pilot would transport five projectiles each weighing at least 20 kilograms, fly at an altitude of at least 650 feet, and drop the bombs one by one in several passages over the target. Should more than one pilot achieve this feat before the deadline, the winner would be the one whose bombs came closest to the centre of the circle. Another prize was reserved for the pilot who – flying at an altitude of 3300 feet or more – would drop his bombs in a rectangle 330 feet long and 33 wide.[7]

There was a paradox here. France's business class was enjoying the prosperity born of industry, whose products now included auto-mobiles on Michelin tyres. And here were the Michelin brothers, calling up lugubrious images of war, when there was no war to speak of. The story that has come down to us is that far from having the effect of a bombshell, the brothers' announcement provoked jeering 'in the cabinets'. ('These Michelin rascals! Success has gone to their head!')[8]

Yet Michelin's point was so evident. Writing about that moment later, André recalled the anxiety of spectators when a plane flew over their heads during an air show. 'Just hope it doesn't drop anything!' 'What could it drop?' 'A spanner would do a lot of damage from that height.' Another day, someone remarked, 'He's well placed up there; he could drop a few shells on our heads'. That, said André, opened his eyes.[9] 'It made us realize what a plane carrying bombs could do. Didn't Renaux fly Senoucque 250 miles? Senoucque, with his fur coat, weighed 80 kilograms. He could have been replaced by the same weight in explosives.'[10]

That the feasibility of air bombing would be comprehended by a civilian engineer and not by the general staff may seem incredible, but history seems to confirm anecdote. In 1914 – the year of the Great War – a specialist in aviation history reminds us, aircraft were still considered by the high command merely as an 'instrument of reconnaissance and illumination'.[11]

Eventually Michelin made its own contribution to the lighter side of the matter by publishing a series of postcards in which the comic figure of Bibendum flies a bomber. And it was inevitable that in a Michelin Monday column André deal with objections – presumably letters that had been received after the launching of the Michelin campaign. 'Hasn't aviation created enough victims, widows and orphans?' asked one reader. 'Young people who die will have a noble death,' was the engineer's somewhat cool reply. 'Their sacrifice will assure the greatness of the Nation and save the lives of hundreds of thousands of fathers' – hardly the way a Bibendum trying to sell more tyres should be speaking, and indeed another objector prodded him: 'In fact, come to think of it, you are tyremakers. What the devil are you getting into?' Replied the engineer: 'Pascal, the great Auvergnat, said, "The heart has reasons of which reason knows nothing"'.[12]

Late that autumn, André again employed humour in the service of preparedness – also in the service of Michelin. At the annual air show held in the Grand Palais the Michelin stand showed a Bibendum Plane, a comic mock-up of an aircraft straddled by a larger-than-life Bibendum. At intervals two human-sized Bibendums, one dressed as a soldier, the other as a sailor, bombarded bystanders with Michelin postcards, but also with flowers and gumdrops. Fun for the crowd, but with a dash of didacticism all the same. It was part of the campaign for 5000 bombers, and professional visitors to the salon would not be left in doubt about that.[13]

Then André was serious again. The lower house of parliament, debating the defence budget, had voted what he considered 'ridiculous sums' for military aircraft. This time he addressed his appeal to popular daily Le Matin; it was widely reprinted. 'A few thousand francs, two hundred and some airplanes, a few men – this is all that they give us for an arm as indispensable for our national defence as rifles and cannon.' He felt that he had to speak out, not 'as a possible supplier, since neither my company nor myself has a material interest in aviation, but as a simple Frenchman who believes that he is doing his duty'.[14]

*   *   *

Earlier in 1911, the attention of the business side of Michelin had crossed the channel, for it was now time to come to grips with its oldest and most preoccupying rival, Dunlop. The offensive took the shape of an ambitious piece of architecture, known even today (when it has passed into other hands) as the Michelin Building, preserved since 1967 as an historic landmark. Space had been found for it on Fulham Road in Chelsea, pivot of London's industrial expansion westward, and the building was clearly stamped with the taste of the time – polychrome tiles framing red bricks, studio windows. Just below the roof, alongside the large engraved lettering for Michelin Tyre Co. Ltd and in letters equally large, the word 'Bibendum' would have seemed incongruous to those not familiar with Michelin lore.

12. Michelin Building, London, inaugurated on 20 January 1911 by André Michelin. An early plan of the building shows that the architect envisaged that each corner turret would be a sculpture of Bibendum. © Philippa Lewis.

Building had been underway during much of the year 1910, under the supervision of a Michelin company architect sent over from Clermont-Ferrand. But if 81 Fulham Road has a place in industrial art history, it is rather thanks to the ceramic tiles that ran around the façade, continuing into the entrance hall and tyre depot, each portraying a victorious racing driver in his winning vehicle. The illustrator Edouard Montaut had acquired a reputation for depicting movement; he had drawn the widely reproduced poster showing an automobile equipped by Michelin beating the fast Paris–Calais railway train.[15]

The whole building was a vast puff, and so it was fitting that André the publicist, and not Edouard the industrialist, orchestrated the inauguration of what he called 'Michelin's Palace'. It took place with due solemnity, on 20 January 1911, in the presence of French ambassador Paul Cambon (known as the ambassador of the Entente Cordiale between Britain and France – and in fact André Michelin titled his own account of the event 'Entente Cordiale').

Everyone who counted in Britain's motorcar universe seemed to be present to hear engineer Michelin apologize, as president of an English company, for not being able to speak in English. (He assured his guests that every educated Frenchman in the generation following his spoke either English or German.) After reminding the audience that auto-mobiles were born on the continent while Britain held back (partly because of laws such as the one that required that every motor-driven vehicle be preceded by a man on foot carrying a red flag and shaking a bell), the British Isles now counted 110,000 motorcars mounted on tyres to France's 60,000.[16] The *Times*, reporting the following day, noted:

> M. Cambon, speaking in French, said that he had much pleasure in taking part in the ceremony, and he congratulated them on showing what an intelligent, energetic Frenchman who was thoroughly businesslike could do. They had shown their English friends that in France could be found energy, ability and an enterprising spirit. Those qualities were not always recognized in them, and that was unjust, for that industry, which now extended through-out the world, and which had made such strides in England during the past two or three years, was essentially a French industry. For that reason he was glad that they had invited him to that ceremony, and glad to find himself amongst Englishmen, whom they looked upon as their friends. He thought, as he was sure they did, that that small gathering well exemplified the Entente Cordiale.

It was not simply coincidence that 1911 saw publication of the first *Michelin Guide to the British Isles*, published in English, printed in London, distributed from Michelin Tyre headquarters. 'The Michelin Guide is the Motorist's Vade-Mecum,' proclaimed the title page. Among other books to be published that year were the *Guide Michelin* for France in separate French and English editions, for Germany in German (via Deutsche Michelin Pneumatik), for Spain and Portugal in Spanish, as well as in French and English. There were also to be French and English editions of *The Sunny Countries* (Algeria, Tunisia, Egypt, southern Italy and Sicily, Corsica and the French Riviera), and French, English and German editions of *The Alps and Rhineland*. 'The Michelin Guides distributed gratis every year would, if placed one upon another, make a pile 60 times as high as St. Paul's Cathedral,' announced the new guide-book. Obviously this was André's familiar conceit, put into English, as we know, by some other hand.

Some of the new guides were acts of bravura all the same. Introducing the new *Guia Michelin* for Spain and Portugal, all three language versions of which were distributed through Michelin's Spanish affiliate, Sociedad Anonimia del Neumatico Michelin, columnist André Michelin at once tried to convince the French that all the clichés about Spain's unnavigable roads were nonsense – and then proceeded to show that there were challenges to confront all the same.

> A still unique exploit: a car was able to cover – without stops or incidents, and with a moderate consumption of tyres, thanks to the dual wheels and tyres with which it was equipped – nearly all the main roads of the country … Henceforth, thanks to the *Guia Michelin*, our countrymen need no longer consider the fact of crossing the border as a brave act requiring the drawing up of a will before departure … On the other side of the mountains they will find one of the most beautiful countries in the world, a friendly and hospitable people who under the influence of a young king, enterprising and courageous, develops its athletic training and business spirit. As for the young Portuguese Republic, tourists will quickly see that it is moving toward a fine future on well-tended roads.[17]

In 1911, the *Michelin* for France was published in 70,000 copies. New sections of the map series were released, and before the end of the year over half of France would be covered. 'It's the only map that recognizes landscape,' André Michelin reminded the hesitant, and from the technical point of view, still the only one that describes as well as numbers all the roads, indicating bad stretches, rapid descents, dangerous curves, open gutters and bumps, etc. Daughter of Bibendum [the map] flirts with obstacles, eliminates disagreeable surprises, and roads hold no secrets from her.[18]

*　　　　　　*　　　　　　*

It was a lively time. Despite André Michelin's forebodings about a war he appeared to see as inevitable, the family enterprise continued to build for peace. It was also in 1911 that André Michelin's son Marcel Michelin, then 25 years old – he who had climbed up the Puy-de-Dôme to inform his father by telephone of the successful Renaux landing – took it on himself to establish another factory-subsidized benefit for Michelin workers, the Michelin Sports Association, nucleus for the development of team activities and individual physical culture. Eventually Marcel would preside over an establishment that encompassed a stadium, gymnasia, a swimming pool, a billiard hall and even a cinema. In its time, the association would field athletic teams worth challenging.[19]

It would have been difficult to fight Michelin then. 'No,' insisted a local union spokesman, 'the union of men and women rubber workers … is not dead, as they claim; it survives'.[20]

Confidence all but bursts forth from a Michelin message published as a Monday column in September 1911, under a headline that must have seemed as unusual then as it would now: 'The House Of Michelin Needs Men'. In what must have been the most prominently displayed help-wanted advertisement of its time, André opened by declaring shamelessly: 'This headline will undoubtedly astonish many people, but it's a fact: we lack personnel to develop our business as we should like to'. Michelin was all but exploding. Of 25 automobiles on the street, running on 100 tyres, between 60 and 70 of the tyres would have been Michelins. The same was true in most of Europe, as well as in Egypt, Java, Argentina, Indo-China and Brazil. 'But in some countries, unfortunately, you'll find far fewer.'

It was, the writer affirmed, because of 'The lack of manpower'. Michelin needed bookkeepers, chief accountants too; and salesmen – and their chiefs, able to speak English or Spanish, willing to work outside France. The kind of person Michelin desired could definitely be found in France, affirmed the writer. Some were presently out of work, others working but insufficiently paid. Michelin required the kind of person who, when asked to ship off to the Transvaal (which had recently become part of Britain's Union of South Africa), would not reply, 'I'm very sorry, but I can't leave my parents'. They needed honest people prepared to work 10-hour days, and be happy with a job well done.

They did not ask for experience – Michelin would do the teaching. 'We just ask for the firm will to learn.'[21]

16

ANDRE'S
BATTLES

He lived at boiling point. But in those days, André Michelin's behaviour was so unlike what one expected of the jolly, avuncular person who liked to play Bibendum. For he really did take this war game seriously. He and his brother backed their conviction by financing the printing of a million copies of a blue, white and red pamphlet arguing the case for airpower, stressing the urgency of being ahead of the enemy in preparedness. 'Our Future is in the Air' was printed on 1 February 1912, distributed free everywhere and in any way André could accomplish it.

It was at once a public document and a very personal one. He did not sign it, but this time it was not quite a 'Michelin' statement, for he used the first person to speak of himself. And in this company whose every scrap of paper was considered to be secret, he actually published two personal letters on the very first page – one that he had scribbled hastily to brother Edouard in October 1906, on hearing of the record 60-metre flight in Paris achieved by the Brazilian Alberto Santos-Dumont, with his brother's reply. 'Since one of these instruments actually managed to rise from the ground,' André had written, 'given the rapidity of the progress we see in the automobile industry and the close analogy between automobile and aircraft motors, suppose we try building birds?' Edouard replied that they had enough to do making tyres. But, like his brother, he could not resign himself to watching the aviation industry develop 'without taking part in it a little'. At his suggestion, they would make their contribution to manned flight by endowing competitions.

Largely a compilation of the work of other experts and opinions published in the press, the Michelin case was summed up at the close by André:

> France needs 5000 airplanes and when we ask for 5000 we ask at the same time for hangars, flying repair shops, spare parts, trucks, everything needed to made these craft not troublesome and useless hindrances but birds ever ready to take flight. France also needs 5000 military pilots... It's for the French people to demand all this from its representatives remembering always that 'The Future of France is in the Air!'[1]

Within a fortnight the pamphleteer would summon the experts of the General Aeronautical Association to the Sorbonne's grand amphithéâtre; out of that meeting came a National Committee for Military Aviation mandated to solicit public donations for air preparedness as if it were the Red Cross or any other national cause.

Michelin archives record that under André's watchful eye as treasurer, the new committee collected sufficient funds, duly turned over to the War Ministry, to create and equip 70 landing fields, and to build 120 aeroplanes.[2]

Meanwhile, the contest for the Michelin Air Target Competition was underway – to see what all those new airplanes could do. An early contestant, who happened to be an artillery lieutenant, managed to get two of his bombs within the target area. The next serious challenger was a French civilian, but he took along Lieutenant Riley Scott of the United States Army as his bombardier, flying an Astra-Wright. The time: mid-August 1912; the place: the training field of the artillery school in Châlons-sur-Marne. Using a launcher of his own making, Scott placed eight projectiles out of 15 within the rectangle; then he dropped 12 out of 15 within the rim of the circular target area, for the grand prize. 'As of today,' announced André, 'the goal we proposed in creating the Air Target prize has been attained. Shelling from the sky is on the agenda.'[3]

He never forgot what he was supposed to be doing. For what was called an automobile tour of France, Michelin was smack in the centre of things during the 2480-mile run through 15 cities beginning on 1 March 1912, only a fortnight after the launching of the latest campaign for air preparedness. It was a matter of making sure that the best motorcars used Michelin tyres, and then nursing both cars and tyres to victory. 'Their precious health was protected,' he reported –

speaking of his beloved tyres – 'and we can say that despite the accumulation of obstacles they valiantly led 27 cars of the 40 eligible to the finish line, representing 68% of the winners'.

Still, these victories were costly, with the special grants, the roving repair teams, not to forget the investment of time on the part of engineer Michelin. Hence the decision, surprising all the same from a company as publicity-bent as Michelin, to pull its support from future races. They'd spend the money on making better tyres. Obviously, the brothers would continue to be solicited by contestants, and would have to justify the decision again and again for a long time to come.

A Michelin Monday column – the 636th – reminded readers of Michelin's strange determination. Once again, wrote André, prices of Michelin tyres had been reduced. This called for eliminating unnecessary spending. And racing was precisely that – 'a heavy and useless outlay'. The amount spent by the company each year to subsidize automobile races came to hundreds of thousands of francs, and it was the customer who paid.[4]

But no expense was too great for André's cherished *Guide Michelin*, now in its thirteenth year, still given away free. From the little 400-page book of 1900 it now ran to 758 pages, including 381 small town maps, but not counting the 12 two-colour maps, and a 60-page four-colour atlas of France on a scale of 1:1,000,000.

In his Monday column, presenting the new edition of the guide-book, its creator called attention to press reports that the police had found the 1911 edition in the possession of highway robbers. 'But, in appropriate revenge, the police were equipped with Michelin maps.'[5]

The 12 Michelin guide-books published in 1912 (a figure that included foreign language versions) totalled 7046 pages, featured 1303 town plans or excursion maps in black and white, 50 in two colours and 184 in four colours; total printings amounted to 274,000 copies. Put another way – André Michelin's favourite way – if stacked together the copies printed that year would rise 20 times the height of the Eiffel Tower, or twice that of Vignemale (highest peak of the Pyrenees chain separating France and Spain) – or they'd simply match the height of Mount Everest. The guide-books, the maps, and Michelin's Bureau de Tourisme in Paris led André to reflect that if the French did not travel enough, as was often said, 'it's certainly not the fault of Bibendum, who spares neither his time nor labours to make travel easier'.[6]

Certainly, users of the travel service, who were invited to submit their needs by post, telegram, telephone or simply by walking over to the Paris headquarters, would not be out of pocket when they were done. 'As free as the public schools,' so André described his tourist information centre, 'it will also become compulsory, by making itself indispensable'.[7]

And as if he needed to justify himself further in the eyes of a humourless, nose-to-the-grindstone brother punching out his sombre tyres down there in Clermont-Ferrand, André now designed a bright pamphlet to enumerate all the activities in which Michelin engaged on behalf of tourists. The jacket showed a merry Bibendum holding the *Guide Michelin* for France, beneath a frame in which five smaller Bibenda in national costumes consult their own country's Michelin guide-books.

And perhaps for the only time in Michelin annals, a series of photographs took the reader inside the *Guide Michelin* – showing how information was sorted by clerks (all of them women, nearly 20 of whom are visible), while men (a dozen at least) drew maps. One also saw how the typesetting, printing and binding were done. In all, the booklet revealed, 1,268,375 copies of the familiar red-bound guide-books had been distributed – gratis – from 1900–12.

*   *   *

Avuncular André Michelin, patron saint of motorists, could also be combative when he thought the occasion called for such behaviour. While he distributed signs to town mayors – each clearly marked as a Michelin gift – he was also ready to join a campaign against advertisers responsible for billboards 'that invade and blemish our roads and finest vistas'. Many of the offenders, he regretted to say, were tyre-makers. And to those who thought Michelin might be responsible for what he called 'road barriers,' he asked: 'Really, could anyone believe that after having worked for so long to facilitate motor touring, we would wish to destroy its charm by stupid signage?'

He was out for blood again; specifically, he was out for the rival tyre company he loved to hate. 'It's true that some of our good colleagues have no reason to spare our country, quite the country. It's not theirs!' Should anyone wonder which particular rival he referred to: 'This is why some advertising shows itself to be so…incontinent'. The alert reader would know that he was denouncing Germany's Continental here.

He blamed those 'unfortunates' who, after selling tyres on the French market for so many years, still had to stand on street corners shouting 'I exist'. But if one should say that Michelin's name was also found on the highways, it was 'on posters of modest proportions' calling attention to addresses of local tyre dealers, or indicating the name of a village one was about to enter, beseeching drivers to be careful as they drove through.[8]

In August he pursued his campaign against the hereditary rival in a circular letter to Michelin customers. Earlier, in May 1910, Michelin had sent out a notice under the heading 'Remove your false nose,' pointing out that 'the Continental Company of Paris is German in management and capital, and sells German tyres'. The notice concluded: 'Contrary to what the Continental Company says: 'THE CONTINENTAL TYRE IS GERMAN'. (It was an uncanny presage of the refrain heard during World War II on Free French broadcasts to occupied France via the BBC: 'Radio Paris is German'.)

Now, announced Michelin, French customs had confiscated tyres from Continental's Hanover factory which lacked any indication that they were imports, and a French court (aided by Michelin testimony) had confirmed what Michelin had always said: 'That in fact all Continental tyres sold by the French company as made in France are imported from Germany, and that they take pains to say, not only to French customers but to Spanish customers as well, that these products imported from Germany are shipped from France'.[9] Having won another round in the battle against Continental and Germany, André could return to some of the positive promoting he did so well.

   *   *   *

In an article on what it called the labyrinth of the French road system, authoritative *L'Illustration* prepared the ground for the next Michelin crusade. France was often said to possess the world's most beautiful roads, although with the coming of the railway they had been less travelled in recent years, and in any case much needed to be done in order to adapt them to the automobile age. Yet, the writer went on, there was another problem – a problem that should not even exist. 'Drivers ask simply to be able to find out where they are on French roads.'

This was often hard to do, despite official signposts, milestones and the best-made maps. Quite simply, roads lacked proper signage.

Conceived not for automobiles but for pedestrians and horse-drawn carriages, they were marked more or less as they had been in Roman times. They were numbered differently depending on type: national, district, major, local – these last the responsibility of individual districts – and country lanes (supervised by villages).

All well and good, but the numbers on these roads, whatever their type, usually could not be read by drivers, and in any event they did not appear on maps, although Michelin was now in the process of remedying this.[10]

André Michelin took up the cause. What good was it to have the very best map if the route numbers it indicated could not be found on the roads themselves? He published a letter purportedly received from a British customer, 'Lord Jimmy'. The correspondent had attempted to drive along the new Alpine road from Evian to Nice, but found himself going twice that distance because he was continually getting lost.[11]

Road numbering was a perfect cause for engineer Michelin. There was a genuine need for it, and it would ensure a favourable image for the person or company proposing solutions. It was an opportunity to associate Michelin with a vast improvement in automobile travel; there was also the possibility of actually achieving the goal, thereby facilitating road use. More cars on the road meant more Michelin tyres.

Closer to our time, an American automobile manufacturer was disapproved for having declared: 'What's good for the country is good for General Motors, and what's good for General Motors is good for the country'. In 1912, certainly, what was good for the country was good for Michelin.

Late in October of that year André was ready with a formal 'Petition for Road Numbering'. The moment was propitious. The air show was just then opening at the Grand Palais exhibition hall in Paris, and when the French president Armand Fallières stopped for a courtesy call at the Michelin exhibit he was confronted by André Michelin holding out an elegant album in the form of a visitors' book. In fact it was the very first blank page of the petition printed in 80,000 copies. Legend has it that it was a ruse of André's, and that Fallières thought that he was only signing a guest book.[12] Whatever the case, the president was recorded as the very first signatory. His name was quickly followed by that of the notables who accompanied him on the tour, senators, senior officers and distinguished aviators.

'Let the decision to number our roads be taken,' argued André in his column,

> and it will be achieved in six months. Then we'll quickly see motor touring develop in a prodigious way, giving a new impetus to our automobile industry, our hotel industry, to all trades, drawing to our nation the wealth that foreign drivers distribute around the world each year and which they'll bring to the country they all prefer, France.[13]

To hear the Michelins tell it, their petition was a sensation. In his Monday column on 16 December 1912, André reported that as of the previous night they had counted 199,453 signatories. Six weeks earlier, the first 180,000 names had been delivered to the Minister of Public Works, with a copy of the file for the Interior Minister – both of whom favoured the plan.[14] They could not have stopped Michelin had they wanted to; fortunately they did not want to, and by next spring road numbering both of national and local roads was underway. And anyone could have predicted who would supply the milestones.[15]

Michelin reigned at the 13th Automobile Show in December. André was quick to point out that 63 percent of the automobiles on show were equipped with Michelin tyres (compare 36 percent in 1906, 50 percent in 1908, 55 percent in 1910). They were also selling new levers that simplified the job of mounting tyres. 'At the Michelin stand,' announced a souvenir leaflet, 'young and pretty girls from the Auvergne demonstrate how marvellous the new Michelin levers are by mounting tyres of all dimensions by themselves, without effort and with a smile'.[16]

17

MORE
SERIOUS
BUSINESS

Pranks could sell tyres; it took a considerable amount of sobriety to design, get the rubber and chemical mix right and then stamp them out, considerable fortitude to live in the dreary ambiance of old Clermont, walking to the factory from a great house on a tame square, and then going home to a dark volcanic town centre. This was the lot of Edouard Michelin, the Beaux-Arts painter, for the rest of his long working life. He seemed to accept it with a stout heart, if not with his brother's gusto. But how do we know that? While all authority came from the top, from himself, he took pains to explain his methods to his immediate subordinates. Later, the principles of manufacturing the Michelin way would be expounded in lectures circulated through the upper ranks of the scattered Michelin plants, later still in pamphlet form to enlighten Michelin's counterparts in other industries, presumably including competing tyre companies.

Thus, in one of the first of Edouard's pronouncements to come down to us (and this one, dated 22 August 1912, would have been a memorandum to his managers and engineers), the chief explained what he called the 'method of five letters'.

A large number of errors committed in the factory come from the following causes, but which the method of five letters can almost always prevent:

a) From not having posed the question clearly. It is extremely rare that a question is well posed at the start. It is wise to indicate one's starting point. One can say that a question well posed is a question already half resolved.

b) From an incomplete investigation, that is to say, reasoning on the basis of incomplete information…

c) From not having considered all possible solutions…

d) From adopting a solution without anticipating the disadvantages and dangers, not to speak of the repercussion on adjacent services.

e) From not having considered the financial consequences. I don't tolerate neglect of this point, since our goal is to produce the best tyre at the best possible price.[1]

He was speaking to insiders, not to the public, and then and later he seemed to mean everything he said. For he believed these things, fruit of his experience and lonely days meditating at the top.

Even the paternalism that would seem hypocritical to scholars and oppressive to militants was a genuine effort to preserve the social peace, to keep Michelin personnel and their families healthy and safe. At that very moment (1912), under the direction of Edouard's wife Marie-Thérèse, a day-care centre for young girls was created – clearly the place to teach principles of morality to the children of Michelin personnel. With a capacity of 150, the patronage would be the nucleus of the Michelin schools founded during the First World War.[2]

Labour unions were not invented to deal with a patron like Edouard Michelin, who tried to do the right thing even if his methods were not of his century, his behaviour not always what was expected of the exploiting class. On one hand, a model community – with living and even working conditions far better than the norm for their time and place. On the other hand, a factory floor where gripes and grunts were not tolerated. It was a place, complained outspoken Alexandre Varenne's *L'Ami du Peuple*, where workers 'can neither speak nor reason nor discuss; they can't show what they are capable of doing'. Edouard Michelin, who would never cease to call for face-to-face dialogue with his best workers, surely would not have understood that particular complaint. 'The Michelin people shouldn't fool themselves,' pursued the critic. 'There are intelligent men among these workers who are kept muzzled, even among the farmworkers who have been lured from the soil by false promises, for their own unhappiness first of all, then for the misfortune of the community.'[3]

Varenne's complaint would have fallen on some receptive ears. For it was the grievance of all simpler societies faced with sudden change – the uneasiness of farmers and artisans displaced by modern methods and social reorganization. Certainly Varenne's brave little weekly was unlikely to move mountains, and perhaps not even Clermont-Ferrand. A social scientist who studied labour mentalities in the first decades of Edouard Michelin's reign decided that the apathy of his workers was a result both of careful recruitment and clever handling thereafter. Edouard was tough – but knew how not to be tough with essential personnel.[4]

And that was only the beginning. For methodical Edouard Michelin was now to find his master in the person of Frederick Winslow Taylor, an American industrial engineer three years his senior. Taylor's principles of scientific management – measuring and then breaking down tasks into their simplest elements, then spreading them along a continuous chain, thereby making it possible for workers to produce more with less effort – had already contributed to the development of the acclaimed Ford Motor Company's conveyor-belt system. The Taylor method, which not only did the job more efficiently but rewarded increased productivity, had actually crossed the ocean several years earlier, tried out in France by avant-garde industrialists (car-maker Louis Renault for one). Some of Taylor's theoretical texts had been translated, and one can be sure that Edouard studied them with his usual concern for a rational organization of the manufacturing process.

In the summer of 1913 he shipped off his brother's son Marcel, then 26 and already a veteran of the Michelin plant – then and later he was in charge of testing new products – to meet Frederick Taylor and his disciples. In the United States, Taylor's stopwatch approach to cost-cutting was keenly attractive to factory owners at a time when economic recession called for a radical revision of old ways. Taylor and his associate H.K. Hathaway, who was serving as Marcel Michelin's guide, proposed that the tyre company begin with a carefully thought-out reorganization of Michelin's Milltown, New Jersey installation. And the Milltown reorganization could then serve as a model for Clermont-Ferrand.

The annals tell us that Edouard Michelin found this to be the long way round; he wanted some action now, and in Clermont-Ferrand. Henceforth, Taylorism was the prescription – not to say the religion. It began with precise timing of individual steps in the manufacturing process, including the gestures and movements of each worker, with an evaluation of their cost.

That of course could lead to paying workers for the specific tasks they accomplished, finding the ideal tempo – and workers who could not keep up would not stay on the payroll long. Increased productivity could also mean making do with fewer workers. All things sure to lead to protest, union intercession and strikes – as had already happened in the United States. But if there was an early walkout over the introduction of Taylorism at Renault, nothing like that was to happen at Michelin.[5]

It was still a time of expansion, with a new warehouse going up at Estaing, near the flagship factory in Clermont-Ferrand. Abroad, the Turin plant payroll kept over 2000 workers busy, and was exporting to Germany and Austria as well as Great Britain (where Michelin production had ceased in 1911). Still, Michelin's international behaviour of the time has been judged conservative. Whenever possible, the company backed away from the establishment of production facilities outside France, preferring exports from the Auvergne to the far corners of the world.[6]

In 1914, which included the first months of the First World War, Michelin sales were estimated at over 100 million francs (roughly equivalent to 260 million euros now). Net profits that year came to over a fifth of turnover.[7] But in 1913 the war could still seem far away. Only the Michelin air prizes contained a hint of the brothers' concern for military preparedness. Introducing the year's trophies, André Michelin reminded readers of his Monday column that Wilbur Wright had won the first Coupe Michelin with a flight of 77 miles; in 1911, the last year there had been a winner, the distance flown had risen to 776 miles. This year the successful candidate would have to fly a minimum of 1240 miles. In fact the winner flew 12,956 miles, of which 9920 counted for the cup.[8]

Preparing the French for another Air Target Prize, a Monday column had Bibendum explain that aerial bombing was equivalent to aerial jiu-jitsu. 'To knock down a giant it isn't necessary to hit him with a sledgehammer; a few well-placed blows, touching a nerve centre and paralyzing the enormous musculature, can suffice.' Concluded Bibendum:

> Imagine, for example, railway station full of trains, soldiers, horses, cannon, and constantly crossed by other trains... Now imagine that a slender bird,

so weak before this colossus of a thousand arms, sweeps over it. A few of its droppings destroy the railway cars, twist the tracks, disrupt the switches and blow up the switchman's cabin that represented the brain of the station. (Don't scream 'Impossible!' A Bulgarian aviator recently destroyed a Turkish radio station by bombing.)[9]

A whole generation later, during the build-up to the Second World War, only madmen dared to suggest that air power could be decisive. The best military authorities, even the so-called precursors, continued to 'scream "Impossible!"'.

But for the moment, Michelin's own favourite target continued to be rival tyre-maker Continental. This time Michelin appeared to have a perfect case: evidence of line-by-line plagiarism of the *Guide Michelin* in Continental's guide to France. The magistrates ordered the seizure and confiscation of all 32,000 copies of the German company's guide-book.

'It would have been too cruel to lose the fruit of so much effort, to discourage our employees who gave us so much patient work and devotion,' wrote André, to explain Michelin's decision to go to court. 'You have to be very audacious and totally indifferent to the laws of the country according one hospitality not only to denationalize one's products and pass them off as French, but to plagiarize a French work insolently.'[10]

But France was still at peace, and there was still much prospecting to do. In June 1913, at the very moment Michelin was taking Continental to court, André engaged a journalist with a Sorbonne degree in literature whose specialties ranged from automobiles to gastronomy to write some of his public messages. Maurice-Edmond Sailland, who signed his writings Curnonsky, would have been 40 years old when André brought him in for an occasional guest column. Later (after the First World War) he would become a professional journalist with a column of his own. Still later he'd become known as the Prince of Gastronomes, publishing a food and wine guide which was at once a competitor to and a validation of the Michelin guides.

In Sailland's own recollection, he wrote a considerable number of Monday columns signed Michelin or Bibendum (but he also recalled that it was he who had invented the slogan 'Le pneu qui boît l'obstacle' – although when André first pronounced that phrase Sailland was still in school).[11]

None of this is important – but it shows the carefree (still carefree) spirit of the times. In December 1913, the 660th Michelin 'Monday' announced to the world (*Le Journal* was now printed in close to one million copies), that Michelin needed draughtsmen to work on its map of France, which was not only regularly reprinted but 'constantly revised, corrected, improved'. The present staff had become 'totally insufficient, and needed considerable reinforcement'. They hoped to recruit professional geographers, but also former soldiers who had worked on topography during their military service.[12]

Whomever they hired as a result of that call would certainly be called up elsewhere within the year.

*   *   *

In April 1914, four months before the beginning of the Great War, Michelin's suit against Continental came up before a Paris commercial court. There was some convincing evidence, seized at the plant that printed the Continental guide-book: entire pages cut out of a current *Guide Michelin*, pasted up to be ready for the typesetter of the *Guide Continental*. The judgment affirmed that while Michelin had more or less kept the same format from the beginning, Continental changed its format and contents each year to approach that of its competitor. The manner in which Michelin was plagiarized by its rival was deemed 'reprehensible'. In its defence, Continental claimed that it had done its copying from an old (1909) edition of the *Guide Michelin*, which it believed to be in the public domain. The tribunal considered that a major work like the Michelin could not be presumed to have been abandoned.

Further, Michelin pointed out that Continental claimed it made its tyres in Clichy, when in fact they came from Germany. Continental's representative admitted that the tyres were German, adding that 'everybody' was aware of that.

Confirming the original seizure of the 32,000-copy printing of the German guide-book, the court ordered payment of damages and forbade Continental from reproducing the plagiarized pages in any future publication.

In his next Monday column, André Michelin was quick to report the decision – but omitted the name Continental (calling it 'X Company of Germany').[13] At the same time he ordered a flyer, to be distributed to automobile manufacturers, garages and Michelin clients, in which Continental was identified by name. The accompanying drawings showed a *Guide Michelin* with its pages cut up; a monkey climbing into a Bibendum costume; Bibendum holding a whip, a cigar between his lips, hauling the monkey into court.[14]

18

OF BOMBS
AND TYRES

There were so many reasons for fighting Germany. Everybody seemed prepared for it, if only in conviction. Yet the immediate cause of war would have appeared remote to all but the diplomats – the Balkan maelstrom, entangling alliances which guaranteed that a war that began there would spread here. Officially, the conflict that would later be called World War I began for France on 3 August 1914, when Germany formally declared war, by which time that country's soldiers were already marching toward France through Belgium. Troops well prepared, and in strength; that and clever strategy facilitated enemy penetration of France and brought the attackers perilously close to Paris; but the line drawn by General Joffre along the Marne would hold – and all this in the first month of combat.

It was not a time to forget that there were two Michelin brothers – the publicist and the maker. The publicist moved faster, with an announcement on 6 August (signed, of course, for both brothers) that the Michelins had established a fund to reward military pilots for heroism and skill – the sums to be distributed at the end of hostilities.[1] But of course André Michelin knew that there had not been time for his campaign for 5000 planes to capture imaginations or affect policies. By his own calculation, the outbreak of conflict had caught France with no more than 120 aircraft, and these of 14 different types, assigned to 21 squadrons, some equipped with five or six different kinds of plane...[2]

So, on August 20 – scarcely a fortnight after the German declaration – the Michelins informed the government that they were prepared to donate 100 airframes for bombing planes, manufactured at their own expense in Clermont-Ferrand. At the same time, they would produce, at cost, as many aircraft as the government needed.

The offer was accepted, the choice of aircraft a Breguet biplane equipped with a 200 hp motor mounted at the rear; acting on Michelin's request, Renault got to work building a similar motor for a second series of Breguet Michelin bombers. For bombers they were – despite the fact that they resembled most other two-passenger warplanes of the day, which is to say that they appeared vulnerable and frail. Based on a prototype flown to Clermont-Ferrand in June 1915, immediately stripped for examination so as to allow duplication of its parts in a new factory building conceived for tyre production, Breguets began to come out of the Clermont-Ferrand factory as early as July – 11 months into the war. In the meantime, the Michelins had begun designing and building bombs and bomb launchers almost as soon as the government gave them the green light to do so.[3]

While Edouard was drafting, then giving concrete form to his designs, André was creating military doctrine. For the Michelins were not just going to turn out bombers in name; they meant to see that their planes were employed effectively as bombers. In a letter dated 19 February 1915, signed simply 'Michelin' and addressed to the War Ministry's director of aeronautics, André made his case for an air offensive:

> Dear General,
>
> Our purpose in donating one hundred planes to the French Army was to give it a tool designed to cut the enemy's communications.
>
> In our view, this tool could only be a group of similar aircraft placed under a single command and conceived for this specific mission.
>
> All the reports we have had, either from officers known to us or from the many company employees now on the front (and who are carrying out their duties courageously, since we have already had 79 dead and some 15 cited for bravery), lead us to believe that the breakthrough of enemy lines can be obtained only at the price of many sacrifices because of the crushing nature of present-day firepower directed to a particular objective prepared in advance.
>
> But these arms – rifles, rapid-firing cannon, machine guns still more rapid – are dangerous only if supplied with ammunition. We are more and more certain that the enemy will be dealt a terrible blow if we can, either on a significant sector of the line or on the entire front, cut his communications, interrupt the arrival of ammunition and thus render its excellent armament useless.

At the time, no French bombers worthy of the name existed. André had learned the sad truth from French aces whose missions took them over enemy territory. At best an observer accompanying the pilot might bring along six small projectiles – but then he'd be carrying them on his knees. Lacking any instruments to guide him, the observer would simply toss them out when he judged that he was over a target. The cleverest planted two nails outside the fuselage to help their aim.

André was to reveal that the officer responsible for aviation at general headquarters, when hectored about the need to find a way to get a bomb to hit a specific target, replied, 'It's unnecessary to aim with a bombing plane, given the dimensions of the objectives under attack'.[4] Michelin's bomb launcher then consisted of two wooden frames, one fixed at either side of the plane; to avoid throwing the aircraft off balance, bombs would be released alternatively. Giving material form to another of their convictions, the brothers put together their own bombsight, to be utilized with tables making it possible for the bombardier to calculate the optimal moment of bomb release from the altitude and speed of the aircraft, as well as wind direction and speed.

Whether or not publicity was among their motives, the Michelin brothers got some immediately. The first 100 planes out of Clermont-Ferrand formed a 'Michelin squadron', also called the division Michelin. The 75 planes sent into combat were divided into three groups, each group containing three flights, while the remaining 25 were kept in reserve.[5]

It should go without saying that much of Clermont-Ferrand was now a defence plant. Army vehicles could use all the tyres and tubes, the chains for driving in mud and snow, that Michelin could turn out. From the start the brothers waived profits on military equipment. For tyres turned out for civilian use – and there were some – pre-war prices were maintained despite the rise in the cost of living.

Shortly before the war, Michelin's research department designed a solid steel wheel which could serve both as protection against enemy bullets and friendly but rough roads; now these wheels were rushed into production. Remarkably, the same steel wheels were put on the market for civilian customers as early as 1917 – the grimmest year of the war. And Michelin's promotion stressed the argument that the tyres had proved themselves in battle – this when the war was far from won.

Launched in the spring of 1914, the Michelin 'Steel Wheel' proved itself in the war. It was adopted by different army services for light vehicles as for heavy ones, as well as for trucks weighing up to seven tons with their loads. Everywhere, in the Orient as in France, exposed on the worst roads to jolts, bumps, and the roughest imaginable jolts, it gave excellent results and proved its solidity and rugged resistance a thousand times over.

This revelatory text – which saved time for enemy agents – was followed by illustrated instructions on how to install the tyre, and further detailed information on its advantages and proper use. All this in a slender three-and-a-half by seven-and-a-half inch brochure (the modest dimensions suggested wartime frugality) with its self-explanatory title: 'Some Advice for obtaining from the best tyre that is, the Michelin Tyre the best results'. Contrary to what one might have expected, the 40-page text did not stress conservation. If the driver's tyres were not the proper ones for the vehicle, 'change them,' advised the manufacturer, describing recent innovations such as a new set of dual tyres recommended for heavier vehicles. Other products still in production were made of solid metals, such as the jack ('1914 model') and the portable air pump. It hardly seemed necessary to add that, despite the war, Clermont-Ferrand was running full steam. Front and back jackets of the booklet depicted a jolly Bibendum, a big cigar in his mouth.

The plant – which from its earliest years had seemed able to make just about anything anyone needed – was now also expected to produce miscellaneous equipment required by the army, including tents, sleeping bags, canteens – even horseshoes.

Everything Michelin did was done in a big way. With the enemy pressing closer at the beginning of September 1914, a recently built tyre warehouse was converted into a military hospital. A wartime pamphlet produced by André Michelin offers a look into the factory as plant carpenters hammer together hospital furniture, while women workers make mattresses and pillows, extra clothing for wounded soldiers, hospital smocks, bandages and other medical equipment that the Michelin hospital might require. At company expense, the hospital brought in the hard-to-find tetanus vaccine from as far away as Britain and the United States.

Twenty-one days after launching the project, Michelin was ready to receive patients. The first convoy of wounded soldiers arrived on

13. Michelin during the First World War: Michelin Hospital, view of one of the wards. Michelin Guides to the Battlefields, *Ypres and the Battle of Ypres*, 1919.

22 September. By the beginning of July 1917 (when André published the brochure on the company's contribution to the war effort), the Michelin hospital had cared for 2914 wounded soldiers.

Michelin's own workers called to arms were not forgotten. Families received special allocations (two francs a day for wives, one franc for each child). Beginning in February 1915, Michelin informed workers then in uniform that in the event of their death pensions would be paid to their children (from 400 to 950 francs depending on the number of children under 16). But surviving families needed more than money – 'A widow and orphans may require moral support,' said the note circulated to plant personnel. 'We are ready, as are many of our senior workers and office staff, to provide this moral support.'

There was a clear intention to encourage large families – part of a pro-birth philosophy which André Michelin would espouse with his usual verve, joining a movement called Repopulating France even before the war began (he had become a board member in May 1914, then a sponsor soon after the declaration of hostilities). The movement's reason for being was the sad truth that France's birth-rate was lower than that of its European neighbours – friends or foes – a handicap in peacetime, a danger in the event of war. Giving concrete form to their beliefs, the Michelins now reduced rentals on their housing sites for families with three or more children. In 1916, the first real Michelin schools were opened in the facilities of the day-care centre – ancestors of the network of company schools which would take Michelin children from kindergarten up to the day they could work – at Michelin, of course. There were special classes to prepare young girls to be future mothers and housewives.

Michelin would later produce statistics to show that its families did produce more children, their birth-rate being 21.2 percent compared to 14.9 percent for 'non Michelin' families of the region. By promoting more births and then nursing the youngsters through school and married life, Michelin was in a sense guaranteeing its future labour supply.[6]

And then, building what was virtually a new plant for a new product – the Breguet bombers – allowed Edouard Michelin to introduce the Taylor system without fear of upsetting old working habits. Scientific management, American style, was credited with making it possible to do so much in so little time, and with such short notice.[7]

*   *   *

Legend has it that Edouard Michelin travelled up to the Camp d'Avord near Bourges to explain his theories to pilots assigned to the new Breguets – and was received with scepticism, if not worse. ('Maybe Bibendum wants to teach us our job!') There had been incidents when pilots ignored wind directions before landing – and so skidded across the strip. So Edouard began by admitting that he knew nothing about piloting; but he did know his tyre. 'In putting my tyres on your planes I wanted them to run and not skid,' he quipped – and won over his listeners.[8]

But there was more to it than that. Michelin did some serious lobbying to influence the way pilots were taught bombing, convincing the high command that for maximum efficacy a squadron would have to string out the launching of its bombs, as opposed to dropping all the projectiles at once in a dive. After a number of test bombings on military terrain, the general staff seemed ready to believe what they had been told.

Next the irrepressible brothers took it on themselves to establish a bombing school. With the support of General Joseph Gallieni, an old and distinguished soldier who had become War Minister, ground was requisitioned at Aulnat, not far from Clermont. To keep his Breguets flying despite heavy mud, Edouard Michelin had the airstrip cemented, thereby creating what was believed to be the world's first paved runway.

'The purpose,' so the Michelins informed the undersecretary of state for aeronautics by letter of 27 January 1916, 'is to present a unit or flight of [Breguet Michelin] planes flown by men trained method-ically, handling equipment expressly designed for the job, and thus to carry out efficacious attacks; in a word, planes truly ready to depart for the front'.

In truth, the Michelin pilots were testing the brothers' theories, and passing on the results so that new military doctrine could be created.

Only on 24 October 1916 did an official body recommend that 'Mr. Michelin's method of instruction and bombing procedures be employed throughout the service'. They called particular attention to the efficacity of string bombing, regretting that because of scepticism in high places two years had been lost. In a letter to the president of the Republic in November, the Michelins made further recommend-ations based on what they had learned at Aulnat. Bombing raids across enemy territory should not exceed 60 miles, to avoid going astray. Any target chosen must be attacked until destroyed, even if that meant returning again and again. While the main objective would be ammu-nition dumps, enemy aviation must be destroyed first, notably by attacking hangars sheltering aircraft, and airfields which remain illu-minated when their planes have flown off on missions, so that on return the enemy planes will be damaged in landing 'on ground pitted with craters'.

Looking back on those labours – looking back 13 months after the Armistice – André Michelin found cause for satisfaction. Aviation had played a a major role in the final, victorious offensive. By November 1918 Clermont-Ferrand was turning out seven planes a day; in all, by the close of the war it had it built 1884 Breguet bombers, 147 of them for the United States forces in France, 8600 bomb launchers, 342,000 bombs of various calibres, of which 27,700 were delivered to the

United States Army. The American Expeditionary Forces moved in to the Aulnat school to train their own pilots and bombardiers.

Faithful to their image and reputation, Michelin quickly produced an English-language brochure on *Michelin Bombing Gear: Bre 14-B²* *Aeroplane*, focusing on operations of the symmetrical frames, each fitted under the lower wing, and which could carry a wide variety of bombs (hand controls inside the fuselage permitted the operator to release the bombs, the launcher powered by a rubber spring).[9]

By now, designer Louis Breguet had perfected his bomber, placing the motor forward as in pre-war models. The first Breguet Michelin XIV B² came out of the Clermont-Ferrand factory in May 1917; when flying in formation the new plane became a formidable weapon, credited with a role in the allied victory.[10]

Fulfilling its pledge, Michelin ceased to manufacture aeroplanes when the war was over, to focus on what it did best.[11]

*　　　　　　　　*　　　　　　　　*

But it was a new Michelin, a Michelin aware that it had been able to transform its physical plant to adapt to a totally different type of production, applying Frederick Winslow Taylor's scientific management not for extra profit, but out of necessity. Edouard had also learned that he could employ more women, discovering just where and how they could do a man's job. He had found new reasons to sponsor a cradle-to-grave welfare system – not simply to attract and retain workers, but because there were times when families needed protection, and one could not be indifferent when they were Michelin families.

Social critics suggested that innovations such as bonuses for large families were introduced not out of charity, but as a way to pacify labour without raising salaries – for salaries would then have to remain at the higher level when peace returned. All the same, while the war was still raging – and far from won – Michelin experienced considerable agitation on the factory floor, attributed to dissatisfaction with wages, notably on the part of newly recruited workers unfamiliar with the Michelin culture.[12]

There is also evidence that, despite the special circumstances of wartime recruiting, and the massive recourse to women, the Patron was not prepared to waive his strict rules concerning loyalty. A woman hired in 1915 found herself confronted by traditional Michelin anxiety about secret-stealing. In her contract, written as an agreement between 'Edouard-Etienne Michelin, manufacturer in Clermont-Ferrand, acting in his name and as manager of the limited partnership Michelin & Co.', and this woman we shall call Mademoiselle X, the new recruit, 'undertakes to give all her time and effort to the Company and to support it in developing its production and sales...'. For her part, she assures her employer that she had never before worked in a rubber or a tyre plant and is totally ignorant of the manufacturing process. She recognizes that any divulging of these processes would cause considerable prejudice, 'given that Michelin & Co. reached the summit in its field only by constantly improving its special and secret procedures which each day form the basis for new inventions and further prosperity'.

Hence, Mademoiselle X pledges to reveal nothing, to take no notes and carry no documents out of the factory while employed or thereafter. On departure, she will neither assist nor work for any other company in France or abroad making the same products, and this for a period of five years; neither will she undertake any such production on her own or file for patents in the field.

Should she violate any of these provisions, she must pay Michelin eight times the sums received in salaries and bonuses in the 12 months preceding her departure, for a minimum of 20,000 francs – and this apart from damages that Michelin might obtain in court.

Her own pay would be 100 francs monthly, plus an annual bonus not inferior to 100 francs (depending on company results). The minimum bonus of 100 francs would be paid in April of the following year, the balance if any to be received in cash or held in escrow for five years after the end of her employment, then remitted only if none of the contract provisions had been violated. (She would receive 5 percent interest on the withheld sums.) Another clause spelled out: 'If Mademoiselle X should die without having violated any of her promises, the sums in her special account and the arrears will be transmitted to her heirs within three months of her decease'.[13]

*   *   *

Michelin had not forgotten how to make tyres, equipping the French military, and (importantly) the Americans as they arrived – for theirs was a young and a famously motorized army. The importation of raw materials – especially rubber – was obviously difficult during the years of hostilities, while exports of finished tyres were encouraged. (France itself was virtually a closed market, with tight government restrictions on tyre imports.) By the end of the war, Michelin had multiplied its workforce by two – reflecting both a boom in tyre sales and the exceptional production of warplanes and other military *matériel*.[14]

19

TOURISTS
ON THE
BATTLEFIELD

In February 1915, German armies continued to occupy much of northeastern France, a region representing both industrial potential and strategic raw materials. The French remained on the watchful defensive. Again and again commander-in-chief General Joseph Joffre sent his troops against German lines east of Paris – with little or nothing to show for it.

It was just then that André Michelin, no shirker, chose to publish a Michelin guide to, of all places, Western Germany. As if there were no war at all. Written in French, the text covered the enemy's heartland as far as Rostock, Berlin and Leipzig to the east, and Bayreuth, Ulm, and Konstanz to the south. (Strassburg – using the German spelling – in German-held Alsace, was not forgotten.)

Although the guide-book bears the indication that it was actually printed in February 1915, a calendar just inside the cover begins in May and continues to the end of that year. There is also some helpful advice: 'When entering Germany, move watches forward one hour'.

When entering Germany? This is precisely what France's general staff would have liked to do, but of course getting even close to the German frontier would be as difficult for a civilian just then as for a man wearing a French army uniform. The little volume goes on to provide an 'Overview of the political and administration organization of Germany', Alsace-Lorraine included.

This German guide-book – largely a revamping of pre-war editions – never actually entered into Michelin's corpus, was not advertised then and never showed up in the historical bibliographies later. It was soon joined by another phantom *Guide Michelin* for Belgium and Luxembourg (printed in September 1915, when both countries remained under German military occupation). One could imagine that an avaricious publisher might compile and print such books in French to sell in neutral Switzerland – but of course patriotic André Michelin would never have considered such a thing, and even a guide-book publisher indifferent to such a sentimental consideration as love of country would not have seen the small Swiss-French-speaking market worth the risk. Nor would any Swiss citizen, whatever his or her attitude toward the war, now be contemplating a tourist romp through Germany.[1]

Surely André Michelin – perhaps on his own, without prodding from the War Ministry – had ordered the publication in preparation for an allied invasion of Germany and adjacent occupied territories, even if nothing inside the books said as much.[2] Issuing guide-books to enemy territory in the usual format, with no indication that they were designed to be used during an invasion, may have seemed as secure an operation as if they were stamped 'Secret'. In a later world war the French *Guide Michelin* was to serve a similar purpose.

*   *   *

Perhaps André Michelin was restless all the same. Although he had passed his 61st birthday some seven months before the outbreak of war in August 1914, he was clearly not ready to retire, and yet the war obliged him to reduce the activity he enjoyed most and did best – preparing his beloved guide-books, his aggressive promotions. One could hardly encourage tourists to use precious resources for leisure-time travel just then.

But he soon found a way to employ his talents and Michelin's unique travel organization in the service of his country. Thus emerged an extraordinary series of Michelin battlefield guides, compiled and written while the war was still in progress, a war not going particularly well for France and its allies at the time.

The precise inspiration for the project is not clear. As an advocate of preparedness in the pre-war years and a manufacturer of military equipment at the current time, Michelin would have been in constant contact with the War Ministry and general staff. Michelin later said that

St. Nicolas   Old French Barracks   School

PANORAMIC VIEW OF THE RUINS
(The point from where this photograph was taken is

an inverted keel. In it were a 16th century altar, large carved pulpit and a fine choir-screen.

Rue de Lille ends at Lille Gate. Before passing through, climb up the

RUINS OF THE HÔTEL DE GAND, RUE DES CHIENS

Post- Bell-   St. Peter's   St. James'
Office Tower   Church   Church

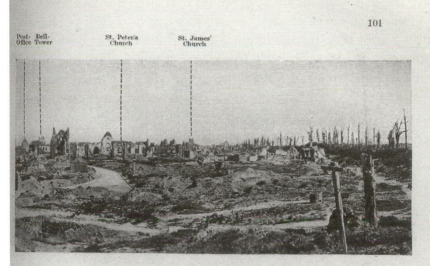

OF YPRES TAKEN FROM LILLE GATE
shown on the plan on p. 72 (at the bottom, on the right).

ramparts, from which there is a magnificent panorama.

Pass through the Gate, the towers of which date from 1395. There is an interesting view over the wide moats, and of the ancient ramparts (rebuilt by Vauban), which were ruined by shells.

Turn back and re-enter the town by the same way. Beyond the Church of St. Pierre, take the first street on the right as far as the Rue des Chiens, where, on turning to the left, the ruins of the Church St. Jacques, and the shattered façade of the Hôtel de Gand will be seen.

The latter fine house, with double gables dated from the 16th century. The transition from 15th to 16th century style is very marked : on the ground-floor is the irregular arch of the 15th century, while on the first floor the arches are full semi-circles, framing the rectangular bays, whose tmypana

THE HÔTEL DE GAND
(Photo, Antony, Ypres.)

14. Illustrated Michelin Guides to the Battlefields, *Ypres and the Battle of Ypres*, 1919. The pages show a panoramic view of the ruins of Ypres, and 'before' and 'after' photographs of the Hôtel de Gand.

the project had been specifically requested by the 'propaganda services', a request that André as a patriot would have been quick to heed.[3]

But what stuns the reader – even today – is the date of publication of the first of these battlefield guides. The three volumes covering the combats on the Marne in the opening year of war were actually printed and distributed in 1917, when much of the country was still occupied by the enemy, and when there was still more bad news than good filtering in from the front. Another set of guides was ready in the early months of 1918 (the war would end with allied victory in November, but the Germans were still launching offensives as late as the middle of July).

The very first volume of the series covered the Ourcq river campaign (with the battles for Meaux, Senlis and Chantilly), one of three covering the Marne valley fought over until the last months of the war. The reader picks up this first, slender (120-page) tome with respect if not awe – it is history, jotted down while history was being made (and who could then be sure that the sites described would not fall to the aggressor soon again?).

Just inside the flexible front cover, one is in familiar territory – with an extract of the peacetime *Guide Michelin* listing towns in which the traveller is likely to find accommodation during the battlefield tour – Meaux, Senlis, Chantilly, Ermenonville and Acy-en-Multien. Hotels are rated with the familiar gabled-roof symbols, garages that stock Michelin tyres are indicated. A warning is included: 'Information published here as of August 1, 1917, may no longer be valid when the reader picks up this book'. In a preface undoubtedly written by André we read:

> We don't see this as a simple promenade in devastated landscape, but as a true pilgrimage…This volume appears before the end of the war, but the territories through which it leads the reader have been liberated for some time. The abundant illustrations will allow tourists who are not yet able to travel to make the trip for the first time in their imagination before actually doing it under the skies of the Paris countryside.

While the war is obviously the central theme of this and the following books in the series, the user was also invited to do some old-fashioned sightseeing. In Chantilly one might visit both Joffre's general head-quarters (occupied by his staff from the time the French stopped the Germans on the Marne until 1916) and the famous ducal castle with its art collections. In a sense, the battlefield series was to pave the way for the Michelin regional guide-books, launched in 1926. Each of the Marne battle guides opened with an historical summary, illustrated with photographs of the commanding officers (French and British, but German too) and maps of the fighting day by day. Under the heading 'Practical Information', automobilists and motorcyclists were advised that the 150-mile circuit can be done in two days; cyclists are given more time.

> The route now to be described covers the terrain on which the fate of Paris was decided in September 1914. In the course of this excursion the tourist will relive the pathetic moment in which the Germans, then within cannon shot of the capital, had to decide whether to pursue their thunderbolt march on Paris, or first to seek to neutralize French and British forces; it will then reconstitute the tragic combat which over five days pitted French generals Gallieni and [Joseph] Maunoury against German general [Alexander] von Klück.[4]

Fittingly, there was no advertising in these invitations to a pilgrimage. That changed as soon as the war was over, and later printings of the early books in the series, as well as new titles, were able to promote Michelin products again. Illustrated with a sketch of a jaunty coupé with a uniformed chauffeur in the outside seat, an advertisement in a 1920 reprinting of one of the Battle of the Marne volumes expounds on the qualities of the new Michelin steel wheels,

> Chic,
>> it adds to the elegance of the finest car bodies.
> Simple,
>> it is held in place only by six bolts.
> Solid,
>> it alone proved resistant on all fronts during the war.
> Practical,
>> it can be replaced in 3 minutes by anybody and can be cleaned in less time than that.
>
>> It extends the life of tyres
>> in keeping them cool
>> And it's the cheapest.[5]

In one of the English-language battlefield guide-books, an advertisement for the same product contrasts two scenes: soldiers in a military vehicle speed along on Michelin steel wheels as a shell whizzes over their heads, and a jaunty chauffeured coupé is parked in front of a great country house. The message is clear: 'THE BEST AND CHEAPEST DETACHABLE WHEEL. The Michelin Wheel is practical and strong [this for the military vehicle]. The Michelin Wheel is simple and smart [this for the chauffeured coupé].'[6] On 27 September 1917, to mark publication of the first volume on the Battle of the Marne, there was a 'pilgrimage' to the scene, sponsored by the government's national tourist bureau and the Touring-Club de France. The 'pilgrims', officials responsible for tourist promotion, were accompanied by represent-atives of the French and foreign press. They were guests at a reception given at Chantilly Castle. 'Three million visitors, in the first three post-war years, could bring France nine billion gold francs, which would nourish all our industries and trades,' declared a Touring-Club official. 'None of us has the right to forget that every encouragement to the hotel industry is an encouragement to one's own industry or trade.'[7]

In his own talk, André Michelin offered what he said was another motive for publication of his little books.

> On the other side of the front the enemy is preparing special guidebooks supposedly meant for 'a visit to the battlefields' but whose secret purpose is to demonstrate that the Germans did not commit the atrocities of which they are accused and that it was the French, Belgians, and British who started it all by burning down homes and raping, and therefore brought on retaliation.

It was the Kaiser himself who had ordered the production of such propaganda in the form of battlefield guides.[8]

Nor was André to forget that the war had brought the Americans to France – Americans who would go home singing the praises of Michelin if he did his job right; Michelin was still small in the United States, but automobiles were big, and more of them could be equipped with Michelin tyres. A scholar who studied company archives on the wartime American market – when (beginning in May 1918) 250,000 United States soldiers were landing in France monthly – found that Michelin men undertook detailed surveys of the strength and location of American soldiers in France, to the point that one of the Michelin commercial travellers was suspected of spying for the Germans. Using the battlefield guide-books as their visiting cards, the Michelin men even thought of making their first contacts with arriving Americans aboard the ships taking them to France, and perhaps back in the United States at college campuses. André Michelin may even have met the American commander General John J. Pershing in order to arrange sales of the battlefield guides inside army camps.

One product specifically directed to Americans was an English-language guide to *Clermont-Ferrand, Royat and Surroundings*, whose points of interest included the army headquarters installed at the Royat-Palace (a four-gabled hotel in the editions of the *Guide Michelin* published just before and just after the war), as well as Hospital Base No. 30. The little book invites American readers to visit the Michelin factory on place des Carmes-Déchaux, for 'remarks or complaints', or servicing of tyres. And then the pay-off message: 'The first automobile tyre in the world was made in 1895 by Michelin et Cie Clermont-Ferrand; Michelin Tires are also made in your country by The Michelin Tire Co. Milltown – New Jersey U.S.A'.[9] This was a book to use on the spot. To take home, American soldiers in France were handed copies of a pocket-sized 18-page souvenir booklet. Inside the front cover, portraits of General Pershing and Marshal Foch illustrate the text of the American commander's message to the French leader. It began: 'I have come to tell you that the American people would consider it a great honour for our troops to be engaged in the present battle...' The following pages offer potted descriptions of American victories – Cantigny in May 1918, Château-Thierry and Bois de Belleau in June, Saint-Mihiel in September – accompanied by the text of President Poincaré's congratulations to President Woodrow Wilson for the Saint-Mihiel victory.[10]

20

AFTER THE ARMISTICE

André Michelin had celebrated his 65th birthday at the beginning of the year that saw the end of the war. But he still gave no sign that he was about to retire. He remained an active member of every professional organization appropriate to his interests and abilities, and never missed a ceremony or a meeting, an opportunity to espouse one of his causes – sometimes more than one cause at a time, as when he turned over the proceeds of his battlefield guides to the campaign for repopulation.[1]

Just two weeks before the Armistice, he was addressing the National Association of Economic Expansion on the subject of the road network that would be required after the war. 'After our victory,' he cautioned, 'our roads will have to support traffic of unimagined intensity, far greater than what we knew before the war…'

He wanted his country to retrieve what it enjoyed 'at the outset of the automobile age' earlier in the century, namely the best roads in the world. It was a matter of surfacing, of signage and of numbering (the better the road, the less petrol was consumed). Road transport would never come into its own until roads were improved so that trucks could match railway speeds. He hoped that municipalities would avoid fashionable street names like Jean Jaurès or President Wilson, keeping more helpful identifications like 'Rue de Paris'. Another thing he hoped to see was the creation of circular boulevards around cities and towns to keep traffic out of congested and narrow downtown streets. Some of his admonitions were heeded.[2]

As soon as the Germans had laid down their arms, the men and women of Michelin gathered up their notes and maps in preparation for the first post-war *Guide Michelin*.

There was a lot to be done. Much of the France described in earlier Michelins had been occupied by the enemy for the four long years of war; some of it was devastated. Then there were so many new cities and towns to add – places that had been under German domination ever since the Franco–Prussian War of 1870–71 – Strasbourg for instance, which at the time the new edition of the guide was going to press still used its German street names.

'We decided to bring out our Guide this year despite present circumstances,' read a title page note – surely from André's pen; it also informed readers that the book continued to be given away without charge. 'It is understood that some information found in this book may not correspond to reality.' After all, some 2350 cities, towns and villages were featured in this first post-war guide-book – while the 1914 edition had covered only 2300. And 75,000 copies were being printed.

In addition to calling attention to the gamut of Michelin accessories like a lifting jack and an air container the 1919 guide-book announced 'Le Câblé', a totally new concept in tyres. Wider, less rigid, it was composed of the more flexible material used for bicycle tyres, yet had been strengthened because each thread was twisted – *câblé*.[3]

*   *   *

Yet the immediate post-war years found Michelin in a defensive position. If the United States had a slow start in the automobile revolution, it caught up quickly, attaining technological superiority even before the war. Just as one looked westward for lessons only a Frederick Winslow Taylor could teach, one knew that the immense American industrial plant was spending more on research and development. American tyres slipped easily into France – or if customs barriers held them up, they could simply be made in a French factory. And for some time to come these tyres would benefit from the prestige of the world's most advanced industrial society. If Michelin continued to grow in the immediate post-war era, with something over 10,000 employees in 1919, and 12,000 a year later, by then America's market leaders outdistanced Clermont-Ferrand – Goodrich with its payroll of 23,325, Goodyear with 22,500 and Firestone with 15,000.

Michelin would triumph all the same; it would grow to be the biggest of them all (and eventually buy out the 1920 leader, Goodrich). Its dominance could not have been achieved through domestic sales alone, or even within the European market, whose size restricted the means available for research and development. Then what did make Michelin?

It would be wrong to underestimate that cautious man down in Clermont-Ferrand. Edouard may have been André's younger brother (he was 60 years old in 1919), but he was still the Patron. And despite his commitment to Taylorism, he believed in some old-fashioned remedies. 'We have customers who came to us at the beginning of our activity – twenty years ago now – and who have never bought tyres from anyone else but us, because they are good tyres.' So he told a meeting of his plant foremen in 1919. 'To make good tyres, you must make constant improvements. You've got to beat last year's Michelin tyre.'[4]

About Edouard there are few anecdotes, only pious recollections. Everything we know of him says that he truly believed that he was running his factory for the general good, respecting religious tenets, upholding the nation. Speaking of Michelin's family support service, which was created 16 years before French law made the system obligatory in 1932, he would say that 'it's proper to help families with many children, and widows too. It's a duty.' It was the kind of charity a churchgoer would comprehend. But patriotism was also involved: 'This duty is even more urgent because France is losing population. We must support and honour large families.'[5]

The end of the war did not signify an end to allocations, or indeed to any of the social services introduced in the recent past. On the contrary, they were now to expand in all directions, concomitant with a new programme of housing for factory and office workers and their families.

Nor did the Armistice allow for a relaxation of vigilance against the late enemy. On 15 March 1919, early in the discussions in Versailles among the wartime allies which were to hammer out a peace treaty and – importantly – to propose means to guarantee against future wars, Edouard Michelin put his name alongside his brother's on an open letter addressed to the French president, Raymond Poincaré, which called for radical measures to keep Germany from rearming. 'The Peace Conference is about to decide on measures required to destroy Prussian militarism for all time,' it began. Germany's armed forces would be reduced to the strict minimum, while its military aviation was to be disbanded totally. But this, the brothers argued, would give the Allies only 'platonic' satisfaction; the danger of air attack would remain 'greater than ever' should defeated Germany be allowed to maintain civil aviation. 'If your generation doesn't shut down Germany's civil aviation fleet [concluded the Michelin message], it will carry the weight of a crushing responsibility before History.'[6]

*   *   *

In April 1919 André Michelin was ready to begin his Michelin Mondays again – only now they were Saturdays, which was the day of publication of *L'Illustration*. His columns would henceforth bear the signature 'Bibendum'. 'Today,' the first column began, 'my papa Michelin is allowing me to talk again and to carry out a weekly conversation with you'. In this magazine read by tourists all over the world, explained Bibendum, he would use his column to give good and reliable travel information on sights, places to stay and roads ('which I know as if I had built them').[7]

Soon Bibendum was reminding readers that in publishing the battlefield guides Michelin was making no money, since all profits would go to a non-profit association promoting French repopulation. After a description of the best features of the guide-book series, Bibendum concluded with a jibe at its potential competitor across the Rhine: 'After that, if you prefer Baedeker!...but in that case there's a chance you'll find some things missing in it'.[8]

In another column André Michelin – or his proxy (who might even have been the travel writer Curnonsky), described a 10-day motor tour from Paris east to Château-Thierry, Rheims and Soissons, following the itinerary of the second Battle of the Marne, the allied counter-offensive of July and August 1918 which regained terrain taken earlier by the enemy.

The writer discovered that the roads were better than could have been expected: 'The battlefield is intact – and sublime, with its decor of trenches, barbed wire, shell holes, abandoned tanks'. But then came the obstacles. Not insurmountable ones, but sufficient to call for in-genuity all the same. The food, for example: 'Don't count on feasting everywhere...But it's easy to bring one's own picnic meat and an old bottle of wine.' As for sleeping: 'You'll find some hastily repaired hotels in Rheims, but they are packed like buses'. Rheims had been in the front line during most of the recent war, and was now in ruins. The 1919 *Guide Michelin* mentioned three modest hotels there, one of which was the Grand Hôtel annex – but there was no Grand Hôtel. Bibendum tells of his own experience:

> ... The Continental [one of the hotels listed in the 1919 guide] sent me to the North Hotel, which turned me over to the Champagne from which I rushed to the Leo to wind up at ... somebody's home – but a friendly and hospitable somebody who let me have the bed of one of his kids.

It was the same situation in Soissons, while in Verdun the writer was told that travellers had to sleep in school dormitories, separated by sex.[9]

One could have assumed that after a full year of peace André Michelin could put thoughts of war behind him; there was more than enough work for one man promoting Michelin in its preferred role as tyre manufacturer to the world.

But now, in the last days of June 1919, after long months of deliberation, the belligerents had convened in the Hall of Mirrors of Louis XIV's castle to sign the Treaty of Versailles, bringing the Great War to a formal close. To the consternation of the Michelins, their 'warning' – expressed in the letter to President Poincaré – had not been heeded. So it was time for André to mount his white horse again. As his prescient 1912 brochure had proclaimed that 'our future is in the air', this time he would declaim that 'our security is in the air'. France had no alternative to building up an air force stronger than that of the potential enemy. And since the public powers could not be trusted to allot sufficient funds – here there was a round attack on the 'inertia' of bureaucrats, 'incapable people' filling important jobs, and 'the abuses of the civil service' – the solution would have to take the form of a French civil aviation fleet, ready for conversion into a military air force.

The Michelins' role? Still another aviation prize, to be awarded to the first pilot to fly a plane both fast (125 mph) and slow (6.5 mph) – and land on a dot (50 feet in diameter). In a postscript, the Michelins insist that they are speaking only as good Frenchmen, and not as aircraft manufacturers. 'In accordance with our promise, as soon as the war was over we ceased all participation, direct or indirect, in the manufacture of aircraft, and our plants have been reconverted to their original purpose.'[10]

21

POST-WAR PROBLEMS

If the story is true (in whatever version one may have heard it) that André Michelin started putting a cover price on the Michelin guides when he saw a pile of free copies propping up a table at one of the garages responsible for giving them away, that incident (or series of incidents) would have occurred shortly after the First World War. For it was in 1920 that the *Guide Michelin* for France and its sister guide-books ceased to be distributed free of charge.

The new edition, running to 815 pages (plus 10 more for the colour maps at the back) went on sale for the equivalent of 5.5 of today's euros; companion volumes for Great Britain, Belgium, Luxembourg and the Rhine valley together, and Spain went on sale at the same price. The total printing of that year's six titles was 400,000 copies; the French volume alone had been published in 90,000 copies.[1]

The advertising pages of the new French volume bristled with offerings of new material from the Michelin tourist office. Henceforth, the folding map of France, originally published in 47 parts, contained a 48th – for the reconquered Alsatian province, with Strasbourg and Mulhouse as the restored treasures.

Not all the promotional schemes worked. Just as the American tyre market was proving to be a more difficult challenge than expected – and the Michelin brothers were not used to doors they could not open – so the Bibendum publicity offensive on American soil got bogged down. One project called for nothing less than a Michelin Touring Map of the United States – a folding map drawn to the scale of one inch for

four miles, produced by 'the greatest touring specialist for automobilists going around the world,' as the promotional text on one of the
first published maps boasted.

In fact, only four sections were to see the light of day: Boston
(and north to Concord, New Hampshire); Providence, Rhode Island
(and north as far as Springfield, Massachusetts; south to New Haven,
Connecticut); New York (Bridgeport, Connecticut is at the top of this
map, Trenton, New Jersey at the bottom), and Philadelphia (down the
Atlantic coast to Atlantic City, across Delaware Bay to Dover).

One can guess that Michelin lacked the facilities to carry out such
an ambitious project. The maps were produced in Paris; the language
seems stilted. Americans could do a better job of mapping their country,
at least for the time being.

Today, as this is written, one can buy a single 'USA Road Map' on
a 1:3,450,000 scale (one inch for 55 miles); published for the first time
in 1996, it presents places of interest the Michelin way and a city index.
By this time Michelin had become fearless: it published a map of the
world in the same format that year.

With peace, the Michelins resumed their campaign for better roadsigns – especially at crossroads. 'They've got to be indelible, as readable
after ten years as the first day,' argued André Michelin at an April 1920
meeting of the Touring-Club de France. Backing conviction with a
material commitment, Clermont-Ferrand began turning out its own
signs, made from lava found in nearby quarries. The Puy-de-Dôme
authorities let Michelin place its crossroad markers at every intersection
on a district road; soon the authorization came for similar signage of
country lanes.

But elsewhere in the country anarchy prevailed – with a proliferation of signs of all shapes and materials, all too often vulnerable to
the elements. Experiments with the Michelin system were to continue
all during the 1920s, with considerable support from the Touring-Club
de France, the Automobile-Club, eventually the bridge and highway
administration and other official bodies. The first decision of national
impact came only at the end of the decade, when the government agreed
to put up crossroad markers all along France's much-loved highway
number 7, running from Paris to the Riviera as far as the Italian border.
Then in February 1931, the French government authorized the placing
of Michelin signs everywhere in France.[2]

Scholars who took the time to look at Michelin's position in the years immediately following the Treaty of Versailles decided that growth was helped in no small part by the readiness of the French government to limit the importation of rubber goods (even if cheaper and better, and apparently American tyres were now both). But tyres produced by the likes of Goodrich, Firestone and Goodyear reached French shores all the same – for a while challenging Michelin on the turf it knew best. Edouard had ordered rapid expansion in Clermont-Ferrand immediately after the Armistice, when at last peacetime goods could replace defence requirements. Some of the new production proved to be premature, the quantities excessive.

That the problem was not simply a matter of competition between French and foreign tyre-makers is indicated by a general explosion of social discontent in the spring of 1920. It had actually begun with railway workers, whose union was caught up in the revolutionary fervour of the moment. The more militant chose as a first objective the celebration of 1 May as a labour holiday. Edouard Michelin rejected that idea out of hand, informing a union delegation that his employees workers were free to stay at home if they so desired, although he was convinced that of his payroll of 12,000 only five or six hundred wished to. 'You will understand that in these circumstances,' he was quoted as saying, 'the duty of the house of Michelin was to say to its personnel: the gates are open; those who want to can go to work. We don't have the right to impose the loss of a day's pay.' Apparently 600 Michelin workers did choose to stay out; the confrontation between strikers and Michelin loyalists was violent, with reported injuries, at least five of them serious. A national rubber strike was scheduled for 3 May at which time the demands included the abolition of contracts and higher overtime pay.

As the largest industrial employer in town, Michelin was the centre of attention, and Edouard asked the authorities for protection. On the day of the strike most workers reported for duty, but one shift was blocked at the entrance by protesters. Troops ordered in by the prefect – the district governor – then intervened, and injuries were reported on both sides. The prefect called for reinforcements, Michelin closed the plant, while a delegation of strikers presented demands through the prefecture, notably for the suppression of piece-work and for better wages.

Before passions subsided, the rubber-workers' union had been dissolved, and Michelin could begin weeding out the troublemakers, setting up its own internal police to be ready for future disorders. There had been a difficult moment, but the unions proved inadequate to stand up to management or to the authorities, and Michelin seemed to have its hands free to reduce its labourforce at will – at the beginning of each winter for example, or whenever economic conditions called for such measures.

That there were more hirings than firings is clear from the severe housing shortage in Clermont-Ferrand in the first years of peace, and a new wave of company-financed homes for Michelin workers and staff – some 600 dwelling units in the years 1920–22 alone – were made available to employees below cost.[3]

*   *   *

The economic crisis turned out to be transitory. French automobiles were in demand the world over, and tyres went with them; France became the world's number two manufacturer in both fields after the United States. Michelin strategy called for a gamut of products, targeted to motor vehicles large and small. Again, we are indebted to students of the industry, who chart rapid development until 1925, a slowing down in the following two years, a new departure in early 1927 but at a slower growth rate until 1929, when the sky was the limit.[4]

In a rare example of negative advertising directed against Americans – whose soldiers and civilians were at the same time targets of a Michelin seduction campaign – 'Bibendum' took up his pen in a Michelin Saturday column to warn that not only good things came from abroad. 'Here is an idea that we don't applaud,' declared the man inside the Bibendum costume, André Michelin. The target was Straight Side tyres, an American import which – according to André, who used illustrations to demonstrate his point – made changing tyres considerably more difficult. While European tyres – and here Michelin certainly had Michelin's in mind – employed flexible padding, these unwelcome American models had rigid sides held by steel cables – making it difficult to slip them on to the rims.

Further, Michelin knew a lot about these inconvenient tyres because it was one of the companies that made them:

I know these 'Straight Side' tyres well because the Michelin Tire Co. of America makes thousands of them daily [so 'Bibendum' confessed]. So it is in full knowledge of the matter that I tell you: the Straight Side does not represent progress, far from that, and European tyres need not yield the road to it.[5]

Then, and for some time to come, Michelin held the lead – for Europe certainly – in tyres designed specifically for trucks, combining the use of heavier tyres with the new principle of dual tyres, and then undertaking tests to show that the new models designed by Michelin did far less damage to road surfaces.[6]

Such improvements may have impressed professionals, but could do little to keep Michelin in the public eye. That would require gadgetry. André Michelin now had a beauty in Michelin's flat-tyre warning device, guaranteed to cause drivers to sit up and take notice. 'The signal includes a blank cartridge which goes off when the tyre loses air,' the instructions read. As soon as the bang was heard the driver was advised to stop, to change a flat tyre or to pump up a deflated one – not forgetting, before driving off, to place another cartridge in the warning system. A sketch showed the strange valve-like device connected to the tyre's inner rim, a puff of smoke indicating the pistol-shot effect.

Of course, the shot might go off while the car was in a garage; drivers were advised to bend down to take a look before starting out on a trip, and if the cartridge had exploded, to change it.[7]

But nothing attracted more attention than an aeroplane flying overhead. Michelin was back in the running on 1 January 1921, with a new round of air trophies, although now the hurdles had been raised somewhat. The winning aircraft would have to fly at a cruising speed of 47 mph, covering some 1800 miles on an itinerary mapped out by the sponsors, beginning and ending at Versailles.

After some false starts, a Frenchman covered the course in a little over 37 hours. But that was on 31 August 1921, and the competition remained open until the last day of the year. Finally – to the consternation of many Frenchmen (many pilots especially) – an Italian laid claim to the title, winning it for the Italian aeroclub after arbitration by the International Aeronautical Federation.[8]

22

ANOTHER
ANDRE

It would be fair to say that the post-war era proper began quite some time after the fighting finished. Even the Paris Automobile Show, always a bracing experience for manufacturers, an event that had been considered so important to the industry – 'a kind of public inventory of its most recent achievements,' in the words of a specialist – had been skipped over in 1919 and 1920, an inevitable consequence of economic crisis, the plunging value of the national currency (by as much as 60 percent) and soaring raw-material costs. It had not been possible to raise the sales price of automobiles accordingly. At the Salon de l'Automobile of 1921, small cars were the crowd-catchers.

For above the gloom, there had been a bright star: Citroën, a name that was to count in the history of French automobiles, and not less so in the Michelin story. Some time before the war André Citroën, a brilliant engineer and inventor specialized in gearing, had been asked to revive a pioneer car-maker (Mors). He earned further respect as a wonder-manufacturer of cannon shells during the years of hostilities, converting his plant and his talents in 1919 to the mass production of automobiles the Henry Ford way. He was 41 years old.

'We have in this country a man whom many would admire were he an American,' a reporter for *L'Illustration* told readers on the eve of that first post-war automobile show,

and I don't know why I shouldn't name him here: André Citroën. In less than three years [the writer pursued] this young industrialist has conquered market leadership. He worked feverishly, delivering an incredible quantity of automobiles under difficult conditions, at the same time mounting an extraordinary promotional campaign through salons, exhibitions, races and competitions.[1]

André Citroën was born in Paris in February 1878, the son of Dutch Jewish parents. His father had been a prosperous dealer in diamonds, and André was sent to a good high school, later gaining admission to the elite Polytechnique engineering academy (he patented his first important invention before graduation). His early successes in industry seemed to combine the technical good sense of an Edouard Michelin with the public-relations flair of Edouard's brother André. It will not come as a surprise to find Edouard and André Michelin linking their fate to his.

Now, at the head of an automobile firm bearing his name, Citroën seemed to sense the mood of post-war consumers. He offered them a truly new low-priced automobile which he called 'Type A' (a term that Louis Renault had already taken over from Ford). 'The first French car in mass production,' his advertisements proclaimed.[2] Before he retired from the field, he was engaging pilots to write his name in smoke in the sky, and spelling it out in lights atop the Eiffel Tower. He got his vehicles into comic strips, gave them away in miniature to children. And when Charles Lindbergh flew solo across the Atlantic, one of his rewards was a tour of the Citroën factory – the first of a series of visits by celebrated aviators.[3] In 1922 Citroën had whittled his basic vehicle down to 5 hp – the official tax designation for what in fact was an 11 hp motor.[4] In December of the same year the Michelins undertook a 'National Survey for a People's Car', targeted to Frenchmen in all walks of life – including workers and farmers – apparently the first market survey of its kind in Europe. 'In the United States there is one auto for 10 inhabitants; In France, one for 150! WHY?' the questionnaire began.

> Because we consider autos a sign of wealth; over there it's a work tool used by everybody ... If instead of 260,000 automobiles France had a million – proportionately this will still be four times fewer than the Americans have – it is easy to see what an impetus that would give the whole nation. The economic crisis born of war would quickly be overcome. It's a matter of national importance.

Nothing was to come of the survey, not just then, but the responses did offer guidelines for designing an inexpensive automobile of reasonably comfortable dimensions, ample enough to carry four passengers.[5]

And the questionnaire was evidence that the tyre-maker was contemplating the immediate future with some anxiety.

All the same, Edouard continued to show exemplary skill in making tyres as good as tyres could be, and selling them well despite the sluggish market. An enquirer uncovered evidence that Michelin wages – combined with cost of living increases – were so generous at that time (undoubtedly for the purpose of attracting and holding the most desirable workers) that union leaders elsewhere in the region were using the Michelin example to obtain better conditions for their members in other companies.[6]

In 1923, Michelin introduced a totally new concept: a low-pressure (or balloon) tyre, noticeably wider than previous designs, thus allowing inflation pressures half that of earlier models; Michelin christened it 'Comfort'. (And Firestone in the United States introduced its own version of the low-pressure tyre the same year.)[7]

The brothers went out for new markets. Odd as it may seem, the public buses of Paris, a component of every street scene, still crisscrossed the city on solid rubber. André decided to order up half a dozen picture postcards to tease the public transport authorities into renewing their equipment.[8] Press advertisements spelled out their argument: 'Pigs are transported on air-filled, not solid tyres, because it's more economical, and they arrive in better shape. Parisians still ride in buses on solid tyres: it costs more and they arrive aching all over!'[9] But of course the main source of revenue would then and forever be automobile tyres. In 1900 Michelin's purpose had been to get more people on the road, and in the mid-1920s that purpose had not changed. 'America now has 15 million cars for 110 million inhabitants, or one car for seven people including women and children,' announced a Michelin publicity release in 1924. France, 'cradle of the automobile', was only in tenth place, with one car for every 100 inhabitants. Wasn't that a pity? Michelin – André certainly – was ready with some convincing arguments, for they had to do with the customer's pocketbook. An automobile cost three to ten times less to 'feed' than a horse, tyres cost less per mile than horseshoes, and one could learn to drive a car faster than to ride a horse.[10]

*   *   *

There was a time for business, a time for a patriot to make his voice heard; obviously gadfly André Michelin believed that. That would explain his presence at a meeting at the Sorbonne that brought together 3000 officials and ordinary citizens on the last day of October 1923, their concern being the potential danger of German air power. The Germans possessed toxic gas, he warned his listeners. Should they be allowed to maintain an air fleet, they could easily spread the gas over French cities. One might object that France could not get her allies – particularly the British – to agree to prohibit civil aviation in Germany. Why not? he wondered. The British were businessmen, practical people. Perhaps they had insufficient imagination, but when they did under-stand something, they acted. He recalled having told English friends that their horse-drawn cabs were obsolete and would soon disappear as France's had. He had been laughed at – 'You don't know how conservative we are,' they had told him. But while there were still a few horse cabs in Paris at that time, not a single one was to be seen in London.[11]

23

THOSE
STARS

Their tyres had smoothed the way for the coming automobile age. Now this tyre-maker's guide-books were to rewrite the history of French gastronomy. Almost without notice, the Michelin star system was born.

The year was 1925; mark it. No ceremony, no raucous publicity campaign memorialized the event.[1]

RECOMMENDED RESTAURANTS

For a certain number of important cities in which the tourist may expect to stop for a meal, we have indicated restaurants that have been called to our attention for good food. These are graded in five categories:

... Restaurants of the highest class.
.. Attractive restaurants – fine cuisine.
. Renowned for their kitchens.
** Average.
* Simple, but well run.[2]

From the first day, the makers of the guide proved to be scrupulously fair – or difficult to please. Not a single star was awarded in Clermont-Ferrand, where one might have imagined that senior plant managers – if not the chief himself, his brother and their families and intimate friends – would have their favourite eating places.

Naturally, particular care had gone into rating the grand restaurants of Paris, some of which would still be in the Michelin, with or without stars, seventy and more years later: Drouant and Bofinger, Lapérouse,

146

Lucas (later to become Lucas Carton), alongside the dear departed Voisin, Foyot and Larue. 'Voisin's has long been known as a rendezvous of the French nobility, of diplomats, and of gourmets and amateurs of wine from all over the world,' an American in Paris wrote in a guide-book of his own not long after that.

> Its cuisine is impeccable, and its cellars are the best in Paris... When asked to name my favourite Parisian restaurant I have to refuse, for I have no single favourite, but Foyot's is one of two or three I always think of first... Naturally the cuisine and service are perfection, and the cellars are of the best, for Foyot's is to the Senate what Larue's is to the Chamber of Deputies... Having considered carefully the questions of where to begin my gastronomic promenade, I have selected Larue's for old memories' sake, and also because, in a sense, Paris itself begins here, at the head of the Grand Boulevards...[3]

Michelin, of course, never explained its choices, and there was no signature, no personal pronoun behind its judgments. The institution that signed its letters simply 'Michelin' signed its guides simply, 'Michelin & Cie'. 'Our goal, in publishing this Guide, is to be useful and agree-able to our clientèle,' explained the unsigned text. 'Thus, to avoid any suspicion of partiality, we accept no paid advertising from hotels or restaurants. We make every effort to mention only establishments recognized as worthy of being recommended.'[4] Recognized as worthy by whom?

We know, because we know how the red hotel and restaurant guides were put together closer to our own time, that a considerable number of volunteers were involved in compiling the Michelin guides – together with professionals such as tourist promotion officials, hotelkeepers and tyre dealers, and – of course – Michelin's own battalion of travellers (tyre salesmen and dealership inspectors). Naturally, Michelin being Michelin, motoring tourists were also asked to contribute: 'We beg readers to call our attention... to hotels and restaurants found to be unsatisfactory'.[5]

We can be sure that André Michelin, creator of the guides, now inventor of the restaurant rating system as well, was taking a personal interest in the Paris listings. Most of the establishments that mattered to affluent and discriminating diners in the capital (and he belonged in both categories) were cited in this first starred guide. We can imagine following him from Paris to Lyon and the Riviera – bypassing

Clermont-Ferrand perhaps – for a great many of the approved eating places are found on the road south.

In Vienne, just south of Lyon in the Isère district, a favourite stopover for travellers en route to Mediterranean beaches, there was the Restaurant de la Pyramide, which at first warranted a single star ('simple, but well run'); under the great chef Fernand Point this simple inn would go on to become one of Michelin's perennials, not only qualifying for the highest rating (three stars) but considered by many the best in its category, meaning the best in France, the nation with the world's best food (under new management and new chefs, it has since descended to two stars).

In Bordeaux, the landmark Chapon Fin received a high (but not the highest) rating in 1925 – for 'fine cuisine', and went on in the years leading up to the Second World War to earn the three stars given to only ten or a dozen restaurants in France. The 1925 edition called attention to the venerable La Couronne in Rouen – 'renowned for its kitchen'; it survives today, earning stars and losing them. In Dijon there were Le Pré aux Clercs and its neighbour Les Trois Faisans, later to be joined together and honoured by Michelin as one, still later (at the present time) rating a star under the single name Au Pré aux Clercs.

Standards were being set; André Michelin could not have imagined how influential he would become. When the star system attained cruising speed, nearly every earnest motorist in France – and of course many food-wise visitors – would know, to cite an early formulation (when cuisine and decor were at last given separate and distinct symbols) that a single star called attention to 'A good table in its community', two stars to an 'Excellent table: worth a detour', three to 'One of the best tables in France; worth the trip'.[6]

Armed with the latest guide, and having familiarized themselves with its multiplicity of symbols, automobilists seeking more than spiritual contentment – a cathedral's rose window, an Alpine view – could set their sights on a new goal: the self-indulging pleasure of a fine restaurant. That was part of André Michelin's contribution to the gastronomic art. But consciously or not, in their choice of language (and symbolic language) Michelin and his inspectors had drawn up a protocol for hotelkeepers, restaurant owners, and chefs in France – in France alone for the time being. One could strive for a star (or more); once rewarded with a star (or more) one would have to study one's every gesture, to make every lunch and every dinner count, for the judges were at work all the year round, and one could be promoted or demoted in the following edition of the guide. When it became a question of better (or worse) business – more or fewer clients – few if any restaurant owners or chefs remained indifferent to their ratings. Michelin was behind every pillar, peering through every window; anonymous Michelin, who might be that passive but observant salesman over there, or the two friends seated over here.

Without any doubt, great restaurants existed before Michelin got around to noticing them. But once the guide existed, with its roll of honour, great chefs had another reason for maintaining standards. Owners who were not themselves chefs made sure to replace a departing cook with his or her equal. And future generations of owners and cooks, in creating their establishments, would be sure to compose their menus with Michelin in mind.

*   *   *

One could, of course, make a meal of the red guide itself, which for nearly every village and town one might care to hear about listed the number of inhabitants, the altitude, the most interesting sights and festivals, nearby curiosities, distances to surrounding cities and towns of significance, then of course the recommended hotels, restaurants and garages; there was also a reference to the Michelin map that featured the locality, and whenever a town was worth it, a small map showed its principal streets and monuments, with the precise location of curiosities, public buildings, and of course the guide's pick of hotels and restaurants.

Then it was time to take another step forward. That step would be the introduction of regional guides – the first descriptive travel books produced by Michelin after the World War I battlefield series. Michelin released the first of the series, *Bretagne*, in 1926, followed in short order by *Les Alpes*, *Les Pyrénées*, *Châteaux de la Loire*, with Michelin's cherished *Auvergne* available only in 1929. These between-the-wars books were published in stiff, red-bound covers, slightly wider in format than the *Guide Michelin* for France but otherwise identical. Unlike the later green series, these first regional guide-books took over a key feature of the *Guide Michelin* for France: the entries for principal towns included the national guide's familiar symbols. (The difference was that individual restaurants were rated only for their comfort; good-food stars were employed exclusively for hotels to which restaurants were attached.)[7]

In the regional guide, as in the national guide, the entry for Clermont-Ferrand (itself a three-star sight, meaning 'of very great interest') did not forget to call attention to Michelin factory sites, clearly indicated on an accompanying map. Yet, as had been made painfully clear in the red guide for France, no Clermont-Ferrand restaurant cited in the Auvergne volume was worth a star, nor did any hotel possess a restaurant whose cuisine deserved one.

Perhaps the single most extraordinary feature of the new regional guides was the care given to presenting roads to be travelled. There was a good reason for that; once seated behind the wheel, a driver was unlikely to find all the information he or she needed on the roads themselves.[8] Hence the appearance (in the regional guide to Auvergne for example) of light and dark lines to indicate the precise turn one must now choose (light lines for the roads to abandon, dark ones for the new choice). Or a hairpin turn is shown, with a small dark point to indicate a café – the café is identified to pinpoint the spot at which the traveller will have to effect the manoeuvre. Every notable incon-venience along the way is mentioned; in those times it was often a narrow trench dug across the roadway to allow drainage – a bane to springs and axles, a rough jolt for motorists.

In sum, these early Michelin itineraries painted a portrait of the roadways the user would confront – along open highways, up and down mountains, through villages and towns. Such step-by-step road guides ceased to exist when rendered unnecessary by better roads and clearly numbered and proper signage to warn of twists, turns, bumps and other potential annoyances.

Later, Michelin's travel office would divulge figures giving an indi-cation of the impact of the regional guides. From 1926 to 1945, over 650,000 copies were sold, as well as 33,300,000 maps; between 1926 and 1940, the *Michelin Guide* for France sold 1,340,000 copies. The last pre-war edition was released in 1939, the first of the post-war years in 1945.[9]

24

PROSPERITY

The post-war decade began with a certain optimism, and surely there were reasons for it. At Michelin, the watchword was expansion.

So in 1924, when Michelin published a pamphlet designed to prove that automobiles were not an expensive toy but a daily necessity, relatively cheap to run, more convenient than any equivalent public transport, it was rather a stimulus to further sales in a time of expansion than reassurance to hesitant buyers. 'With a car, no more 5 a.m. trains,' read the caption under a drawing of a traveller being jolted from bed by an alarm clock marked 4 a.m. 'With a car, there is more opportunity for the pleasant things in family life.' Here man and wife are depicted in bed together (ostensibly snoozing).[1]

It was the first of many such brochures dedicated to the automobile industry, which moved one writer to call the Clermont-Ferrand tyre-maker the unqualified leader of the between-the-wars automobile lobby.

Soon Michelin would begin distributing an annual survey of this industry on which it depended, dedicated to the proposition (as spelled out in its first edition in 1927) that automobile development was 'an unmatched factor in the nation's prosperity'. France was number two in world production when the pamphlet went to press – but a distant number two, with 190,000 vehicles against 4,480,000 in the United States.

Still in all, no amount of bravura could exorcize a business cycle. The final years of the 1920s saw an abrupt industrial slowdown. Nevertheless,

Michelin continued to expand its share of the market in France, improving its position in Britain with a new factory at Stoke-on-Trent, maintaining its activity in Turin, Italy, and even in the United States (thanks to the large plant in Milltown, New Jersey). Michelin installations in Clermont-Ferrand sprawled over 125 acres of urban and suburban land, which happened to be the surface occupied by one of America's giants, B.F. Goodrich, in Akron, Ohio, the rubber capital of the New World.[2]

*   *   *

Whatever the ups and downs of tyre-making and tyre sales in those years, there was no slackening in the production of promotional matter. Take the readable little pamphlet whose title translates as 'Prosperity, or Sam and François', a tribute to the American way of manufacturing. The jacket drawing tells us that more lessons are about to be learned, for here again is a stern-looking Bibendum, haunted by those productivity devils 'Lost Time' and 'Waste'.

'Many people speak of America without knowing much about it,' the text begins. 'That's not our case. We make tyres in Clermont-Ferrand. Our subsidiary, the Michelin Tire Co., makes them at Milltown, near New York City.' So they were well placed to compare the lives of workers in the two countries, and the differences were all too evident. In Milltown, many employees – even typists – come to work in their own automobiles. In Clermont almost everybody arrives on foot or on a bike.

Sam is an American worker, François his French counterpart. With two days' wages François can buy a pair of shoes; Sam can buy shoes, a shirt, and two hats. In 43 days, François can purchase a small motorbike, his American cousin a four-seater automobile. In 500 days, François can afford a small two-room house, Sam a four-room cottage with central heating and a bathroom. 'Sam, compared to François, is rich.'

But François would also be rich if he produced more, and more cheaply. 'More production does not lead to unemployment,' Michelin assures the reader, 'when it is cheap'. And that is achieved by avoiding lost time – say by arranging tools so that they can be found immediately, reducing waste too – say by planning so that more patterns can be cut from the same piece of leather. Further examples are given on following pages – each sweetened with comic-strip sketches. Little streams make big rivers, we are told. Which means that a single minute lost each hour adds up to eight in a day, 2400 minutes in a year – or 40 hours per worker. If a factory employs 20,000 workers and each loses that minute per hour, that is 800,000 hours in a year – the equivalent of 333 years of work.

The scene switches to bespectacled Bibendum, notepad in hand, watching a team of workers as they go about their daily routine, jotting down the time spent in work, stoppages, or just plain waiting around. Next, the rubber man (scratching his forehead) asks himself, concerning each movement – or lack of movement – 'Is it necessary?' For waste, instead of looking at the worker, look at the material. Each time you see merchandise going to waste, ask yourself the question: can't we eliminate or at least reduce this waste? and then do it.

It was Taylor again – and Taylorism. The back cover listed a set of pamphlets for further reading (posted in single copies free of charge). They included a treatise on how Michelin had 'Taylorized' its machine maintenance shop; a lecture by Taylor to young engineers on 'Success'; a pamphlet whose title translates as 'Is it Worthwhile to Use the Taylor Method?'

Edouard Michelin was in Paris in 1927 for the first International Rubber Exhibition held at the inevitable Grand Palais; for a souvenir book distributed on that occasion, he put his name to a recapitulation of his company's worker benefits. 'We have often heard,' he began, 'that it isn't possible for a company that is not prosperous to carry out social work... We believe, on the contrary, that our company prospers because of its social work.'

He pursued his exposé with a rundown of these benefits, from the introduction of profit-sharing in 1898, to the health service launched in 1902, allocations to large families and widows initiated during World War I, antenatal, birth and postnatal care. Then the housing programme, legal aid, the co-operative stores and athletic activities.[3]

And of course this text became another Michelin booklet, available on request. The cover had a bountiful Bibendum holding in his bulging arms a house, a baby, a lawyer, a doctor, a carton of goods from the co-op and a bag of money for the profit-sharing plan. The back cover showed another Bibendum, bowing modestly, holding a lighted cigar. Inside, humour gave way to practical detail; a typical sketch is captioned: 'At the nursery young mothers learn how to bathe their infants'.[4]

It was easy to forget that the brothers were in business. Only one of the stack of Michelin pamphlets that saw the light of day at the time seemed to have anything to do with the exchange of goods for cash. This was a brightly written brochure, 'Used Cars',[5] addressed to would-be motorists who would love to own a car but did not have the cash. Simple, says the anonymous writer: get a used car. Saving money for customers was not a new idea at Michelin, but suddenly it had become urgent, as if the astute brothers had foreknowledge of what was coming. In a remarkable message to his senior staff late in 1927, Edouard Michelin showed how insufficient briefing of a designer had led to the production of an air pump that was too expensive; the misguided man had understood that he was to develop a pump 'functioning better than that of the competition, and costing no more'. But the point was not to align Michelin with the competitor's high price, which would limit sales, but to make it cheap enough for massive purchases. 'It doesn't have to fill the tyre very rapidly,' explained Edouard. We can imagine Edouard behind the drive to improve manufacturing processes with the help of his personnel. It was now that Michelin set up a system to collect ideas, appointing a suggestion engineer whose mission it was to meet with workers and office staff in an attempt to convince them to speak out.

In a memorandum to his top managers, Edouard described the visit of the suggestion man to the Michelin tyre depot in Lyon; of the 33 office staff and workers there, 29 came forth with a total of 76 suggestions, a result better than Michelin had obtained in Clermont up to then – why? It was because the managers in Lyon had under-stood the utility of the project.[6]

We hear Edouard's voice again in a no-nonsense message to his senior staff on command procedures. There were three elements in command, he said: order; the chief; the worker or executant. Young engineers (clearly he was thinking of some on his payroll) did not know what a worker was; their school had not taught them such things. There were even chiefs who hardly knew their personnel.

But there were encouraging examples too – or examples of honest workers whose errors were well-intentioned. He cited the example of a young woman seated at the belt whose job was to affix labels on passing tyres. Eventually she pushed back her chair and walked up to the tyre to stick on each label, returning each time to get another one.

Asked why she took those unnecessary steps, she answered, 'I can't just sit and do nothing'. Edouard's conclusion: the belt was not quite what it should be. 'But also, we have to find an active role for this active young woman.'

He cited his wonder-worker Michel Arnaud, then in the testing department, who proved so observant and attentive to scientific management that he eventually commanded 300 men.[7]

In another message Edouard returned to one of his favourite subjects – economy. Saving both time and money was one of the principal concerns of chiefs, but those who carried out instructions also had a role to play, for they could see things that their superiors had not noticed. Then there was what he called 'new eyes' – specialists whose only job was to find simplifications and economies. All three categories of people were important. 'Our purpose is to make a tyre each year that is a little cheaper than last year's,' he summed up. It was what the Michelins called 'beat the tyre of the year before'. Yet they did not intend to save money on quality – nor on wages.[8]

There is no doubt that Edouard, now entering his 70th year, was prepared to devote as much of his energy to communication as to execution of work. A remarkable document survives to prove this: a message to his senior staff on the need to give the performer of a task sufficient responsibility – since this person knew a lot about the job, and would become more involved with it. Furthermore, 'this often reveals abilities ignored until then'; finally, 'it avoids wasting the time of the chief'.

25

DOWNTURN

The best historians of the era will say that France only began to hurt in the early years of the 1930s. The global depression, best remembered through such watershed events as the Wall Street crash of October 1929, picked off the major economic powers one by one.

Michelin was one of the companies that had wagered on international development. Tyres moved easily from market to market, in good times at least, even across the widest seas. Much of Michelin's growth in the late 1920s came from abroad, so that it was bound to be affected by a downturn in the business cycle in any significant economy. Still more alarming was the dramatic fall in prices of American tyres – giving American manufacturers a competitive advantage even in France.

The consequences at Clermont-Ferrand can be seen in the inexorable decline in profits, from 126 million francs in 1927, to 118.7 million in 1928, to 93.7 in 1929 – a figure more than halved the following year.[1]

A letter has been published from Louis Renault to Michelin, warning him that foreign tyre-makers – he meant Americans of course – were offering better terms for equipping newly manufactured cars with their tyres rather than Michelin's; he and his fellow French car-makers expected Clermont-Ferrand to match them.[2]

The record should also show that the Michelins were well aware of their handicap; they admired the United States and wished to emulate it, but knew how far they'd have to go. On 21 January 1929,

André Michelin, who had turned 76 less than a week earlier, addressed
a meeting called to discuss that most avant-garde of industries, aviation;
he made no attempt to conceal his enthusiasm for that country so far
away – even further away, he said, by its achievement. Imagine! he
declared: a country whose workers earn between three and four times
more than France's, but whose finished goods usually cost less than they
do in France (all that thanks to Frederick Taylor).[3] 'A country where

PROSPÉRITÉ

ou

SAM et FRANÇOIS

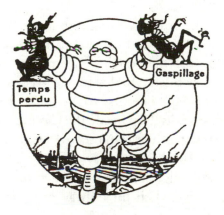

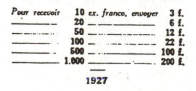

15. 'Prosperity, or Sam et François', with Bibendum collaring the productivity devils of
'temps perdu' ('lost time') and 'gaspillage' ('waste'), Michelin pamphlet, 1927.

the boss talks in a friendly way with his workers…A country where, of 38 million voters, you don't have 90,000 Bolsheviks.'

The burden of André's message, of course, was the danger of German rearmament; he reiterated his conviction that even to allow Germany a civil aviation fleet would be to render France vulnerable to a future air offensive.

For his part, home in Clermont-Ferrand, Edouard was also preaching peaceful competition with the United States. Lecturing to a local audience in July 1929, he lamented,

> We have too many people here who work at a Senator's pace – and I dare say at a civil servant's pace. One is not in a hurry, one enjoys life – it's intolerable…All that must be done away with. We've got to move faster – we've got to gallop.
>
> Our direct competitors are the Americans. Everything you've read about that country shows you that they don't lose time, and that as soon as they see there is progress to be made, a reform to accomplish, execution follows decision very rapidly.[4]

It was the theme of the year – 'we've got to move faster'.[5] Speed went hand in hand with research and development, for the record should also show that 1929 was the year that Clermont-Ferrand completed its basic research on air-filled tyres for train carriages and filed the first of many patents for them. The first trial used a Renault 40 hp automobile, which rode on rails deep inside the Clermont factory grounds. Among the problems that had to be solved were finding a means to keep wheels cushioned by pneumatic tyres from slipping off the tracks, and redistributing the weight of the vehicle to reduce the load on each tyre. The first operative Michelin railway car – to be baptized the Micheline – was only two years away.[6]

While Edouard kept tyres in the forefront of progress, André was assuring the durability of his beloved guides. It was now that André gave the go-ahead for a questionnaire addressed to travellers – detachable from the guide, making it all the easier to use – asking for the user's evaluation of hotels and restaurants visited during a voyage. This invitation to more direct participation was bound to make the familiar red book a true friend of the family, a friend with whom one could share pleasures as well as disappointments – occasionally even rage.

The questionnaire was decorated with a small O'Galop sketch already familiar to users of the guide: a hotelkeeper with cloth cap stands at

his threshold, offering a tray carrying a sack of money to Bibendum –
who holds up both hands in indignant refusal of the bribe.[7]

More wondrous still was the launching of a *Guide Aérien*, heralded
as 'the first aviation guidebook for tourists'. It covered France, North
Africa and French West Africa.[8] For this very specialized directory,
Michelin's travel department had the help of Air Ministry's safety
division, and one can understand why, in an area where life and death
hung on the right choices, the Michelins had not left the picking and
choosing to the enlightened amateurs who compiled their guide-books
to *terra firma*.

The new volume provided information on equipment, flying rules,
existing airlines and how to obtain and make use of weather information. There were sketches of airfields in France and French Africa,
with an indication of their dimensions and the nature of the terrain
(for example, for Montpellier: 'not very stable in winter, especially the
southern part'). For each site, a small map showed the positioning of
the field with respect to nearby towns, and each town entry included
recommended hotels and restaurants. Hotels were graded according to
comfort, but in this very particular Michelin guide-book, restaurants
were not rated.

The prefacer noted that advances in aviation, with improved
security and the relatively low cost of equipment, made it possible to
predict a rapid development of air touring as well as the use of private
planes for business travel: 'Soon the density of airplanes cruising in the
sky will be as great as that of automobiles on the roads'.

There would be one more edition of the *Guide Aérien* (in 1935) –
and then no further volumes. If the spirit of adventure remained in
the hearts of Frenchmen, pockets were empty.

Perhaps a more appropriate decision, in this first of the bad years,
was the reprinting of the Michelin roadmap series (1:200,000) in a
cheaper paper format. 'The map on canvas costs 12 francs; you use it
for several years as it grows out of date,' an advertisement pointed out.
'The map on paper costs 4 francs; it is brought up to date every year.
Buy the paper map.'[9]

*   *   *

Half a century after the event, Edouard Michelin's grandson, the next
Michelin to run the family empire, had a confession to make. 'We were

on the edge of bankruptcy in 1930,' he told an interviewer, 'for the simple reason that our products were no longer the best'.[10]

As for Michelin abroad, it was time for a painful choice. The oncoming crisis struck first and hardest in the United States, and there seemed less and less reason for a French manufacturer to attempt to confront the competition of the American giants on the giants' home ground. There were simply fewer customers to share. In 1930, the decision was made to close down Michelin's New Jersey plant, which in effect shut down Milltown.[11]

For local residents – workers and their families, and all the local business drawn to Milltown by the plant – it was the end of a world. Yet in retrospect, a local historian discovered that the Michelin decision to terminate its American operations brought surprisingly little bitterness. Townspeople liked the Michelins too much for that. They blamed a cruel world, so instead of throwing rocks at the departing French contingent, Milltowners looked for ways to limit the damage.

And four decades later, the same local historian found old-timers who remembered the Michelin years as 'the good old days'. By then there was little to remind them of the distant past. Most of the Michelin families had returned to the mother country, although some streets named for eminent French personalities retained their names, as did Our Lady of Lourdes church.[12]

If Milltown hurt, what of Clermont-Ferrand? For massive firings began in 1930 and were continued as the bad news flowed in. Before conditions improved, over half the company's personnel had been set adrift – in figures: 16,554 people were employed by Michelin in Clermont in 1929, 12,585 in 1930, 9542 in 1931, 8403 in 1934, 8085 in 1935 – the lowest figure before the payroll began to rise again. Many Michelin families went elsewhere – the locals to their rural villages, while most of the large foreign contingent simply abandoned the district.[13]

Henceforth, there would be bitterness; Michelin could no longer, considering the circumstances, preserve its image of paterfamilias. It was the beginning of the era of combative trade unions, the clash of ideologies leading to the rise of the Popular Front. Michelin was soon to hear itself accused of firing fathers of large families, in order to reduce its commitment to household benefits – an accusation made by union leaders and confirmed by the prefect (provincial governor).

Confronted with the allegation, Michelin director Jean Callies, husband of Edouard Michelin's eldest child and father of eight children himself, insisted that bachelors were the first to be fired; the company was paying out as much in family benefits as ever it had.[14]

All sources comment on the plight of workers and senior staff alike, fired by Michelin, prevented by their contracts from taking jobs at other manufacturers in the very fields in which they had experience at the risk of losing profit-sharing benefits.[15]

Edouard Michelin himself favoured a reasoned response to adversity. He met that first year of downturn, 1930, with an outpouring of memoranda to senior staff. It was as if economies could do it all. It was as if the little things would add up and make the big difference he so desperately needed now. He had seen, he told his foremen,

> working men and women who are poorly installed for their jobs – Example: their benzine pail is placed out of reach, sometimes on the left when it's the right hand that uses it. I saw one who had two steps to take in order to dip his knife into water.

Surely the world outside, aware of the global and national crisis and of Michelin's particular crisis, would have been surprised to hear how the Patron had decided to deal with the problems of the firm.

A note entitled 'Little Streams Make Big Rivers', in October, began with the affirmation that forms did not cost much to print – about ten francs for 1000. But it was also true that at the present time the company was stocking 2515 different types of form, costing 485,560 francs. A good many of them could be replaced with sheets of blank paper. The note said: 'I ask that we join the campaign against this waste'.[16]

Soon Edouard had ordered the regular publication of a newsletter called *Economies*; it had reached issue number eight in January 1931 when Edouard returned to the rostrum with a severe attack on laxity in the handling of materials; those responsible were – his language – 'guilty'.[17] But he drew the line when a suggestion came in – anonymously – that all salaries – of workers and white-collar employees alike – be reduced by 10 percent. 'We must fight against the Americans. In our view the ordinary Frenchman, the bureaucratic Frenchman, will be beaten by the American. But the elite Frenchman will beat the American.' And so he wished a company filled with men of the elite, but that meant paying them adequately.[18]

It would probably be a mistake to say that the Michelins were drowned in gloom; there is too much evidence of building for the future. In the first bad year, 1930, Edouard Michelin stepped in with cash for brilliant, unlucky car-maker André Citroën (when his banking partners of Lazard Frères withdrew); world depression was not to stop the Michelins from pursuing their new commitment to the Paris manufacturer, which was at once a token of confidence in the future of both Citroën and Michelin.[19] In 1931, a large Michelin tyre factory was opened in Karlsruhe (on the German side of the Rhine), while another sprawling factory site was being readied for production in Lasarte in northern Spain (inaugurated in 1933).[20]

And now, as the global slump reached France with all its dead weight, Edouard and his men moved ahead with plans to put tyres on railway carriages. Their hope was to build single-carriage trains as well as the tyres to equip them. 'The Micheline, or the marriage of rail and tyre,' to cite a Michelin presentation of the project in July 1931.

France's railway deficit had been blamed on smaller regional lines deserted by passengers because of their slow speeds and unsatisfactory schedules, and yet which had to be continued as a public service. But just as tyres transformed road travel, they might now revive rail travel. Tyres would reduce jolts, providing greater comfort for passengers. Greater adherence to the track would make it possible to accelerate more rapidly – and to brake in a tenth of the distance usually required. Because of this manoeuvrability, Michelines could even be driven without signals.[21]

On 10 September 1931, a Micheline carriage with space for ten passengers – utilizing a Hispano-Suiza engine – pulled out of the Gare St Lazare for a trial run to Deauville on the Normandy channel coast, accomplishing the trip in two hours and three minutes at an average speed of 66.5 miles per hour. Soon Micheline carriages would be carrying 24 passengers on the eastern French rail system, and in 1933 a new series was put on the tracks carrying 36 passengers, then 56 passengers the following year. By December 1936, 90 Michelines were operating on French tracks, 10 more in the colonies. Soon a 100-seater went into service (carrying 40 more standing passengers), its cruising speed 75 mph, with a maximum speed of 85 mph.[22]

26

DEATH OF A MICHELIN

André Michelin had celebrated his 78th birthday in January; his list of achievements, published in the *Guide Michelin* – another omnipresent monument – credits him with production of the first map of Saharan desert trails in the year of his death. A friend remembered meeting him for the last time at a reception in the salons of the Automobile Club: 'Steady on his feet, André Michelin didn't at all give the impression of being an old man. His features, his tone of voice had the vivacity of a man both vigorous and mature.' Then in late March he was confined to bed with bronchitis, and a week after that he was dead.[1]

'For the first time in 32 years,' read the announcement in the form of a black-bordered 'In Memoriam' in the next edition of André's little red book, 'the Michelin Guide appears without its creator and constant inspirer having been able to take a last expert look at the proofs...'[2]

*   *   *

He was buried beneath the haunting Puy-de-Dôme, that curious cone he had done so much with, in a humble village cemetery at Orcines some five kilometres east of Michelin-Ville, close to La Bosse, site of the large, unimpressive mansion that served as his brother's country residence.[3] André, who had only recently built a house of his own alongside his brother's, was survived by his widow Jeanne, their two sons and a daughter. Of the sons, Marcel, now a mature 45 years old, was the more active; an organizer with traits inherited from André, he would leave Clermont-Ferrand for Paris to replace his father in sales and promotion.

What is certain is that no son of André would move into the chain of command held by André's brother Edouard and Edouard's sons. Nominally, Edouard 'retired' in the year of André's death; he turned 72 in June.

That was the official story.[4] To the rank and file of Clermont-Ferrand, the old man was still at the helm; to the Communists, he was still the devil. 'Michelin, the philanthropist with a false nose, is one of those insatiable sharks, without scruples, who would stop at nothing to exploit the sweat and the blood of their victims.' So began a typical attack, in an article called 'At Michelin', in the local Communist Party weekly on 20 August 1932. 'A kind of sadist' was Michelin – or the Michelins; until then they had been speculating on the ignorance of the masses, explained the Communist periodical, although from now on they'd be exposed, to reveal 'their true nature as vampires and drinkers of blood':

> What is Michelin, judging from its acts? The height of hypocrisy, a mountain of lies... It builds collective housing for its workers. Well and good... but what is behind that?... A Jesuitical infiltration into the intimate lives of its salaried slaves. By the priests in its pay, who by confessing their wives, allow it to reach into the bedrooms of its robots. By its cooperative stores, it knows what its workers eat and drink. With its schools it instils a one-way education in the next generation, made up of religious debasement and submission. By its apprenticeship training, it manufactures workers by the belt system, just as the boss wants them and the country needs them...[5]

Just a week after that philippic, a gem of Communist pamphleteering, patriarch Edouard lost his presumed successor, his first son Etienne, 33 years old and the father of three children of his own. (One of them was François, who was to become chief in his own time.)

Etienne had been known, if we accept the account of his death published in France's most authoritative newspaper, not as a chief or even a crown prince, but simply as the elder son.[6] He was an ardent flyer, piloting his own plane nearly every day, and a serious contestant at air shows. On the fatal day, he taken off from Aulnat – the airstrip that his father had developed for training of wartime bombing crews. During his brief flight a thunderstorm trapped him, while fog reduced visibility. The precise reason for the crash was never determined, but rescuers who approached the debris found that he had died on impact.[7]

Always ready for another diatribe, Clermont-Ferrand's Communist weekly featured the accident on its front page. Etienne, it charged, 'did not die a victim of progress and science,' as a local paper favourable to the family had it, but 'having fun'. (Thanks in part to aeroplanes, the Communist organ added, the Michelin family got rich during the war.) Etienne had died virtually in sight of his parents' castle. Returning again to respectful accounts of the accident in the local press, the Communist writer did not see why the death of a Michelin should be more moving than that of a homeless worker. During the economic crisis, so the Communists alleged, Etienne had recommended closing down his cousin Marcel Michelin's athletic facilities for company personnel. Edouard Michelin had had to intervene to save them. Michelin personnel did not like him, said this polemicist, because he would walk into the factory, chronometer in hand, and begin talking to a worker; but should the worker pause in his or her work to reply, Etienne would note the lost time, and then report it to the nearest supervisor.[8]

*   *   *

Etienne was dead; long live Pierre. Edouard's second son had turned 29 just a fortnight before his elder brother's fatal accident. Too young, evidently, to take over this empire constructed so carefully, laboriously, over four decades, and ruled for so long by seniors.

The logical successor to the chief would have been Marcel, André's son, who had grown up in the factory and had been in charge of its strategic testing department. He had proved himself as an organizer, and at 45 seemed to be of the right age for the job. But old Edouard was not to let the succession slip from his own line to his brother's; better that he himself continue to preside over the destiny of the empire, even if he sometimes had to drag himself across the factory floor to do so. He would nurture his second son as successor; surely Pierre would be ready to take command in a very few years.[9]

In 1932, the worst year of the decade for industry,[10] Communist militants kept Michelin in their sights. 'Nine thousand unemployed in less than three years, doubling and even tripling individual worker output, reducing salaries up to 50% and even more for certain categories of workers, does not suffice for the insatiable Michelin,' declared a tract distributed by the Communist union and reprinted on *Le Cri du Peuple's* front page. Now there was talk of a further 10 percent reduction of wages…[11]

Yet nothing in the *Guide Michelin* during the depression years was there to remind a traveller that there was a depression. Unless it was this bit of news in the 1933 edition: 'Hotel prices are falling…Only the present year's guide will tell you that!' 'The guide is brought up to date yearly,' explained another notice. 'In 1933: 144 hotels deleted, 544 new recommended good hotels, 391 hotels that have changed category, etc…' 'Don't rely on an old edition'. On another subject: 'Bibendum does not accept a cent from the hotels it recommends!'

This 1933 edition, put on sale at 25 francs, ran to 1156 pages, not including a supplement sewn in at the back consisting of 52 pages of maps in colour showing large French cities and their surroundings. There was a set of four-colour maps pinpointing localities in which one or more restaurants had been given Michelin stars. One star meant 'Good cooking available in the town', two 'Excellent cuisine; worth a detour', three 'One of the best in France; worth a journey'. The maps made it easy to locate the three-star restaurants: in Paris, at last (for this year Michelin was handing out its first in the capital of the country), in Rouen, Bordeaux, St Gaudens (a village in the Haute Garonne), Roanne; then Lyon, Col de la Luère, Macon, Priay, Belley and Sassenage – all located on a smaller map of the Lyon region; finally, Strasbourg and Moosch (a village in the Haut Rhin district).

Since 1932, the red guide had been listing specialities at restaurants which they had awarded stars; one likes to think that this was a decision – the last or one of the last – made by André Michelin. (It would be the kind of thing he would have enjoyed working on.) The 1933 guide added the warning that some listed specialties might be available only on the highest-priced menu, or à la carte, and occasionally only upon special request.

There were of course the dishes one expected. Already the Tour d'Argent in Paris, with its three stars, featured the famous Caneton Tour d'Argent (along with filets de sole Cardinal, a soufflé Valtesse, a white Château-Yquem 1900 or a red Romanée St-Vivant 1911). In Rouen, the three-starred Couronne on the Place de Vieux-Marché facing the site of Joan of Arc's burning had not yet realized that visitors to that city expected duck; they would instead be offered chicken roasted on a spit (or, as a fishy alternative, a brill in hollandaise sauce), then for desert a very Norman apple pie.

High up on the Col de la Luère (at an altitude of 2200 feet), 13 miles east of Lyon, Mère Brazier simplified with a three-star house-style chicken, then crêpes flamed in Grand-Marnier; below, in Lyon, the same owners suggested dumplings of poached fish for a starter, chicken with a white truffle sauce, house patés and local wines. A little further south, in Vienne, chef Fernand Point would have one begin with a gratin of crayfish tails – the same first course suggested in the guide when the present writer visited the venerable and still thrice-starred establishment exactly 25 years later.

The Michelin red guide for 1933 offered another symbol: a minute sketch of a waiter carrying a platter, signifying 'Waiters in white waist-coat'. But was this not too much for the tyre manufacturer pledged to cost-cutting to ride out the economic downturn? Perhaps, because that symbol would never be used again.

16. André Michelin, 1853–1931. Photograph by H. Manuel in *L'Illustration*, 1931. Reproduced by kind permission of the Mary Evans Picture Library.

By now, much of the world had got to know that one could eat one's way around France, and famously, thanks to the ubiquitous red-covered Michelin guide. In what may have been the first significant description of Michelin guides in the New World, a writer in the *New Yorker*, a weekly magazine tailored to sophisticated Americans – the very kind of American likely to be travelling with a specific objective such as tracking good food and wine – provided a laudatory guide to the *Guide Michelin*. He called Bibendum 'a benign and clairvoyant angel' who understood what motorists need and what they like. Then followed a kind word for the Michelin company – tyres and tourist information both – and a compliment that pertinacious André Michelin would have liked to hear: 'Michelin tires are presumably good tires, but one is apt to assume it because the Michelin maps and guides are so good, not the other way round'. The reporter went on to enumerate the wealth of detail contained in each annual volume. The Michelin, he explained, covers everything 'that a man lost, broken down, sleepy, hungry, or curious can possibly want to know…The stupidest tourist alive can't go wrong…'

*   *   *

Clearly, the *New Yorker* was taken with the thoroughness of a book that could tell a traveller whether a resort is quiet or crowded, whether a beach is covered with sand or pebbles; for dining rooms, whether the surroundings are pleasant, whether wine is included or extra. The writer was intrigued by the importance of Lyon and its surroundings to gastronomy. If nine of the restaurants accorded three stars were in Paris – the author was using the 1934 edition of the guide – most of the others were on the way south.

It was apparent that the *New Yorker*'s gourmet had done the trip, for he knew at least some of the recommended places to stop, such as a tiny inn at Priay (six rooms, of which two boasted hot and cold running water, so the guide of that year tells us). It was run by 'Madame Bourgeois, one of the great cooks of France, and so far as I know the only woman so distinguished'. And, of course, she had her three stars.[12]

27

REVOLUTIONARY FRONTS

However different they were in approach – André Citroën appearing recklessly extravagant alongside the prudent Edouard Michelin – there was no doubt that each side respected the other's workmanship. In bad times, Citroën's flair for innovation seemed ever more necessary to Clermont-Ferrand, for the seemingly indefatigable, boldly innovative car-maker had found a new public for automobiles, hence for tyres. But sometimes the versatile car-maker moved too far too fast, and then he was hard to follow.

Just now, for instance, in 1934, when Citroën had stretched his credit to breaking point, and the country's economic health seemed to offer little hospitality to new products, the Citroën engineers were getting ready to unveil the automobile of the decade, the *traction avant*, or front-wheel drive, an innovation making for a safer vehicle, one easier to control on the road. 'It is so new, so audacious, so rich in original solutions, so different from anything that has been made until now,' wrote a convinced editorialist in the authoritative *L'Auto*, when at last the 7 hp version was put on show in April 1934, 'that it produced an impression that really deserves the adjective "sensational".'[1]

Front-wheel drive would be André Citroën's swan-song. Henceforth, the bankers would not let him out of their sight, nor could the new concept, however revolutionary and potentially profitable, turn his financial situation around quickly enough – even had the first automobiles on the road proved to be flawless.

An ailing Citroën – he had only a little more than a year to live – turned for help to Edouard Michelin, who happened to be his chief creditor. That Michelin came through for him indicated, of course, that he felt confident about his own financial position. Old Edouard had been reducing production and slashing his payroll – not in despair but to be in a better position to face the future. Citroën could be part of that future. Indeed, Citroën's historian and biographer reveals that it was not Edouard but his son Pierre who seized upon André Citroën's offer of voting shares as additional collateral; he did it with an option valid for 10 years. That was on 3 January 1935; eight days later Pierre Michelin picked up the option, thereby taking control of 50.91 percent of the votes in Citroën with only 22.27 percent of the capital.[2]

It was time to apply shock treatment. Armed with their experience of measuring everything, Michelin men clocked day-to-day workings at the vast, up-to-the-minute Citroën plant on Quai de Javel along the Seine. Their remedy would be severe. Citroën had built for a world market that never materialized, and had floated an inordinate amount of stock to pay for successive expansions of manufacturing capacity; now the engines had to be reversed. Surplus labour had to be let go, but also surplus management (or salaries greatly reduced).

The next tug of war was with the banks, and this time Michelin and Citroën stood together. Then, in November 1934 one of Citroën's creditors, a small steering-wheel supplier, went to court to demand payment. Citroën filed for bankruptcy, and the court ordered judicial liquidation to permit the company to survive. Edouard Michelin's son Pierre and two other major creditors were appointed to a management committee.[3]

The context was popular revolt against the harsh, seemingly boundless economic crisis; Citroën could not be allowed to founder. In parliament the Socialists were calling the Citroën affair 'one of the most ominous dramas of contemporary social history'. The company's payroll of 19,000 (far larger than Michelin's) represented 50,000 family members, not to forget the smaller companies that supplied parts to the manufacturer.

Down in Clermont, Citroën's historian Jacques Wolgensinger lets us know, Edouard Michelin was directing the crisis from the wings. Yet Michelin, in order to protect his position with his other automobile manufacturer customers, could not show himself to be at once their supplier (of tyres) and their competitor (as car-maker). Citroën's sales position also had to be preserved with respect to consumers – but without making Citroën so attractive that creditors would refuse a settlement. The drastic cuts in costs had to continue, and cars actually produced had to be better.

Meanwhile, the genial founder of the company, diminished by illness, had become a liability. Early in 1935, Pierre Michelin asked André Citroën to step down; six months later he was dead (of stomach cancer). And the banks were ready to support a Citroën empire run by a Michelin.[4]

One business analyst would later reckon that the combined sales of Michelin and Citroën, if considered as a group, raised it to the position of number one manufacturer in France, ahead of the legendary de Wendels and Renault.[5]

*   *   *

The social climate is measured not only in business results – their rise or decline – but in the temper of the public, and these were volatile years. On 6 February 1934 a violent demonstration at the gates of parliament by right-wing extremists shouting the slogans of moral order left 17 dead and over 2300 injured (of which 1664 were from the ranks of the police and other government forces). The shock provoked both the resignation of the government and a momentous general strike that mobilized moderate republicans and the left.

The events of 1934 had had a predictable echo in Clermont-Ferrand, predictable also in their moderation in the face of the Michelin mono-lith. On 12 February, the day of the counter-demonstration in Paris against proto-Fascist movements that had marched on parliament, there was a certain effervescence in Michelin's town, visible not inside the plants but at the gates. The local Communists were dedicated but ineffective, and more moderate labour leaders had yet to come to the head of the line. It took another two years before rival left-wing unions joined forces, making many things possible.

But not everything. Until 1936, labour unions signified little at Michelin; the astute carrot-and-stick tactics of the company guaranteed that, with high rewards for loyalty, abrupt dismissal for the others. Then, when unions gained strength in the plants, Michelin did what it could to ensure that they remained moderate.[6]

In June 1936, French voters placed their country in the hands of a Popular Front, in this case a Socialist-Radical Socialist parliamentary coalition supported but not joined by the Communist party. Now it was worth going out on the streets, or disorganizing production inside the plants, for there was a chance that grievances would be heard, demands for higher wages honoured. Strikes quickly paralyzed strategic industrial sectors, beginning with aviation, and spread through the country. Most often they were sit-down strikes, effectively shutting down production. Before they were over, nearly two million workers were involved.[7]

The trouble began in Paris when Citroën workers laid down their tools. Michelin – with Edouard's son Pierre directing operations – sought to head off the movement with a lock-out, declaring an eight-day paid holiday with an immediate pay rise of 40 centimes an hour for men, 30 for women.[8]

That was on Sunday 7 June; on Monday the bulk of the Michelin workforce struck all the same. Michelin wasted little time before launching its counter-attack. Convinced that they knew how to talk to workers, factory emissaries sought them out at their homes to convince them to stay away from the plant – above all, not to participate in a sit-down strike. While the main factory buildings remained empty, workers caught management by surprise at a suburban annex, and maintained a round-the-clock occupation of that site.[9]

On 19 June, management was back with an offer – less than workers wished for, but all agreed that the time for compromise had arrived. In addition to a modest hourly raise, there was a company pledge that no strikers would suffer prejudice – nor would non-strikers. And family allowances for the strike period would be paid.[10]

Eventually calm was restored; all seemed as before. But in fact it was not. At Michelin, as nearly everywhere else in France, union membership soared. The position of the Communist Party and the unified Communist-Socialist CGT labour movement was strengthened. By December 1936, nearly every worker in a Michelin plant was a union member, and three out of four had chosen the Communist-led CGT.[11]

If in the past Michelin's labourforce had been among the last to join a protest movement, henceforth it would be in the avant garde. For the first time, the interior of factory buildings had been the scene of merriment as well as of ardent militancy, with red flags flying. One no longer need be afraid of the chief: this too was new. 'The moral order upon which Michelin had built its empire until now – this unilateral power wearing the mask of paternalism – was demolished forever,' a young militant was to say in retrospect.

*   *   *

Two bombs exploded near the Arc de Triomphe at the top of the Champs-Elysées in Paris on a Saturday night in September 1937 – and all France shook. The precise targets were the headquarters of France's employers association on Rue de Presbourg, where four floors collapsed and two policemen standing guard were killed, and on Rue Boissière, the headquarters of the federation of metal industries, where there was heavy damage but no victims.

These objectives were centres of industrial power; in the minds of good citizens, and the press that represented them, the bombers necessarily came from the radical left. The authoritative afternoon daily *Le Temps*, virtually a spokesman for right-thinking Frenchmen and the business community, reminded readers that 'you can't multiply the diatribes against money... against the oppressive upper classes, without breeding dangerous ideas tending to translate into direct action, into pure and simple terrorism'. Extreme right-wingers blamed premier Léon Blum for favouring a climate propitious to violence.

When the true culprits were found, France was shaken again. An underground of terrorism existed, all right, but it was composed of a heterogeneous grouping of right-wing extremists, some of them drawn from the ranks of militant royalists. This was the clandestine movement branded 'Cagoule' (literally 'hood'), especially by its adversaries; its formal name was the no-less odd Secret Committee for Revolutionary Action (CSAR), founded by a dissident royalist, Eugène Deloncle.

In the minds of Deloncle and his inner circle, a series of terrorist acts against the leadership class would necessarily be blamed on the Communists, thereby convincing right-wing Frenchmen and the military to take power and rid the country of leftist influence.[12]

The Cagoulards, as they were called, were rounded up in January 1938 – four months after the fatal bombings near the Champs-Elysées. The chief author of the attack was a certain René Locuty, who had studied chemistry before entering the Saint-Cyr military academy, coming out a second lieutenant in 1935, after which he was hired as an engineer by Michelin in Clermont-Ferrand. He was soon active in The Children of Auvergne, a front for the local Cagoule section; three of his fellow Michelin engineers, Henri Vogel, Roger Mondereau and Gustave Vauclard, belonged to the same group.

In his confession, Locuty revealed how he was ordered by his Cagoule chiefs to proceed to Paris on 10 September 1937; there he found (among others) François Métenier, whom he had first met in the latter's villa outside Clermont-Ferrand. In Paris, and in the presence of the mysterious Deloncle, the ways and means of the planned bombings were explained to him, and above all the motive – to stir up anger against the 'reds'.[13]

In fact, the Paris bombings were a godsend for those reds. The arrests made the top of the front page of the French Communist Party's national daily *L'Humanité*: 'The Infamous Plot Against The Nation'.

The accompanying story left no ambiguities: Locuty's confession, it said, proved that Michelin had harboured 'a veritable nest of Cagoulards enjoying the full confidence of the king of rubber'.[14]

There were more arrests of Michelin men – apparently including the chauffeur of an influential member of the Michelin family.[15] An arms cache was uncovered in Clermont-Ferrand; another front page of the Communist organ headlined a question and provided its own response: 'Who Financed The Plot? Michelin? That's certain!'[16] The day after that, the Communist organ reported that the union was given evasive answers when it asked Michelin management whether it would dismiss the Cagoulards. And would Michelin confirm that they had paid 10 million francs to arm them?[17] In fact, the only word from Michelin was a refusal to answer these 'insinuations and libels'.

Incredible as it may appear, the case against the bombers would have to wait through the short war and long enemy Occupation before being heard in court, in 1949.

*   *   *

The French business community would have had copies of *Le Temps* shortly after lunch on the last day of the year, Friday 31 December 1938 (actually the newspaper bore the next day's date, 1 January, as was the practice of this paper whose style, typeface and traditions were inherited after the Second World War by *Le Monde*).

It was a small item, buried in one of the narrow columns on the fourth page of the large-format, colourless and official-seeming paper:

> We learn of the accidental death in Montargis, on December 30, 1937, of Pierre-Marc Michelin, industrialist, co-manager of Michelin & Co., president and managing director of the André Citroën Co. His funeral will be held in the St. Jeanne d'Arc church in Clermont-Ferrand on Saturday January 1, 1939 at 9:30 a.m…He will be buried in a private ceremony the same day at the Orcines cemetery. No flowers or wreaths.[18]

Nothing here suggested that the successor to a throne had disappeared, and with him the immediate hope of carrying on a family dynasty.

Edouard's first son had died in his aeroplane; now his only other son became a victim of the automobile on national highway 7, some 70 miles south of Paris; it was a Citroën front-wheel drive at that.[19] Until then, he had been firmly in charge of the perilous, promising Citroën empire, with a larger payroll and broader industrial activities than the parent company in Clermont-Ferrand. He had been more than ready to step into his father's shoes.

Would the old man never be able to rest? Patriarch Edouard was now 78 years old, active as ever on the factory floor, still able to identify the problems that his company would have to resolve to keep pace with the future, even if he continued to deliver his proposals as Sunday sermons.

He had made his own decision on a successor by the time Pierre was laid to rest, not far from the family's great house in the little cemetery of Orcines. No question of leaning now on his brother André's son, Marcel – that matter had long ago been decided. Nor would a nephew or great nephew be chosen; like so many others before it, the Michelin dynasty would be legitimate only if an heir was chosen in the direct line of succession. And that could only be young François, Etienne's only son, born on 3 July 1926 – who was just 11 years old when his uncle Pierre was killed.[20]

His official biography has the venerable Edouard telling his doctor then, at the beginning of the new year 1938: 'You've got to keep me alive for another two or three years. The factory needs me.'[21]

28

CLERMONT
AND VICHY

We know now that before his premature death Pierre Michelin had given the green light to a model that would keep Citroën alive for many decades. This was to be a small, super-economical people's car, in a sense the logical outcome of the survey ordered by the old Michelin brothers in 1922, a survey conceived long before the founders could have imagined that the family firm would one day be in a position to build its own model. During his brief reign at Citroën in Paris, Edouard's second son had devoted his energies to the perfecting of those streamlined front-wheel drive vehicles – automobiles that more than any other marked the 1930s decade in France, a black, ground-hugging machine familiar to film-goers, used by cops and robbers, and by Gestapo squads and Resistance fighters (when they could find one).

Pierre had posed the problem of a 'tiny' car (calling it the 'TPV' for 'tout petit vehicule'). François Michelin remembered that as a child he had watched his uncle picking up pieces of his toy construction kit to put together a crude model of the simplest car ever. 'That's what I want our engineers to understand,' he told little François.

Simple, yet it would have everything one really asked for in a car, not excluding heating and decent suspension. An early prototype was put together at the Michelin plant – not at Citroën – some two years before his death on highway 7.[1]

Pierre Michelin's successor at Citroën, resourceful Pierre Boulanger, now drew up specifications for his designers: 'Build a car able to transport four persons and 100 lb of potatoes or a small cask at 40 mph for a consumption of three litres per 60 miles, very cheap maintenance and selling for a third of the front-wheel-drive model'. He told his engineers that he wanted them to be able to transport a basket of eggs across a field without breaking them; as for 'aesthetics and speed, I don't want to hear about such things'.[2] Make way for the 'deux chevaux'.

Through it all, one thing never seemed to change – the wonderful *Guide Michelin* – although of course change it did, and that is what travellers eagerly looked for, and the reason they rushed to buy a new edition each spring. But look at these books in the mid-1930s to try to discern hints of the social climate – the cries for justice that led to the Popular Front, the strikes, the growing war between political extremes. The red-bound Michelins remained mute, focusing on succulent dishes and velvety wines, irresistible curiosities, breathtaking views.

Yet in a short while the principal preoccupation of the Michelin travel department would be to publish maps for the military. In fact, the familiar maps on the 1:200,000 scale used by tourists in every corner of France were adopted as roadmaps for the French Army, with a special edition (lacking colour) distributed to all theatres of operation. Michelin maps were, after all, the best one could get. At the request of the War Ministry, Michelin put its cartographers to work on nearby countries not heretofore covered – such as the Netherlands (until then only the southern region of that country had been included in a map series with Belgium and Luxembourg) and even Norway. Later, say Michelin's historians, the Germans occupying France asked for similar help – and did not get it.[3]

There was a *Guide Michelin* for 1939, of course (printed in March, six months before the declaration of hostilities). Is it only imagination? The curious observer who stares at a shelf of old Michelin guide-books has the impression that the 1939 edition stands out – the colour brighter, the stiff cover less worn. After all, it was the one edition that was used for only half a year: an only partially worn-out guide-book is one of the best-preserved monuments to a France that was and could never be (not quite) again.

If it did get read, its pages thumbed till they were worn out, its cover nearly in tatters, it was in a very special reprinting of the 1939 *Guide Michelin* five long years later. That was when the Military

Intelligence Division of the United States War Department, preparing its armies and those of its allies for the Normandy beachhead landings of June 1944, reprinted the 1939 *Guide Michelin*, not forgetting the jacket drawing of Bibendum running after a spinning tyre or the starred restaurants inside, reprinted it with the warning: 'For Official Use Only'.

It is easy to see why. All the landmarks a soldier might need to find his way were included in it, such as distances between localities. Further, the tiny town maps highlighting significant buildings and sights, such as the town hall, post office and principal churches, would provide unmistakable markers that no camouflage could conceal.

                *   *   *

We have seen that purchasers of the 1939 *Guide Michelin* at Easter had only a few precious months to enjoy it. By August it was no longer a matter of if, but of when, and then Hitler's invasion of Poland at the beginning of September led to a declaration of war against Germany by France and Britain. Over the following eight months there was little action on the front that divided the belligerents; the Germans, joined by their new Soviet allies, were able to complete their absorption of Poland with little opposition. One could almost – almost – be a tourist in France.

That was until 10 May 1940, when Hitler was ready to turn against the West. His offensive was mapped through the Netherlands and Belgium, although the obvious target was France; the *Blitzkrieg* would not slow down until Paris had been taken. In the night of 12–13 May the first German troops tramped on French soil – rode over it would be the better term.

Between that moment and 14 June, when German soldiers marched through Paris on the way south, there was little evidence of hostilities in the capital of France. Panic there was, with the flight of refugees from the north, their route through Paris, following the main highways toward what were presumed to be safer territories in the French heartland. Soon the escapees were joined on their trek by an exodus of Parisians. In that period of waiting, only one enemy bombing raid broke the silence, striking inside the gates of Paris. The sprawling Citroën plant was then turning out military equipment of all kinds; that facility and nearby Renault on the edge of Paris were the chief objectives of a German air assault on 3 June. Some 200 enemy bombers were counted, launching an estimated 1000 bombs in a raid that lasted nearly an hour and caused sporadic but scary damage in contiguous residential areas.

The destruction at Citroën was considerable; the raid also left dead and injured workers. By the next morning, officials insisted, the plant began producing 75 millimetre shells again.

Eleven days after that, the Germans were present on the ground. The Citroën plant stood intact but silent, its workers having been evacuated in anticipation of the invasion. When Citroën's manager Pierre Boulanger and his staff sought to enter the plant at the end of June – a fortnight after the invasion of the city – German army sentries turned them back; on a second try, Boulanger was ushered into his own office to find a German automobile manufacturer, a man he had met at pre-war auto shows – seated behind his desk. 'You've got to get the Citroën going as rapidly as possible, and bring back your workers,' the German instructed Boulanger. 'You'll be making trucks and rolling stock to transport supplies in France and for other uses... I count on your collaboration, that of management and labour both. If not, we'll proceed without you!'[4]

*   *   *

Meanwhile, in those last days of June 1940, Clermont-Ferrand – obscure, quiescent, insular Clermont-Ferrand – had become the capital of France, if only for a moment. The new French cabinet in Bordeaux, presided over by Marshal Philippe Pétain, had been declared unwanted by the invading Germans, for whom that Atlantic port was strategic. So the Pétain government, for whom Paris was also now out of bounds, would have to find another place of exile – preferably in a city with existing government buildings, but above all in a place possessing a considerable stock of hotel rooms.

Clermont-Ferrand did not have many hotels to offer, but the Auvergne capital was wedged in the centre of a thermal resort region, with many small spas possessing hotels worthy of a cabinet minister. Premier Pétain himself was given rooms at a private home on Clermont's elegant Cours Sablon (within sight of the Michelin family compound).[5] And, to believe one historian, already in Clermont-Ferrand the plot to transform the French Republic into a dictatorship was ripening in meetings between Pétain, Pierre Laval and their evil genii.[6]

But Clermont's moment of glory faded quickly. By 1 July, the government had packed up again to settle in Vichy, less than 40 miles to the northeast; it was actually a smaller town than Clermont, but as a resort devoted to thermal cures, it could offer enough hotel rooms to serve as offices and lodgings for nearly everyone who counted in what would become Pétain's authoritarian French State.[7]

Edouard Michelin was by this time 81 years old, still at the helm of his family firm, assisted by a trusted son-in-law, Robert Puiseux, now also by Pierre Boulanger, who after the arrival of the Germans had joined Michelin in the Vichy zone. But there is evidence that the patriarch was still the boss. A remarkable document survives from the last full year of his life, 1939, when the Patron was in his eightieth year: another homily, the last that has survived. 'I should like the principal goal of this House in 1939 to be to move faster,' old Edouard began. 'Slowness is the special defect of large companies, and a cause of their ruin.' It was not enough to say that something would take so much time, one had to specify a delivery date, to find the points in an operation which are holding up everything else, get the advice of workers who are going to do the job and get a completion time when giving an order of execution.[8]

He died on 25 August 1940. No attempt has been made to link Edouard's death to that of the Republic, although certainly the fall of France and enemy Occupation – not to speak of the tumultuous hours during which Clermont-Ferrand was the capital of Pétain's government – would have affected this old man, who had watched the Germans win an air war that he and his brother had conceived a generation earlier.

One cannot of course document the deathbed scene; we know Edouard must have said what he is credited with saying, simply because it really happened that way. Thus, he ordered things so that his daughter Anne's husband Robert Puiseux would succeed him, and on his deathbed pledged Puiseux to place a Michelin at the top as soon as that became possible.[9]

Of course, he could have annointed another Michelin at once, had either of his brother André's sons been co-opted; André's second son, Marcel, for instance, who had been introduced into the family business by Edouard himself, learning his job in the United States and Britain, taking charge of the strategic testing department as early as 1913.

Marcel had participated in the development of steel wheels, and of all the innovative tyres, had been in charge of launching Michelin train carriages. (Family legend has it that Marcel was furious that the company worked for the Germans during the Occupation – but that was another story; he himself would be arrested by the Gestapo and die in a concentration camp.)[10]

Better let the Michelin name slip into the shadows for a while.

But if the Michelins were discreet – men and women trailing no stories behind them – the new managers Robert Puiseux and Pierre Boulanger were not much more helpful to their would-be biographer. Long after their disappearance, Edouard and André were remembered for sociability, for the chandeliers one might glimpse through the windows of the Cité Chabrol, the family's cluster of houses hidden behind the sober façades of Cours Sablon in the centre of Clermont. In Robert Puiseux's time, the chandeliers ceased to glow. Puiseux was not a misanthrope, decided genealogist René Miquel – only a busy man.

For there was work to do in 1940, and in every successive Occupation year. Most heavy industry continued to function under the Germans, and this for a variety of reasons, most of them well-intentioned – such as to keep workers on the job, which could also mean to shield them from deportation to factories in Germany. As a consequence, factories produced what the Germans asked for – more or less speedily, and of varying quality. For some did dare to slow up the German war machine.

In Paris, for example, according to the best evidence we have, Citroën turned out trucks, as the Wehrmacht demanded, but ever so slowly – using whatever pretext could be found to slow the machines. Vehicles came off the assembly line at the rate of 30 a month, says one business historian, instead of the pre-war 400. On its side, Citroën management endeavoured not only to prevent the transfer of workers to Germany, but also to keep them nourished and clothed.[11]

Boulanger's biggest secret, however, was the 2 CV – an incarnation of the pre-war dream of a 'tiny car' that had been on the drawing boards for the past four years. Unknown to the public at large, perhaps unknown to the German occupying authorities, a near-final prototype of the ugly duckling had been developed and even registered as acceptable by the authorities on 28 August 1939 – less than a week before the declaration of war. Photographs survive, and one must say that the 'tiny car' did look ridiculous – but not terribly different from the final version, with its absurd chassis of corrugated sheet metal and that fragile canvas roof; worse still, to make it really cheap, this early proto-type bore a single headlight (on the driver's side).

On 3 June 1940, when Paris's sole air raid targeted Citroën, the design office had been hit, and a heap of plans for the 2 CV were scattered about. After the fall of Paris, Citroën's historian tells us, Boulanger resolved to take up the programme again – keeping it hidden from the Germans who virtually shared his offices. The prototypes were stashed away, and when the Germans got wind of the project Boulanger refused to talk about something that was not their business – or so the story goes.[12]

*　　　　　　　　*　　　　　　　　*

And that was only the half of it. Down in Clermont-Ferrand, which was perhaps less subject to indiscreet inspection by the Germans (who in theory were not to occupy the Vichy zone until November 1942), the Puiseux team had its own deep secret, the designing of an all-new tyre for the post-war world they would call the X. Drawing on lessons learned during the development of an an innovative pre-war tyre, when it became clear that the use of steel made possible a thinner casing, thereby reducing the accumulation of heat, the developers decided once for all that rubber and steel need not be incompatible.

There is a story behind the X tyre and its inventor, the kind of story one likes to hear about Edouard. Marius Mignol was a clerk in export sales when Edouard Michelin walked in one day, and noticed a curious object on a table. It turned out that Mignol had devised his own slide rule to do quick currency conversions. 'But this man's a genius – he should be working on the technical side!' exclaimed the chief, and soon he was.

At the time, Michelin engineers were looking for ways to reduce overheating and energy loss in treads and sidewalls. Amateur engineer Mignol now put together what became known as 'the fly cage': he replaced the sidewall – an element considered essential for holding the tread to the bead – with steel wire running from bead to bead to main-tain the tread in place. (The bead is that part of the tyre that is sealed to the rim.) It was seen that the tyre heated less, which signified that the rise in temperature was caused not by the tread but by the sidewall.

The answer seemed to be to eliminate the sidewall, but that caused the tyre to lose directional stability. Pierre Bourdon, husband of Edouard Michelin's second daughter and a company executive, then applied know-how acquired in the development of the earlier metallic tyre, making use of a steel-cord belt under the tread. The new test tyre was stable, ran cooler, and had lower roller resistance, keeping tread wear to a minimum.

What came out of it – but remained a deep secret during the Vichy and Nazi years – was the radial tyre, the tyre that would ensure Michelin's post-war renaissance, but there was no question of even trying to protect it with a patent at the time.[13]

29

MICHELIN'S CHOICE

The Nazis could not have imagined that the Michelin plants were producing their war material with enthusiasm. In the absence of evidence to the contrary, we must repeat what Clermont-Ferrand has always believed, that during the German Occupation Michelin did only what it had to do, maintaining as priorities the continued employment of its workers (thereby saving them from forced labour in Germany) and the procurement of essential raw materials to keep the machinery rolling. Conceivably, the managing partners could have chosen to shut down the plant – with easily imagined consequences: their arrest and possible deportation, and the transfer of their workers to other factories producing war material – perhaps in Germany.

Instead, and from the first days of the Occupation, Michelin accepted a *modus vivendi*. As part of the arrangement, German authorities allowed Michelin access to essential supplies of cotton thread produced in German-occupied northern France in exchange for Michelin's stock of raw rubber. The 'deal' was an expensive one for Michelin, manager Robert Puiseux privately assured the new Vichy government, but it would save the jobs of the firm's 10,000 workers.[1]

The claim would be made that tyres produced for the German army with synthetic rubber furnished by the occupying authorities were sabotaged by Michelin engineers so that they would fissure at low temperatures, putting army vehicles out of commission on the cold Russian front.[2] It is a good story, but apparently not a true one. Our best authority on wartime Clermont-Ferrand was assured by Michelin's chief engineer of that period that the firm continued to produce 'only the best tyres', in order to preserve its reputation. Sabotage, when it happened, was co-ordinated with the underground Resistance to destroy tyres in the course of shipment to the enemy. There was no sabotage inside the factory.[3]

Another story that has had a long life assures us that the Nazis were wary of the Michelins not only because of their historic anti-German campaigns, but also because the Michelin family had some Jewish ancestry. In the most thorough study of the Michelins, Barbiers, and Daubrées over the centuries, their unofficial genealogist put it this way: 'Their family... through the origins of some of its ancestry, and despite its Catholic religion, would be subject to the [Nazi] racial laws if it had not resided in the southern [Vichy] zone'.[4]

The genealogist gives us no further clue, unless it be in tracing the family surname to the Gallo-Roman era and the early Middle Ages, when Michel – from which Michelin is derived – was often a Jewish name.[5] Yet, closer to our own time, polemicists who took delight in uncovering Jews hiding behind gentile family names found no Jews at all among the Michelins, Barbiers and Daubrées.[6]

The Nazis would have been more justified in worrying about what family members were doing after office hours. The most notable activist was André Michelin's son Marcel, who was 54 years old when the Germans drove into Clermont-Ferrand. In charge of the company's technical studies and testing, he had been the driving force behind the Michelin athletic association, and it was almost as if an extension of his social work that he went about creating a refuge in the forest, a little over 20 miles from the city, for workers who risked being sent to Germany. He was also credited with organizing groups that made their way to London or to Algiers to join the Free French under Charles de Gaulle. Two of Marcel's sons, Philippe and Hubert, succeeded in reaching London and became Royal Air Force (RAF) fighter pilots.

Then in July 1943, Marcel and still another of his sons, 26-year-old Jacques, were denounced and arrested. Family history has it that Jacques was able to get rid of a compromising document by passing it on to his 11-year-old brother before disappearing behind the walls of the Clermont prison. A fourth son, Jean-Pierre, was one of the first

Free French soldiers killed on French soil during the liberation of Corsica in 1943.

Marcel and his son Jacques were detained in the notorious Buchenwald camp, Jacques to be transferred from there to Flossenburg, where his services as a doctor were utilized; he was one of the few survivors when General Patton's army liberated that camp in April 1945. As for Marcel, after working in the Buchenwald quarries he was transferred in December 1944 to another concentration camp, Ohrdruf. His execution took the form of a cold shower, after which he and other prisoners were left standing in snow and icy wind; he died in January 1945 of double pneumonia.[7] It is useless to speculate on why there were so many Resistance activists on André Michelin's side of the family. On his side, Edouard had no male descendants of fighting age.

*   *   *

So Michelin's doors stayed open, and that almost until the end of the German years. By 1941, Michelin and other rubber companies in the region were turning out tyres made from buna, a synthetic rubber supplied by the Germans.[8] At the same time, the company – its personnel roster reinforced by a large number of women – was producing a variety of goods needed in the harsh everyday life of Occupied France – from rubber shoes to truck trailers.[9]

Characteristically, the company continued its *pro bono* activities, notably in such publications as a Vichy government reissue of an old Michelin handbook for young mothers, *Comment Alimenter vos Bébés*. It contained the preface signed by the since deceased Edouard, marked by his predilection for systems; one could almost say that he was introducing an assembly line for tots. 'A capital point,' he had written, 'is to train the infant, to discipline it for its feedings…Go to visit the factory nursery, spend a day there if necessary. You'll see 25 or 30 babies who are fed every three hours and aren't touched in the interval…and who don't cry (save perhaps for some new-born babies who arrived with bad habits).'

Even Michelin's promotion of athletic activities was exploited by the Pétain regime – paradoxically, these were activities for which the doomed Resistance militant Marcel Michelin was responsible. Vichy's education and sports commission issued a booklet in which Marcel

Michelin assured readers that the club's organizers were 'inspired by the pure spirit of the [Pétain] National Revolution'.[10]

Prominent left-wing militants, who might have been considered natural leaders of the Resistance to Pétain and the Germans, were easily identifiable in the small town Clermont-Ferrand was. Most Communist leaders, including Robert Marchadier of the CGT, were interned, and suspected Communists among factory workers were closely watched. But resistance there was. Most of the national underground movements carried out operations in and around Clermont-Ferrand, if only by distributing the Resistance press. The meeting of clandestine activists that led to the founding of the movement called Libération took place in Clermont-Ferrand, and Michelin workers were active in a strong local unit of the Franc-Tireur Resistance organization. One of the irregular underground publications distributed by trade unionists of the region was actually called *Bibendum*.[11]

*   *   *

The Germans moved south across the lines separating the German and Vichy zones in November 1942, their pretext the allied landings in North Africa, which brought the war closer to France's Mediterranean coast. There is a strange story – truth or legend – that when the Occupation troops arrived in Clermont-Ferrand, Michelin's Robert Puiseux received them in the unimpressive reception area at the entrance to the Michelin plant and offices on Place des Carmes. 'Gentlemen, you are here in a private home,' he is supposed to have said. 'Traditionally, as you know, no one visits our factories. That being said, you can come in. But I take you for men of honour. The decision is yours.' In the anecdote, the Germans left without a word and never tried to get inside the plant.[12] Whatever actually happened, a student of those tense times was able to say that Nazis and Western allies both felt that (in the words of a British intelligence report) 'one of the strongest leaders of resistance in the country was Monsieur Michelin'.[13] Perhaps the official meant 'Monsieur Puiseux'.

Michelin saw its first direct war action in the final year of Occupation, when on the night of 16–17 March 1944, RAF Lancaster planes, equipped with six-ton bombs known as 'factory busters', made Clermont-Ferrand and Michelin a specific target.[14] That these bombers crossed France to hit Michelin – the only other RAF raid on France reported that day struck Amiens, considerably closer to the English Channel and to England – does suggest that there were sound strategic reasons to cripple this particular tyre plant.

We now know something else about that raid: it might have been avoided. Our source is the man responsible for the united Resistance movements of the Auvergne region (MUR, for Mouvements Unis de Résistance), Henry Ingrand, who had been chief of the Combat movement for the province; at the end of the war he was appointed regional governor by the Gaullists.

Ingrand had been contacted by an agent of British intelligence (actually a member of the British organization responsible for European underground work, the Special Operations Executive or SOE). If the local Resistance, aided by Michelin, would sabotage the factory on the ground, an air-raid could be avoided. Ingrand got his people to try to start fires in the factory with incendiary bombs tossed through a window into a tank of benzine, without result. His SOE contact warned that he had only one week to accomplish sabotage from within before the aeroplanes received their orders.

Through Ingrand's contacts among higher-ranking Michelin exec-utives, he met the general manager, to whom he explained that the point was to 'destroy the minimum indispensable to halting production'. The answer was no; Ingrand remembered the phrase 'indecent and useless'. In any case, the Michelin director said, officers of the company were already in touch with the British secret service in Lisbon, and he would work through them to head off the air attack. Ingrand's own response was to attempt further sabotage by workers inside the plant – but his best efforts did not cause significant damage.

So the RAF came.[15]

The March raid was the subject of a meticulous inquiry carried out soon after the liberation by the United States Strategic Bombing Survey, an inquiry not as revelatory as it might have been, since Michelin was back in full command. RAF investigators went only where manage-ment let them, getting much of their information not from examination of records but from plant managers. At the time Cataroux was turning out tyres for automobiles, motorcycles and light-weight trucks, bicycle tubes and incidental goods such as baby carriages, stoves, rubber soles and heels, while heavy truck tyres were being produced at Carmes. The Germans had been allowing Michelin to pursue operations under its own management with a minimum of German supervision, the company said. 'The Survey team was unable to obtain definite figures regarding production for the German account'. the report said, 'but a Michelin representative stated that 50 percent of their production went to the Germans and the other 50 percent was allowed to be retained for French civilian consumption. The Germans demanded truck tyres only.'

The British had sent 21 Lancasters over the city that night, releasing bombs at an average of 10,000 feet. The mission of the post-war survey team was to assess the effectiveness of 12,000 lb bombs – ten of which were dropped in the attack, along with 50 1000 lb bombs. They discovered a considerable amount of structural damage, affecting over 30 percent of the built-up area. The investigators also wanted to find out what British 30 lb oil incendiary bombs could do against rubber manufacturing. The answer was that just under 8 percent of the con-structed surface had been destroyed by fire.

Without intending to, the team did learn something else about Michelin. Although the company had compiled 'a very complete record' of destruction of machines, tools and other equipment to justify its claim for war damage compensation, management was being difficult. 'The members of the field team were not permitted to enter the operating departments, mixing plant, wire shop and textile mill at Cataroux, nor any part of the Carmes plant, except the office,' the report complained. Speaking of the company's proverbial secrecy, it added: 'Even their own workmen were not permitted to travel from one department to another'.

But investigators being what they are, they were able to give a hint of what was going on:

> A tyre using metallic fabric, a speciality of Michelin, was made at the Cataroux plant. The process included the drawing of wire, the weaving of it into fabric and then the moulding of the metal fabric into the final tyre. The process was considered secret by the management, and no information was made available.[16]

The X tyre was about to be born.

30

NEW
BEGINNINGS

The annals of Michelin provide a sympathetic story to explain why American officers landed on the beaches of Normandy in June 1944 with the *Guide Michelin* in their kits. It seems that the United States military carried out a wartime survey – one guesses it was as informal as it was discreet – among Americans who had lived or travelled extensively in France before the war. Its conclusion was that most respondents – the figure given is 85 percent – agreed that Michelin guide-books and maps were the most helpful one could find. Hence the labour of Hercules – for some surely a labour of love? – by United States Military Intelligence, which reproduced all 1107 pages of the 1939 edition of the red guide, not forgetting a facsimile of the cover with its listing of the volume's highlights – the best food, the good wines, peaceful hotels etc.[1]

As the allies fought their way out of the beachhead pocket to pursue their drive south and east toward Paris, life went on as usual in occupied France. In retrospect, the surprising thing is that many of the French who collaborated with the Nazis did not understand that only a few more weeks or months remained before their individual routs. The hardest of the hardliners in Vichy exercised power through the militia, a native French version of Nazi stormtroopers.

Once again, our source is the historian of Clermont-Ferrand during the German years. He reports abuses of legal processes by militiamen, including an incident in July 1944 – little more than a month before the Germans withdrew from the city. Two militia troopers in search of subversive elements marched into the Michelin plant without first notifying the factory's management. When threatened with a reprimand, they insisted that a revolution was underway, and they would enter the factory whenever they needed to.

Michelin complained to Vichy's regional prefect, who in turn contacted the militia's operations commander in Clermont-Ferrand, who agreed that in future – in future! – a representative of the Michelin company might be present when an arrest was made.

And then it was all over. Under pressure of the Allied forces moving north from the Mediterranean landing beaches, the enemy withdrew from the Auvergne with as much decorum as could be marshalled under the circumstances. The local German commander had made preparations to blow up strategic industrial facilities in the region, but in the end agreed not to destroy Michelin. The occupying forces had, actually, achieved their mission; they had kept the factories humming.[2]

Archives of the post-war purge contain no files on the Michelin family hierarchy or on any of its non-family directors, suggesting that a case could not have been made against anyone in charge – or simply that their good deeds outweighed the bad, as so often happened in the German years. The only complaints directed to the post-war purge commission involved a dozen or so lower-ranking employees who took advantage of the particular circumstances of the Occupation to abuse their authority.[3]

*   *   *

That the victorious Free French bore no grudges is proved beyond any doubt by the formal visit to Clermont-Ferrand on 30 June 1945 by Charles de Gaulle, then head of the provisional government in Paris. Much pomp surrounded the visit of the living symbol of French resistance to Fascism, and Robert Puiseux himself greeted the convoy of official limousines as they pulled up at the courtyard entrance of Cataroux. 'Owners, engineers and workers,' declaimed de Gaulle, 'who knew how to set an example of courage and sacrifice, I salute you'.[4]

Again, legend has it that the company's fabled secrecy kept General de Gaulle on the outside of the factory looking in; he was duly honoured, said one source, 'but he too would not be able to walk through the door to the workshops'.[5]

Those who lived through that day in Clermont-Ferrand remember it differently. After the exchange of polite words in the decorated court-yard, the general and his party began a visit inside the plant, with a motor tour of the reconstruction. They got a brief look at ovens currently in use, before going on to the flagship factory at Place des Carmes. There the party was given a walking tour of the mixing chamber where rubber was prepared, and the shop where tyres were pressed.[6]

It took nearly two years to come to grips with the damage done on that terrible night in March 1944. The whole job would be terminated by the end of 1946, by which time Cataroux would be producing more than it ever had, and with more up-to-date machines.[7]

New tools, traditional caution. In a solemn message to personnel published in the company's internal bulletin in March 1945, in the first full year of liberated France, Puiseux described the visit of an American officer to Clermont-Ferrand in January (perhaps as a prelude to the contract for delivery of tyres to American troops still fighting in Europe).

The American visitor had been shown how a tyre was removed from the mould after baking; himself a former specialist in an American tyre company, he had expressed astonishment at the near-perfect condition of the finished tyre, and asked that a sample be given to him for shipping to the United States. The incident confirmed that Michelin possessed ideas, processes and machinery that others did not have. 'It is essential that we keep them for ourselves,' concluded Puiseux.[8] Left unsaid was the reason for heightened concern about security. This was the year of the final urgent efforts to perfect and test the tyre that would take Michelin through the second half of the century.

Bringing it to market was another story. As Robert Puiseux later told the story to his successor, François Michelin, both the engineering and sales departments had come to the conclusion that it would be a mistake to put such a superior product on sale. Since it would last three times longer than existing tyres, they would be able to sell only a third as many as before. Puiseux's reaction was to put a set of radials mounted on his own car, and to try them on a route with which he was familiar. The improved road safety and lower energy consumption were imme-diately obvious.

What was good for the customer today, he decided, would be good for the company tomorrow. Recalling that conversation at the beginning of the 1990s, François Michelin added his own thought. Had it not been for the X tyre, today's world would not now have sufficient rubber – natural and synthetic – for its needs.[9]

Perhaps Michelin's BM wheel (BM standing for 'bon marché', 'value'), was more appropriate for that time. Launched in 1946, it had been put together with the most readily attainable, least costly materials, making use of the least expensive manufacturing processes. Nearly two years had gone by since the liberation, and yet rationing was still the order of the day, with tickets required not only to buy food and coal, but petrol and tyres as well. Michelin was still making and selling its pre-war standbys. Yet if the revolutionary radial was not ready to be launched that year, it definitely had to be patented.

The operation was carried out with the precautions one has come to expect from Michelin. The tyre had a code name, CAM – standing for 'cage á mouches', or fly cage, because the post-war model continued to resemble amateur engineer Marius Mignol's wartime prototype. Wrapped in canvas to protect it from the indiscreet, the tyre was smuggled into Michelin's photographic laboratory on 13 February 1946 to be stripped and photographed, layer by layer. The application for a patent was filed on 4 June at the industrial property office of the Ministry of Industry and Trade.

It was a new way of thinking of tyres, explained the Michelin engineers in their presentation, and the result was greater resistance to wear and enhanced security. The layers of rubber were rigid to render the tread inflexible, and thus to maintain the stability of the tyre on the road. Then the innovation: 'The rigidity of the layers is obtained by the fact that each sheet consists of metallic threads buried in a coat of rubber and that the diverse threads are arranged to form inflexible "triangles"'.[10]

The new tyre was baptized X only in 1948, and in June 1949 the green light was given for rolling the Xs off the assembly line. The *Guide Michelin* for 1950 was the first to publish recommended air pressures for the wonder-tyre, listing them for no fewer than 12 types of automobile, including the Citroën 11 hp and 15 hp and the Chevrolet Fleetmaster.[11]

*   *   *

This struggle for a perfect X tyre was in a sense young François Michelin's rite of passage. He was just turning 20 when the patent application was filed in Paris,: he was 23 when the first radials began coming out of the ovens, not always as perfect as his mentor Robert Puiseux or the finicky engineers would have liked them to be. Michelin's unofficial genealogist paints the portrait of a young François growing up in a joyless environment. He had lost his father (founder Edouard's first son Etienne) when he was only six, his mother when he was ten. If he had lived in a cocoon, it was nonetheless a reasonably comfortable one, as the crown prince groomed to succeed the regent (but not just yet).

31

THE GUIDE
IN A TIME
OF SCARCITY

The Second World War came to a close – at least in the European theatre of operations – on 8 May 1945, less than nine months after the liberation of Paris and of Clermont-Ferrand. When the first post-war *Guide Michelin* was printed in April, the Western Allies were still fighting their way through Germany, which is to say that the publication of the 1945 edition was a *tour de force*.

At first approach, one hardly sees the difference. The same red covers, Bibendum happily rolling his tyre through the flourish of the Michelin signature. The quality of paper and printing seems identical to that of the last published edition, 1939 – and where the pre-war guide ran to 1106 pages, the new one came in at a respectable 1012. The price announced on the cover had more than tripled, but the decline in the value of the franc was even greater – making the new edition a bargain.

Scarcity remained the order of the day – in paper and printer's ink as well as food, electricity and fuel for heating, cooking and everything else; driving could hardly be a pleasure then. The very idea that a new *Guide Michelin* could be produced under such conditions is a wonder.

Of course there was an apology, the new guide being 'less complete' than its predecessors. Indeed, the Atlantic coastal towns of Royan and La Rochelle were still in enemy hands – and were to be heavily damaged during the siege. The notation 'Without information, late 1944' was the editors' succinct warning in such cases, used also for Strasbourg,

Colmar and smaller Alsatian towns such as Riquewihr closer to the German border.

To deal with such uncertainties, as well as the inability of the Michelin team to visit every village and town in France for verifications, the editors opted for leaving the listing of hotels and restaurants essentially as it had been in the last, pre-war, edition. But for hotels, the usual symbols designating their class were replaced by the same symbols in outline, simply to indicate what the hotel had been worth. Travellers were advised to reserve rooms in advance.

As for the celebrated stars honouring excellence in cuisine, Michelin dealt with the matter with a sabre-like stroke. On an explanatory page, titled, as in pre-war editions, 'Les Bonnes Tables', and illustrated with the familiar sketch of a smiling Bibendum wielding knife and fork as he attacks a chicken, an editor recalled the traditional one, two, and three-star system. That was 'the past'. 'The present' had a sketch showing Bibendum in a towering chef's cap, looking at a list of foods currently available and those that were not – the first running only a few short lines, the unavailables a couple of dozen. 'We have had to give up stars for good food in this edition,' the editor announced rather calmly. 'At the moment we go to press choice foodstuffs don't arrive or arrive irregularly, fuel lacks; finally, and this is worse, good cooks sit in German prison camps waiting for return to their ovens.'

Truly, everything had to be done. 'While the engineers reconstruct roads and bridges good hotelkeepers have been hard at work and are making an effort to preserve the world reputation of the French kitchen.'

Not only were the stars missing, but there were all the new, more sinister references. The simplest was 'destroyed', alerting travellers that a bridge or some other feature would have to be 'totally rebuilt'. The label 'damaged' offered hope that some rooms might already be available while repairs were in progress; 'requisitioned' was the notation for establishments still in the hands of the authorities, although in some cases the original owners had given Michelin their pricelists anyway, anticipating an early return to normality. Among the requisitioned were nearly every luxury establishment in Paris, among them the Crillon, Ritz, George V and Meurice (many of them had first been taken over by the invading Germans; some now served the liberators).

A great number of the accompanying maps were poignant reminders of what battles and bombings had done to strategic regions of France.

For readers in places that had been spared, and of course for visitors from abroad, this 1945 *Guide Michelin* might well have brought the first detailed information about the fate of cities and towns and particular streets or structures dear to them.

For cities like Caen – an Allied target before, during and after the landings on the nearby channel beaches – and Rouen – a vital hub whose bridges and adjacent quarters were heavily bombed – signs and symbols were hardly enough; the editors had to write it out. In Caen, 'Only the western and peripheral quarters are more or less intact; all the rest of the city, some 8000 of its 10,000 buildings, are destroyed or heavily damaged'. The fine arts museum no longer existed (although the paintings had been evacuated earlier and were therefore preserved), the city hall had also vanished, the railway station and post office had been seriously damaged.

In the list of monuments and other curiosities that followed, 'seriously damaged' and 'damaged' and 'heavily hit' appear frequently. An ancient restaurant survived but had been requisitioned; only the railway station restaurant was apparently open (and recommended). All hotels and the one other restaurant previously recommended were destroyed or heavily damaged. Caen would still be showing its scars to Michelin readers a full decade later.

'Nearly the whole centre of the city was annihilated,' begins the entry for Rouen; 'on both sides of the Seine, damage is immense'.

But the guide was there, with its maps in colour, its rich detail, and whatever could reasonably be included had been (such as the map showing where France's best wines could be found). The 1945 edition was also advertising a new Michelin map (on the 1:1,000,000 scale) called 'Roads and Bridges', whose essential features were 'Destroyed Bridges – Roads Broken Up – Poor Roads'.

'Finally…' cries Bibendum, watching as a little car bursts out of a garage, 'you can drive, but pay attention, tyres are still rares…For yours to last, they mustn't be overloaded or poorly inflated.' Thirteen pages of advice followed.

Concurrently with the publication of this incredible guide-book to practically nothing, there were new roadmaps. One of them was a necessary revision of the fold-out map of France – particularly that part of Normandy covered by sheet number 54 of the series of 90, a collector's item today, with its dots and circles and patches in red ink signifying bridge or ferry crossings destroyed, locality or part of locality heavily damaged, or a mined sector, mines in the course of being removed. The two sections having Caen as their centre are so blotched with red ink one imagines a printer or printing machine gone wild, or a newspaper that has been used to wrap raw meat.

Then the war was over, the enemy gone – but scarcity remained daily reality. Food shortages persisted, leading to abusive pricing; trains were overcrowded and 10 percent of the country's hotels remained unusable. Yet tourists did want to come to France, and there were regions in which they would be well and comfortably received.

Michelin's anonymous inspectors had recently revisited 3000 establishments, mostly in regions hit by the war. No, they could not yet give out stars – not the expected ones. 'We nevertheless thought it would be helpful to indicate with white stars those establishments whose well-ordered kitchens appear to give satisfaction for a reasonable price...'

'It's a beginning,' Michelin summed up, as if to reply to puzzled or disappointed travellers. 'We are persuaded that other establishments deserve a star. Let us know about the ones you find.'[1]

*   *   *

For the 1947 guide, Michelin visited 10,000 hotels and restaurants, accepting 8000 of them into the fold. But the editors were still not ready to award traditional stars; once again they were replaced by light-printed stars. 'This sign,' noted the English-language explanation, 'refers to hotels whose catering seemed to us satisfactory, allowing for the prices'.[2]

It still created odd situations. During the war, Lyon had been a relatively protected site, deep in the Vichy zone, closer to the agricultural heartland of the country than Paris, yet it continued to be deprived of its stars – as Paris was. So the guide had to apologize again. 'In Lyon there are many places where one can dine well,' the notice began. 'The present difficulties, the inequalities in distribution of supplies in the major cities make it impossible for us to make a selection this year.'[3]

At last a second star crept into the Michelin in 1948, and specialties offered in one and two-star restaurants also returned. Michelin made a particular effort to bring devastated regions back into the fold; there were stars at the Normandy towns of Caen as well as Lisieux and Le Havre (single stars, then signifying 'well-made food which in composition and quality justifies the price'). As for two stars, they were defined thus: 'One comes close to the excellent food of prewar days, but of course the prices are postwar'.

Shortages there may have been, but the guide was growing again. In 1948, confronted by the monster it had created – 1035 pages, despite a determined effort to save space wherever possible – Michelin's tourist department looked around desperately for a solution. The company had always lost money on the annual red guide, publishing it all the same as the best publicity one could have, since nearly every reader was a rider on tyres. But the costs of producing this compendium in an economy of shortage – of rationed tyres and inhibited tourism – had become punishing.

So Michelin set up a task force to re-examine the basic tenets of their creation. One product of the deliberation was a new questionnaire, in which users of the guide-book were asked not only what they should like to find in the volume, but also 'what information seems superfluous to you'. The result of all this – reader suggestions surely, but above all hard thinking by the editors themselves – was a 1949 *Guide Michelin* reduced to 839 pages – another *tour de force* – of which the editors were sufficiently proud to include a five-page introductory section explaining how they had accomplished the feat without divesting the book of the qualities that continued to make it unique.

'Bibendum' revealed that his staff had undertaken a page by page, line by line revision of the famous, seemingly immutable guide-book, deliberating over each detail to decide whether it was really necessary. Among discarded elements, for example, was an explanation of how to get someone to open a locked church, and the habit of indicating the altitude of beach resorts.

32

BAD TIMES AND GOOD HOPES

The month of October 1948 had begun badly. At long last, the criminal prosecution that should have taken place 10 years earlier, following the arrest of the Cagoule plotters who had set off the bombs near the Arc de Triomphe in 1937, was ready to begin in Paris. Among the defendants were other members of the same CSAR organization accused of the brutal murder of Carlo and Nello Rosselli, anti-Fascist Italian intellectuals exiled in France, in the year of the Arc de Triomphe bombings, and still others implicated in the cold-blooded assassination of Marx Dormoy, who as Interior Minister had investigated the Cagoule at the time of the Rosselli murders and the Paris bombings. Dormoy had been arrested by the Vichy regime, and was killed in 1941 while under house arrest.

Much grim history had been made since those crimes. Some of the defendants were present, others were fugitives; one who did stand before the jury was François Métenier, who had guided the hand of Michelin engineer René Locuty and his friends in the Paris bombings.[1] (One who had not been found was, precisely, ingénieur Locuty.)[2] The trial allowed another airing of the allegation that the Michelins had been behind CSAR. 'Did Michelin and Lemaigre-Dubreuil Finance the Cagoule?' was how the widely respected *Le Monde* headlined one day's report of the proceedings. 'Where did the money come from?' the story began, reporting the testimony of defendant Gabriel Jeantet, who told the jurors that a letter of introduction signed by the arch-Conservative Marshal Louis Franchet d'Esperey had made it possible for the conspirators to meet sugar king Jacques Lemaigre-Dubreuil and Edouard Michelin's son Pierre. Questioning in this direction went no further.[3] On 26 November the jury acquitted 11 of the 38 defendants present at the trial; six were sentenced to hard labour, either for life or for fixed terms, four went to prison and 17 others received suspended prison sentences.[4]

The Michelins could not have liked that kind of publicity, but fortunately the press was still operating under conditions of scarcity, news items were brief and printed in small type. The big story in October 1948 was down on the floor of the Automobile Show. While government planners had decided that Renault and Renault alone would be the authorized maker of small cars, the Michelins chose to defy that regulation.

Taking care not to reveal his hand in advance, Michelin's man at Citroën, Pierre Boulanger, defied the planners by unveiling his super-secret cheap car, the 2 CV, smack in the middle of the crowded Grand Palais. It was the latest reworking of the prototype, but now equipped with two headlights like all the other vehicles in the exhibition hall. And that funny tin-can form (with its roll-up top reinforcing the resemblance to a sardine can) intrigued a considerable portion of the 1,300,000 visitors to the show. Boulanger had delivered three of these 'sardine cans' to the exhibition floor, so one had to be patient to get a turn at the wheel.

On the eve of the surprise unveiling, Citroën's chief Pierre Boulanger had looked straight in the eye of France's leading automobile journalist as he said that he was not showing a new model this year. Stung by the deception, the journalist (and some of his colleagues) retaliated. The man whom Boulanger had misled decided to give only passing attention to what he called the 'mock-up' shown on the floor. 'I say mock-up because the car shown on the stand lacks a motor,' he wrote ironically (actually it had one, but it was under a bonnet that was bolted down).

Yet one witness to the event, who happened to be editor-in-chief of the Swiss Revue automobile, apparently got it right. 'Citroën seems not to care about public or press opinion,' he wrote. 'They can speak well or badly about us, as long as they speak! And indeed they were speaking. Because the new creation of the vast [Citroën] establishment is in truth a revolution of a kind not seen in several decades.' The little 2 CV, he exclaimed, was 'an entirely different car from all those in circulation today'.[5]

Nobody would forget that show. But they would have to wait a while to see the ugly duckling waddle. They were told what to expect: front-wheel drive the Citroën way, with independent suspension for each wheel, a speed of 40 mph, 65 miles on four to five litres of petrol. To be spartan to the nth degree, the vehicle lacked an ignition key, and to find out how much petrol remained, the driver simply dipped a slender rod into the tank. All that ugliness and inconvenience had its reward: the duckling would be cheap, if one could get it.

A new post-war generation could afford an automobile now; a new class could move up from bicycle to enclosed space on wheels. And from the outset they were not making them fast enough.

Scarcity whetted appetites, a lengthening waiting list. They would never be able to make enough of them.[6]

*   *   *

The Michelins also found their own way to slip the X tyre into circulation before they were sure they were ready; they did it by catching the public unawares. So favoured clients found themselves using, and apparently getting good mileage from, a new SP tyre. In fact this was the radial, half disguised as a traditional rubber and textile model already a dozen years old.

The new product got a name of its own only in June 1949, when the first tyres came rolling out of the most secret assembly shops. Choice was limited to the two sizes already submitted to tests and trial runs, to be fitted on already existing rims and some other wide-base wheels.

Only at the 1949 Automobile Show would aficionados actually get a chance to see the X under its own name, mounted on those reliable and familiar 11 hp front-wheel drive Citroëns. The first automobile sold with Xs as standard equipment was the 1950 Lancia Aurelia, and Italians would also put the new Michelin marvel on their Alfa Romeos and Ferraris before it became a must in France itself.[7]

It was probably difficult even for Michelin men to realize how far ahead of the pack they were. They seemed not to mind being teased for their conservatism, their paternalism, each time digging deeper into the bunker they had erected down among the volcanic cones of France's most mysterious province.

And yet at Citroën they had tweaked everybody's nose with the 2 CV, building the automobile any believer in the Popular Front would have liked to be able to offer the little people. All the same, to maintain their reputation for thriftiness, Pierre Boulanger and his associates in Clermont-Ferrand preferred to keep customers waiting rather than invest in expanded plant capacity. And since priority was accorded to farmers, doctors, social workers, even country priests and nuns, the waiting list for everybody else grew longer and longer – at times up to a ridiculous four years.[8]

For customers on a faster track, there was Michelin's own radial – the X – to become everybody's tyre in France (and elsewhere on the Continent) before the Americans even dreamed it existed. In 1947 Michelin became the first company in Europe to be equipped with an electronic microscope, the next year the company was innovating again by utilizing butyl synthetic rubber for inner tubes, reducing the loss of air (they called the new product Airstop).[9]

In 1949, in its internal bulletin, intended for plant personnel, Michelin did not hesitate to publish photographs of the old vulcan-ization process for finishing tyres in pressure-sealed moulds, and the new way, in what was called a 'wrist-watch case'. Both methods were still in use at Cataroux, but the old method required 145 workers, the new one only 24.[10]

In 1948 there was a new tractor tyre with extra-deep grooves. The following year the company went to market with the 'biggest tyre in Europe', the so-called 21.00-24 model designed to be used with earth-moving equipment imported from the United States.[11]

*   *   *

This company that lived by the road now gave another hostage to the road. Driving down from Paris to Clermont-Ferrand on 11 November 1950 – and only some 28 miles from his goal – Pierre Boulanger veered off the road near Gannat to smash into a tree – one of those towering shade trees along France's main highways that have killed again and again. He had been driving his company's pride, a front-wheel drive, but it was a dank day of the Auvergne autumn.[12] Boulanger, number one at Citroën and co-managing partner of Michelin with Robert Puiseux, had just turned 65, yet without giving a sign that he was ready to retire. Robert Puiseux was seven years his junior.

One direct consequence of the death of Pierre Boulanger – not part of Michelin's collective memory but of Citroën's – was a relaxation of the spartan, penny-pinching, corporate culture at the Citroën factories. Boulanger had wanted a cheap car that looked cheap. No petrol gauge, as we have seen, but also no way to indicate a change of direction (the driver simply held open a small window flap – no elaborate roll-up windows for this car – while making the appropriate hand signal). Need space to haul heavy goods? Simply remove the rear seats and leave them at home. Need an emergency repair – say a broken shift on a motor trip to Communist Eastern Europe? Some rubber bands found at the bottom of one's tool kit might suffice.[13] One young driver in the early 1970s dropped off a troublesome 2CV for a repair and returned to the garage to be presented with a bill for one franc.

Eventually the 2CV got a few additional amenities, and then a more powerful motor. Production was stepped up, as if satisfying demand was a reasonable notion. Finally, in 1959, buyers were given the timid choice of another colour, blue, besides the uniform battleship grey of all the other 2CVs on the road.

It was the kind of thing Boulanger's successor, Pierre Bercot – another self-made industrialist, who had been more of a scholar and jurist until Boulanger saw him as the perfect number two – now dared introduce, along with a light-spirited advertising campaign to go with the new will to sell cars.[14]

*   *   *

It was not being said, not publicly, but surely the stepped-up effort to claim a significant share of the transatlantic market was one of the motives for the innovations. Robert Puiseux saw the radial tyre as an excellent calling card in this new approach to the American consumer. Within a month of Boulanger's death, Michelin had dispatched a sales representative to New York to recreate a Michelin Tire Corporation there.[15]

33

THE GUIDE
AT FIFTY

Decidedly, an André Michelin was needed, on this fiftieth anniversary of the *Guide Michelin*. The editors of the 1950 edition did try to deal with the event in their own ponderous way, comparing the manner in which towns were handled in the 1900 edition with today's entries. 'The *Guide Michelin* pursues the mission set for it by the great precursor André Michelin,' declared a slightly pompous Bibendum. 'Fifty years separate the two editions: fifty years of study, effort, prospecting on the roads of France, in the quest for the whatever is better; fifty years of labour at your service.'

For all its exclamation points, and liberal use of red in town maps and page layout, it was a sober, no-nonsense guide in those days. One can almost hear André Michelin storming around the office, demanding to know why that other great event of the past year and this one, the unveiling of the X tyre, was not given more attention in the guide.

André Michelin had made promiscuous use of the press, often with his own style of personal journalism – but as paid publicity. Compare the austere, pictureless, five-and-a-half inches of unreadably small type that announced the fiftieth anniversary edition of the guide. 'With the fiftieth anniversary edition just published, motorists travelling in France, in examining the wealth of documentation contained in this work and remembering times past, can measure the importance of the evolution that has occurred in automobile driving and travel conditions.'[1]

*   *   *

Yet perhaps there is something to say for publishing a dull guide-book. How appropriate for a tyre-maker: surely there is nothing less inspiring, less comely, about an automobile than its tyres? Drivers purchased those annular black excrescences only because they were necessary to get the most out of a beautiful car. One picked up the red guide-book because it contained the key to some magical experiences, opening the door to truly fine hostelries, tables set for superb meals; it was also a guaranteed time and money saver.

By the 1950s, worldly-wise travellers were already keen users of the Michelin. Tourists in France – whether American, British or Continental – simply wanted the facts, distances, prices, stars. Now more than ever, Michelin was the tourist's bible, as the magazine *Time* called it on publication of the 1952 edition.

The magazine gave facts and figures that French people were not getting, probably because travel and food writers there never bothered to ask. Thus, *Time* could say that the guide's print-run was 200,000, double that of the pre-war figure; the current edition described some 8000 hotels and restaurants in its 880 pages. 'Michelin loses some $57,000 a year [or nearly 20 million francs of that time] on its little red guide book, but it has spread the company's name all over the world.'

Time's reporter talked to the editors of the guide, to learn that Michelin's travel department then counted on 92 of its own regional sales representatives to keep its information fresh, plus five full-time inspectors who spent their year eating their way across France. When dining, they remained anonymous 'until the meal is over, and woe to the chef who is having an off day'. The inspectors reported what they saw and heard and even overheard in considerable detail; if the word was going around that the professional problems of a certain chef had to do with his home life, that too went into the file.

Reader suggestions were important too. Some time before release of the 1952 edition, Michelin's travel department had opened a mal-odorous package to find an obviously inedible slice of ham and some sad-looking fried potatoes, backed up by a reader's letter complaining that Michelin had recommended the place. An inspector dispatched to the restaurant found that the complaint was justified, and scratched the establishment from the book.[2]

We have to turn to America again for the first eyewitness account of a Michelin restaurant inspector at work. It also happens to be the most respectful and perhaps the wittiest piece ever published about the guide. André Michelin might have appreciated it, and would conceivably have written something similar. The chief of Michelin's inspection team, who at the time was a Monsieur André Trichot, had agreed to allow the *New Yorker* to have its writer accompany a seasoned inspector on an important mission in preparation for the next edition of the guide.

Late in April 1954, the *New Yorker's* man was summoned to Arles at 9 a.m. on a certain morning, where he was to meet Michelin inspector Jean Lasbugues in a hotel lobby. The reporter found a conservatively dressed gentleman in his early forties, 'with a restrained – or, rather contained – joie de vivre'. (That he was one of Michelin's finest is proved by the fact that when the writer of this book visited Michelin's editorial offices a dozen years later, the spokesman who received him was the same Monsieur Lasbugues, by then the dean of inspectors.)[3]

So the reporter tagged along while Lasbugues did some routine inspecting of hotels in Arles – four of the five listed in the 1954 edition (the fifth was where Lasbugues was staying – and he'd save that inspection until after settling his bill the next morning). After that, he looked in at an establishment that had been omitted from the guide but had asked to be reinstated, and finally visited a building then being converted into a hotel. Inspectors did not call at hotels anonymously; in each case the Michelin man asked for the manager and showed his credentials (with photograph) before proceeding – explaining to the reporter that, despite such precautions, imposters continued to extort money and free meals from anxious hotelkeepers.

As he made the rounds with the manager, Lasbugues filled in one side of a form (the other side was reserved for his comments and criticisms – and he saved that for later). He asked to see an example of every category of room, peered out of windows, into closets, made sure that bathroom facilities were in working order. 'The managers often gave away what they were most worried about,' he observed – like insisting that the hotel was clean by unmaking bed after bed. In hotels with restaurants, Lasbugues checked the tableware, 'sniffing at bits of food'. He told the reporter that he did not have to eat at all the hotels; if something was wrong, he would find it out for himself in the kitchen.

They lunched at the best restaurant in Arles from the point of view of comfort; it rated two spoons and forks in the guide (no restaurant in town had earned a star). After giving the lavatory the once-over, the inspector chose a table with a view over the Place du Forum, asked for and ordered the specialties. During lunch he told the reporter that he inspected between 1200 and 1400 hotels each year, and as many restaurants as he could, as one of six full-time inspectors who spent from eight to ten months of each year on the road.

When the *New Yorker* man expressed admiration for their main course, a seafood patty, the inspector agreed it was tasty – but felt it a bit overdone. He liked the fruit sherbet. After they had split the bill Lasbugues talked to the *patronne*, wife of the owner-chef. She invited the diners into the kitchen to meet her husband, who did not conceal his irritation at being taken by surprise. But the inspection went well.

Next morning they drove over to Les Baux, that curious ruin of a fortified hilltop town, a spectacular tourist site worthy of the three stars it gets in both Michelin's red hotel and restaurant guide and its green travel guide. 'Looking up at the stark gray ruins,' the reporter mused, 'I was struck for a moment by the seeming incongruity of our coming here to judge a sauce'. But they were to call at Raymond Thuilier's already famous Baumanière, the only restaurant that had been pro-moted to a third star in the new (1954) guide, stars it wore alongside four sets of spoons and forks – the next-to-highest rating, meaning 'deluxe' but not 'great luxury'; moreover, the symbols were printed in red, signifying exclusive company (Michelin's own definition – 'pleasant' – hardly seems adequate in the circumstances).

Lasbugues had shown the reporter a file card containing notations from a number of tourist's letters praising Baumanière, and one negative one (complaining of small portions, slow service, rude wine steward, dirty napkins, lavatory lacking paper – even cheating on the bill). The inspector confided that users of the guide who contributed comments often became regular correspondents, and after the third such reader's report, the sender would be typed by the Michelin people as sympa-thetic, testy or reflective. The *New Yorker* man wondered whether the person who complained about Baumanière had been one of the testy.

It was half past noon when the two men reached the main entrance, passing a man in chef's cap and apron, whom the Michelin man guessed was patron Thuilier. 'He is out of his kitchen during lunch,' he added disapprovingly. It would be a rigorous inspection; Lasbugues looked at everything, lifting up a straw placemat to scrutinize it (remarking that he would have preferred a tablecloth). He also examined his napkin, as he if were thinking of the complaint in his briefcase. Then he opened the guide ostentatiously and read out the three listed specialities (as if he did not know them by heart); the two men decided to order them all and to share them, with the two recommended wines. They voiced judgments as they went along: a surprising but not entirely satisfactory small local wine, not quite perfect sweetbreads in the pastry, too much flour in the sauce, too long a wait for the crayfish. But that dish turned out to be splendid and the American mopped up his share, ignoring Lasbugues's warning that the meat was yet to come. The reporter liked that as well, but Lasbugues would only say that the accompanying wine was excellent. After they settled and split the bill the Michelin man waited for the last guest to leave; he was confident that he had not been recognized, for inspectors never covered the same territory more than once every seven or eight years. But now he would identify himself and inspect the kitchen.

The reporter was not invited to join him in the kitchen. Later, he would learn what transpired later from Thuilier himself, who confessed that he had wondered why the Frenchman and the American had stayed so long. Then when Lasbugues flashed his card Thuilier thought, 'Monsieur, you are a cow'.

Lasbugues, it became evident, was still puzzled by Thuilier's role; was he or was he not the chef? He had not been in the kitchen during lunch, yet told Lasbugues now that he had gone alone to prepare dishes at a gastronomy festival in Switzerland. Thuilier then gave the American his own tour of the kitchen. 'Above all, service and courtesy,' Thuilier called out as they left – his motto, he said. ('Above all – food,' Lasbugues murmured to the reporter.) He had his doubts about the place.

That night in Lasbugues's room he asked the *New Yorker* man what he thought frankly about their lunch. The inspector had been ruminating on that unexceptional meat, that good but not sensational pastry *hors d'oeuvre*; as for the cheese and the wine, the chef did not cook those. Thuilier had been making progress year after year, and it was hoped that he would continue to do so. Removing a star was a grave matter, and in any case Michelin had become less finicky about details like white tablecloths. As they parted, Lasbugues admitted the decision would be a difficult one to make, and the reporter hated to think that he would have to wait a year to see if Baumanière kept its third star.[4]

It did keep it, and that for many years to come. It was down to two stars again in the 1990s and since.

*   *   *

A new period of expansion was underway in the travel department. In 1956 the first red guide for Italy was launched – actually covering only northern Italy ('from the Alps to Siena'). It contained all the familiar symbols save one – for who would have dared to award stars outside familiar territory? There was a first hotel-restaurant guide to West Germany in 1964, to Spain and Portugal together in 1973, Great Britain and Ireland in 1974 (with a separately published booklet for Greater London). The series was completed in 1978 with a three-in-one Benelux edition.

Gradually, as Michelin's foreign tyre companies became surer of themselves, and Michelin became surer of them, the first stars appeared alongside the names of restaurants – a single one at first. And even these timid stars proved to be relative in the early years. A fine provincial restaurant in Italy might merit high praise, but if its fine chef quit, there was no guarantee that an equivalent one would be found and hired at once. (In France, where the sacred nature of Michelin stars – not to forget their commercial value – were known, one could be sure that no restaurant owner would leave him or herself vulnerable for very long.)

In 1982, Michelin published the first Michelin red-jacketed hotel and restaurant guide to Europe – to Europe's principal cities, those that business travellers as well as tourists would be likely to visit (the book was slim enough to tuck into an attaché case). It was surely the first Michelin to contain, in the same volume, differing sets of criteria for judging food. The section on France, with its long history of Michelin ratings, described restaurants with one, two or three stars, but other countries attained only a maximum of one or two stars, while restaurants in still other countries were not being rated at all. In 1997, Salzburg and Copenhagen moved up from their previous one-star maximum to two stars (an honour Vienna had earned earlier); Athens got its first star, a single one. Italy and Britain had long since attained three-star ratings.[5]

*   *   *

But back in the 1950s, Michelin's secrets continued to be leaked, if in small doses, to the foreign press. In 1958, by which time the print run of the French *Guide Michelin* had soared to 300,000 copies – making it, in the words of a *New York Times* writer, 'France's most dependable best-seller' – some 10,000 copies went to Britain, 20,000 to other European countries and 4000 to the United States.

Not all Americans knew who the sponsors were. The *Times* critic Pierre Schneider told of an American admirer of the guide who while in Paris decided to congratulate the editors personally for its excellence; after a few minutes in the Boulevard Pereire salesroom he exclaimed, 'What? You also make tyres?'

When Schneider visited the Michelin guide, its total staff numbered 150 people, and some 12,000 copies of the questionnaire slipped into each copy of the guide were being posted back by readers annually, each containing an average of five pieces of information. These comments were verified by 'the seven most dreaded travellers on French roads – the Michelin inspectors'. Note how slowly this team expanded – from five inspectors in 1952, to six in 1954, to seven in 1958.

Schneider got a look at their evaluation form, which rated details such as quantity of food, quality, originality, presentation, service, friendliness, cleanliness, speed and comfort on a scale ranging from zero to five – the final decision being based on all these elements. Reports were then condensed into one-letter symbols in blue, green, brown or red pencil, depending on how each quality had been graded, so that a general idea of the quality of an establishment could be seen at a glance. They were filed alphabetically by locality; each year in December, final decisions were made in committee.

The inspectors themselves continued to come from the ranks; they were not professional gourmets but 'super-tourists', who had worked in other parts of Michelin before joining the guide. Only two things were asked of them – a critical sense and honesty. They were certainly aware, as a chef told Pierre Schneider, that 'Michelin can make or break you'. In the provinces, a star could represent a 50 percent increase in business; 'losing a star is like being stripped of stripes to a soldier'.[6]

34

THE FUTURE
AND FRANCOIS

Antoine Barrière was a quality control checker, author of one of the rare memoirs attempting to describe life and work inside the high walls of the Michelin plant. At times naive, at others iconoclastic, Barrière's report always impresses with its honesty. He remembers having been asked to inspect a newly vulcanized tyre, brought to him by a tall young man who seemed to be Barrière's own age. The stranger, accompanied by the director of the workshop where the new radials were being made, was introduced as François Michelin, then doing part of his apprenticeship in that department.

Barrière knew, of course, that François Michelin was able to follow the making of an X tyre from the first step to the last, something none of his fellow workers would be allowed to do. But Barrière's impression of his future chief was favourable, and he had to admit that the tyre he presented showed no defect whatsoever.

Another time, Barrière had the privilege of a visit to his shop by Robert Puiseux, who walked in silently, then stood near a wall as Barrière and his comrades continued their work. Puiseux remained there, without speaking, for what seemed like half an hour, leaving without having opened his mouth. 'Was it deliberate?' Barrière asked himself. 'Or shyness?'[1]

Shyness or not, it would still be Robert Puiseux's show for some time longer, the time it took for Edouard Michelin's grandson, son of the hapless Etienne Michelin, to learn to be a boss. We've seen that it started badly for this almost-orphan. Family legend shows François growing into adolescence in ill-fitting clothing, his ready-made jackets inevitably decked in mourning, as if someone close had died every day. It was said that he dreamed of becoming an astronomer like Robert Puiseux's father and grandfather, but he also adored sports and hiking. He was placed in a religious boarding school, and later deliberately kept away from the Paris schools that turned out the country's leaders and engineers, for fear of evil influences – and friendships that might prove awkward for a Michelin.

François had begun to make the rounds of the Carmes factory in 1951, when he was 25 – the year Antoine Barrière also began – but under a false identity, working as a machine fitter, filing metals. He tried all three eight-hour shifts; at another point in his training he travelled around France with tyre salesmen. He would wait until he was nearly 29 before joining the management group (on 28 May 1955).[2]

Surely he would be able to change the way things were done in Clermont-Ferrand. But for the moment, the operating procedure continued to resemble that bequeathed by Edouard Michelin, as reviewed, and only occasionally renewed, by his son-in-law Puiseux.

In July 1951, the still new and eager Barrière had been re-commended by his union to join a contingent of workers leaving for a study tour of American industrial plants, part of a productivity project sponsored by the Marshall Plan. Barrière readily accepted, and got in touch with the American Embassy in Paris to arrange his departure – in vain, because his superiors said no. The management feared that if Michelin workers visited American factories, the door would be opened for American visitors to Michelin – and that of course was out.[3]

Perhaps Michelin could have used some help in increasing pro-ductivity in the 1950s. In Paris, its Citroën affiliate was the number two automobile manufacturer (following Renault), turning out 117,674 vehicles in 1952, of which 88,626 were passenger cars – and 21,123 of these were the little 2 CV.[4] Yet it was estimated that the waiting list of would-be buyers of the elusive little vehicle now numbered 100,000[5] – clearly a productivity problem.

At Michelin itself – to quote a popular magazine of the time – these were boom years. 'You only have to question dealers about the waiting time for deliveries,' the reporter added ominously – as if increased demand necessarily implied a long waiting list.

With the opening of another French factory in Bourges in October 1954, the company informed its personnel with evident pride: 'Once again the Michelin tradition of building a new factory each year has been respected'.[6]

So they were not exactly sitting on their hands at Michelin. They seemed to have plenty of ideas, like putting subway trains on rubber tyres, a programme launched at the beginning of the 1950s with a panache resembling André Michelin's crusade to rubberize horse-drawn carriages at the end of the nineteenth century. A subway train equipped with test tyres took a bevy of cabinet officers on a trial run in Paris in autumn 1951. 'Surprise: the silence is almost absolute,' a popular daily told its readers – again reminiscent of what another Paris daily had said about André's tyres for horse-drawn cabs in 1896: 'One slides softly, without jolts, without the hammering of wheels on tracks. At a station, one looks with pity at passengers boarding one of the old trains on the next track.'[7]

*   *   *

He was five weeks short of his twenty-ninth birthday when he was co-opted to the board. Henceforth, François Michelin (Edouard's grandson) would be a managing partner of Robert Puiseux & Cie, an almost-equal and foreordained successor to his patient mentor and uncle. No-one could have doubted that François had been everywhere, seen and done everything in the scattered Michelin empire, or that he was qualified for the succession.

A photograph of François taken in December 1957 shows an eager young man as he addresses a meeting of over 400 senior employees who had entered the company in 1907, 1917 and 1927, and were now about to receive suitable medals. 'You all have over 30 years of the factory,' he told the veterans, most of whom were probably seeing their new master for the first time; surely they found him deferential in demeanour and in language. 'The man speaking to you only has six years.' He could also have said that he had turned 31 earlier that year.

Was there not something strange about a young man addressing his elders in this way? 'I don't think so,' he answered his own question. 'On the contrary, doesn't it say something about the continuity of our plant?' A continuity that had been assured by constant concern for quality, regular investment in what was newest and best. 'Everyone of you knows perfectly well that we cannot neglect putting aside part of the harvest needed for future sowing.'[8] It was as if he knew how many of these old-timers had come up from the farm to join the factory – and continued to potter around in their gardens.

It was almost two years after that public appearance that a sober François Michelin confronted an extraordinary general assembly composed of family owners of the company and their associates. François, who was now 33, reminded his listeners that in 1955, in order to assure continuity in leadership, Robert Puiseux had asked that the ownership be reorganized so that he could retire when he was ready to do so. (It was the 1955 arrangement, of course, that brought young François in as co-manager of the holding company.) Now Puiseux, at 67, had informed the younger man that he was resigning as co-managing partner, leaving François to run the company all by himself.

François confessed his emotion at the thought of taking over from the man 'who, after having presided over the destiny of the house since the successive deaths of Edouard Michelin and Pierre Boulanger, called me to his side to prepare me for his succession'. They had worked together for eight years. The assembly voted to call the group 'Michelin & Co.' once again.[9]

*   *   *

So, what was he like, this man who through his origins had a foot in each of the Michelin centuries? Truly he was taking on a nineteenth-century enterprise, with its antique corporate structure and archaic notion of labour relations, to produce twentieth-century products, and some of the most advanced at that. Yet again and again he would be found moving ahead of the pack, not letting go until this company, dug into an isolated volcanic region of rural France, was world market leader in its field. His risk-taking was to give him a position in the United States few European firms could match, a voucher that would be cashed in on the eve of the twenty-first century.

All the evidence tells us that this machine-age man was also an old young man, an old-fashioned industrialist entrenched in his fortress city and factory fortress, an unreconstructed capitalist who would never change his views about big government and big unions.

He was the right fit for Clermont-Ferrand. A churchgoer, he was married to Bernadette Montagne, sister of the lawyer and politician

Rémy Montagne – another Michelin-style marriage, for François's elder sister Geneviève happened to be married to Rémy Montagne himself. Montagne, former president of a national Catholic youth association, had just won a bitter electoral fight in the Eure district, taking the assembly seat of Pierre Mendès France, leaving the impression in Mendès' camp that he (Montagne) had not tried as hard as he should have to distance himself from bigots who opposed Mendès not for his politics but for his Jewish origins.[10] François and Bernadette would have six children; Rémy and Geneviève had six more.

One of his antagonists on the labour side was to remember François Michelin as an 'ascetic', a modest dresser who spent his days in a gloomy office ('in the manner of a police station in a provincial capital'). A legend grew up about his parsimony. He would get his staff to send out memos on the reverse side of defective printings of roadmaps.[11] Another Edouard, truly.

Had he studied his grandfather's life and gestures? For François was so much like him, and from the start, a hands-on manager who apparently enjoyed walking the factory floor to get his information fresh. Without any doubt he was his own man, wholly devoted to his family enterprise. Even his closest associates described him as unsocial, preferring familiar faces. By living simply, wearing frayed suits and 'ageless raincoats', flying economy class and using the Paris subway, he was personifying the virtues he wished to apply to his managers and workers.[12]

He began at what seemed like an auspicious moment in Michelin's history. Announcing the group's results at the annual shareholders meeting in June 1960, signing the report alone for the first time, François Michelin offered reasons for optimism. Business was up, thanks to a good year in the United States as well as in Europe, thanks to a liberalization of exchanges between Common Market countries that facilitated exports and helped improve Michelin's market share in neighbouring states, thanks also to a rise in tourism and a more stable franc.

Speaking of North America, he made it clear that this was still a small market for the firm. 'Any important commercial effort in that region,' he warned, 'calls for costly means, and becomes more risky as the competition wakes up to the challenge. In reality our results are too new and need to be consolidated.' An important early statement of a preoccupation with the American continent. Later, at least to his detractors, his willingness to engage 'costly means' would seem a dangerous obsession. But then he would prove that he was right.

Elsewhere in Europe, Michelin was watching developments closely. In Germany the old Karlsruhe plant reactivated in July 1958 had reached its cruising speed by the end of 1959 – but there was a lot more to do before Germany counted again in the Michelin constellation. In Vietnam the Société des Plantations et Pneumatiques Michelin reported record production and good results thanks to a boom in rubber prices. It had opened an affiliate of its own, the Manufacture Saïgonnaise de Pneumatiques Michelin, which would begin by building a plant for bicycle tyres. A new tyre factory was in the planning stage for Algeria. Vietnam, Algeria – it was still possible even for a prescient manager to bet wrong when it came to overseas territories and areas of influence.

But François Michelin knew which way his business would have to go. 'The only enterprises that will succeed in future,' he declared, 'are those which know how to improve quality constantly, while reducing production costs and improving management and investment policies'.[13] He could not know it, but France was smack in the middle of a growth phase, a period of expansion which began almost as soon as the war was won and would extend over three decades. The economist Jean Fourastié invented a term for the period: 'the thirty glorious years'.[14]

35

AMERICA
MA PIANO

Rarely did a financial paper focus on Michelin without mentioning its tradition of secrecy, and yet at the beginning of the 1970s it would have been difficult to ignore that the close-mouthed giant of Clermont-Ferrand was in an expansive mood. Soon after the May 1970 shareholders' meeting, a business weekly outlined Michelin's plans for expansion not only in France but abroad, where sales already exceeded domestic turnover. Yet at the time, Michelin's market share in the United States was only 4 percent – and it was clear that the firm had a lot of catching up to do.[1]

That year – 1970 – group profits increased again, in the context of the continued good health of the French economy: rising production, declining inflation, automobile and tyre production both up by at least 12 percent. Domestic Michelin turnover soared by 23.6 percent (to over three billion francs), and this despite controls which kept French tyre prices artificially low – a situation Michelin naturally deplored.

To a question from a shareholder – what precisely was the Michelin group's total sales last year? – François Michelin replied that the figure would be communicated later (to the questioner perhaps, but certainly not to the world outside, for he was not about to give away more figures than the law required).[2]

Clearly the Michelin empire – as a Paris news weekly described it – remained an enigma. Investigative journalist Pierre Péan had travelled to Basel in Switzerland to discover that world headquarters of the Compagnie Financière Michelin was only a four-room suite, more of a letter-box than anything else, a convenient address allowing the movement of tax-free funds between Michelin headquarters and its foreign holdings. Much of this market was potential. Before the end of the decade, radial tyres, now representing no more than 3 or 4 percent of the total United States market, were expected to hold a 90 percent share (although this did not mean that Michelin would be the only or the main supplier). Reporter Péan quoted François Michelin, referring to the Americans, as saying 'I'm going to colonize them'. Certainly he would begin well armed, with a $100 million investment in Canada, creating factories that would sell most of their production to the United States just across the border.[3]

But the build-up to what the *Financial Times* called 'a U.S. bridge-head' was a long-drawn-out process, giving Michelin's American competitors time to make a case in Washington for placing prohibitive customs duties on tyres imported from Canada. The major tyre-makers of Akron also complained that Canada was engaged in unfair trade practices by according financial aid and a customs tariff holiday to the invader from France.[4]

It seemed time for Britain's leading financial daily to take another close-up look at Michelin, so the Paris correspondent for the *Financial Times* journeyed to Clermont-Ferrand for an update on 'one of the most mysterious companies of its size anywhere'. He found, as today's visitor would, that there was no indication on factory buildings, or on the trucks that ran between them, as to whom they belonged; the same was true of the housing estates: 'Socially, too, Michelin men have the reputation for keeping to themselves...' The reporter published his own estimate of Michelin's foreign affiliate sales – 2.5 billion francs, or close to $470 million – a figure approaching the turnover of the French manufacturing company.

But he would never get further than that. 'Our interest in life is to make the best tyres in the world, and we are already doing so,' a senior executive told him. 'Our rivals are scared of us. Why should we tell them something that's going to change that?'[5]

*　　　　　　　　*　　　　　　　　*

François Michelin's conquest of America may have been his finest hour, and he went about it the Michelin way – with prudence, but also with a keen sense of where the future had to take him. His forebears had conquered all France from Clermont-Ferrand, and of course they had been among the rare French entrepreneurs daring to manufacture a French product on American soil.

Let history render justice to François Michelin's elder and teacher Robert Puiseux, for it was during his tour of duty as supreme manager of the family enterprise that a new Michelin Tire Corporation was established in New York City in 1962 (a humble beginning, that smallish office in an old building run by a sales manager sent from Clermont-Ferrand). By the time the first radials reached American soil in the 1950s – XZZ truck tyres – the company had moved to more practical quarters across the river in Brooklyn. The mysterious Michelin Investment Holding Company Ltd, headquartered in Curaçao to facilitate financing of more ambitious American ventures, became operational in 1963.[6]

Mystery contributed to the excitement. An influential New York business magazine, aware of Michelin's turn toward the American market, offered Wall Street a profile of 'enigmatic' François Michelin: 'Secretive. Suspicious. Even paranoid. Those are the adjectives Frenchmen use to describe the Michelin dynasty…' François Michelin himself, warned this Dun & Bradstreet publication, compounded his company's unwillingness to communicate with his own reclusive personality.

And yet, after his successful arrangement with Sears, Roebuck in mail order and retail sales of Michelin tyres under an American brand-name, Michelin now planned to step up its sales effort in the face of the American giants – Goodyear, Goodrich, Uniroyal and Firestone ('David tackling Goliath' the reporter called it). Nor would the mystery man make any concessions to other people's ideas about how to go about his offensive. He would advertise only via the *Guide Michelin*, and let superior quality and longer wear rather than low prices do the rest.

Indeed, Michelin's chief advertising medium was the green guide to New York City, the first of the familiar guide-book series to deal with an English-speaking city (and it had sold over 150,000 copies within a year of first publication in 1968). The interviewer took pains to point out that the book was produced at a loss ('although the guidebook sub-sidiary typically refuses to give out actual figures'). Michelin officials in Paris who asked that their names not be used said that the New York City book was designed 'to increase Michelin's standing in the U.S.'.

Still, Michelin came to the United States with a built-in handicap, since its radial-ply tyres cost up to 20 percent more than a roughly comparable American brand (in part because of duties paid on imported tyres); they would not cut prices, but they did offer a money-back guarantee – 40,000 miles – that no domestic tyre-maker was prepared to match.

In summing up, the business journal stressed the Auvergne firm's proverbial secrecy. It was thought, but not known for sure, that the firm's earnings came to a healthy 14.7 percent (better than any of America's 'Big Four' tyre-makers); it was known that Michelin controlled Kléber-Colombes, but no-one then knew how much of Citroën-Berliet was held by Michelin, or whether it was true that Citroën owned part of Fiat-controlled Pirelli, or that Michelin controlled Germany's Continental Gummi. The chief, François Michelin, was known for his paternalism and anti-unionism. 'Any company that has operated in that almost feudal manner for some ninety years will have some adjustments to make in fighting for a larger share of the U.S. market,' so this analyst concluded.[7]

*   *   *

It would indeed be an uphill struggle, but the Michelin men proved shrewd strategists. Building their first plants in Canada – whose government had offered grants and loans that no prudent manager would have refused – also gave them a toehold in the United States. Michelin was already importing some 2.5 million tyres a year via a depot at Lake Success, Long Island. These were all radials, deemed safer than standard models at a time when American consumers were becoming acutely conscious of the role tyres played in road safety. And although Michelin by then held no more than 5 percent of the United States market, that was already enough to alarm the major players of Akron, Ohio. Soon they would be making their own radials.[8]

There would be another year of such sparring before Michelin was ready to dive off the high board. The announcement in December 1972 came not from the Auvergne but from Long Island, via a transplanted Michelin man, Marc de Logères, president of the Michelin Tire Corporation. In its biggest investment ever, Michelin would attack the American market from within, constructing new plants for radials.[9] They'd get a helpful $150 million of credit from New York's finest banks – Morgan

Guaranty, First National City and Chase Manhattan[10] – and pump in $250 million of their own cash that had been waiting to be used.[11]

In their earlier American adventure, the Michelins had created a replica of Michelin-Ville in a small northern town just across the Hudson river from America's business capital. This time their choice was South Carolina, specifically the northwest Piedmont region best known for textile manufacturing, and where factory wages reportedly ranked a low 46 out of 50 in the nation. South Carolina went after industrial investment aggressively, via a development board that proclaimed in national advertising: 'South Carolinians want industry'.

The Michelin scouts who explored and then recommended South Carolina would not have been indifferent to the evidence that there would be no labour problems here. The state was listed forty-ninth – next to last – in unionization of workers. 'The Greenville-Anderson area where the plants will be located has a great many low-paid textile workers and no labour unions,' a liberal American weekly pointed out in an editorial called 'Michelin Go Home'.

But despite appearances – and its title – the editorial was not an attack on Michelin; on the contrary. Hostility to the French tyre-maker came not from American liberals but from textile manufacturers in South Carolina. For Michelin was known as a high-paying employer, and its presence in that state would raise the average wage scale considerably. It would also draw away workers in a tight job market, and might even encourage unionization – sure to lead to a sharp hike in pay. The head of a large textile company in Greenville, which was to be the site of Michelin's principal activity, had expressed the opinion that a trade union at Michelin would resemble a cancer – likely to spread. And South Carolina's most influential newspaper had suggested that Michelin go elsewhere.[12]

But the French company's invasion of South Carolina would be unhurried (or seem so). A year and a half after those expressions of local hostility, the new plants were far from operational, and the business monthly *Fortune* in December 1974 predicted that the rubber-mixing facility at Anderson would only be ready the following summer, after which the first tyres could begin rolling out of the assembly plant in Greenville. The magazine reported that Michelin had invested close to $300 million in the project, and was already considering expansion, as Americans pursued a 'massive transition' to belted radial tyres.

Five years earlier, only one out of every 50 tyres sold in the United States was a radial; in 1974, the ratio was one in four, and in half a dozen years it was expected to be two in three. All this, said the writer, was belated recognition that Michelin's innovation had changed the industry 'as profoundly as the transistor changed electronics'. Since the French company made only radials, its chief American rival Goodyear would have to convert at least half of its production to catch up.

Still, mixing Michelin and American was at times an uphill struggle. Later – two decades later – some of the locally hired managers were to remember how it felt to work for this French company in South Carolina, involved in processes that had French code names, in plants guarded by former American soldiers hired as security police. For here, as in France, Michelin kept its manufacturing processes secret even from its own personnel. Test tracks were restricted to those who needed to be there, and even some senior executives would not be allowed to visit them.

'Some information, even if you needed it you couldn't get it,' a Michelin plant manager recalled in an interview. So far as middle managers knew, there were no budgets, so they would have to apply systematically to higher echelons for authority to invest, making it difficult to control costs or even to know how much things cost.[13]

And yet this stubborn man, François Michelin, seemed to know where he was going. The recession had struck the United States at the end of 1973, and was most damaging in 1974 – at a time when Michelin poured over $100 million into the South Carolina wager; another $100 million or more was ready to be poured in the following year. There would be criticism and debt, and criticism of the debt, but François Michelin held firm. In all, he would sink $600 million into the American venture in the years running from 1975 to 1979, or 35 percent of the group's total investment (compared to 25 percent for France) – and, as Michelin's French unions noted, that meant creating jobs elsewhere than in their country.[14]

Eventually the American adventure began to pay off. By the summer of 1976 the Greenville plant was working to capacity, producing at an estimated rate of six million tyres a year, fed by the Anderson rubber-mixing and cord plant. Construction was about to begin on a new facility for truck tyres in Spartanburg, South Carolina (to become operational in 1978), while still another installation – this one a deserted factory in Littleton, Colorado – was being rehabilitated to make truck tyres (to be ready in 1979). There would be a research and development centre in Laurens County, South Carolina, on land recently acquired by the company, while in Lake Success outside New York City Michelin was building a new headquarters for American operations.

Reporting these raw facts, *Business Week* noted that Michelin's moves were making the American giants Akron 'more than a little nervous'; what bothered American tyre-makers was 'Michelin's single-minded emphasis on quality and innovation'. Its products were expensive but that had not stopped it from dominating the European market. Among the French company's advantages, noted one of its Akron competitors, was the absence of unions in its American plants – giving it greater operating flexibility, thus 'a competitive edge'. For its part, Michelin was counting not only on radials – the old X tyres – but also on a new TRX, a broad-tread, flat tyre with an oblong cross-section that would not skid in curves; it would be particularly well suited to large cars – thus American ones.[15]

In June 1979, describing soaring production and sales in the United States – although Michelin was still exporting more tyres to the rapidly growing American market than it was producing on the spot – the chief informed shareholders that the United States was now a bigger market for Michelin truck tyres than France. Real development – real market expansion – was now possible only in America, and future profits there would be greater than they could be in Europe. America was Michelin's best bet.

Still, François Michelin was not about to relax his guard. He released the figures that the law required – sometimes a little more of them than the law required – but there were limits. His principal competitors were diversifying, whereas Michelin made tyres and only tyres, and so – felt Michelin – was more vulnerable to prying eyes than they. As a consequence

> neither our Group nor the people who make it work, including our shareholders themselves, would find it in their interest to 'undress' our companies.
>
> This is why, for example, we don't have the right to give facts and figures on our American operations. We regret not to be able to satisfy the curiosity of our shareholders on this important matter; it would be too dangerous.[16]

Michelin had not become too American after all.

36

THE RED AND
THE GREEN

Using the new green guide to New York City 'to increase Michelin's standing' in support of future American operations surely made sense, although at the time of its publication in 1968 it is likely that most users of Michelin's touring guides to the principal cities, regions, and countries of Europe were in fact French or continental neighbours of the French. But that would change. By 1976, the same slender volume – updated of course – was selected by the City of New York as the official guide for the bicentennial year marking the two-hundredth anniversary of America's Declaration of Independence. Users of the New York guide (in English) were exposed to some convincing reasons why 'America's sold on Michelin radials', among them that 40,000-mile warranty.[1]

Shortly before that, the writer of this book paid another call at Michelin's Paris headquarters. Nearly everybody who travelled knew, used and cherished the red hotel and restaurant guides, and some sophisticates even had an idea as to how they were put together. The point of this visit was to see that the green travel guides were also given their due. By that time a total of two million copies of these books were being sold each year, and the most popular principal ones in the original French were selling over 100,000 copies annually. The English-language edition for Paris sold an incredible 80,000 copies each year, and the others in English for France, its neighbouring countries, and New York City, averaged 50,000. It was possible without flattery to say that these guides came out virtually flawless; at least one writer who thought he knew the traveller's Europe could not remember encountering an error in any of them.

But facts were one thing, judgments another; one could question the latter. It was fair to ask, for example, whether Italian churches, Portuguese beaches and Dutch canals – signalled by one, two and three stars just as restaurants were – had all been rated by French inspectors.

This time the writer expected to be able to conduct a normal interview, even citing sources by name, but was quickly set to rights. Here, as in the department that published the red guides, editors and inspectors worked in a climate of secrecy, for even a green guide's star was worth money. 'Some museum curators tell us their jobs are at stake because they have no stars; if we gave them a star, they'd get a promotion,' the editor-in-chief of the green guides explained. 'Don't forget that when we list a privately owned castle that charges admission fees, both cash and the owner's *amour-propre* are involved. Give a star to a grotto with a seven-franc [$1.50] entrance ticket and it draws 30,000 visitors a year – that adds up.' In order to protect writers from pressure, they had to remain anonymous.

The English version of the Normandy guide was shorter, since descriptions that would not be of interest to non-French visitors were omitted. At the same time, it contained an expanded section on the Normandy invasion of June 1944, considered to be of particular interest to Anglo-American readers. In the English version, itineraries in Normandy began at the ports of Dieppe and Le Havre to help British travellers; in the French original, all voyages began in Paris.

In the New York City guide, the original draft called for a three-hour stroll up Fifth Avenue, but Michelin's American editors warned headquarters that no American would walk for three hours. The itinerary was reversed to follow one-way traffic from north to south, so that tourists could hop on and off Fifth Avenue buses.

Each green guide was the work of a single person. The guide writer did not have to be a specialist, although a diploma in history or geography was desirable. Stars for recommended sights were decided upon in Paris, and were identical in all language versions. But if stars did not vary from country to country, impressions might. A French person might remark with distaste that a monument had been subjected to conspicuous restoration; of the same monument a German might say, with admiration, 'restored with much care'.

The editor revealed that his department did not recruit writers who could be transformed into Michelin men; on the contrary, they preferred to find people already in the company known for objectivity and integrity. The important thing for these 'professional tourists' was to be free of influences. They were to remember basic definitions. 'Three stars hit you on the head.' They indicate 'international significance'. Two stars signify something of importance on the national level, while a single star called attention to a local curiosity. Should a sight be listed without a star, it might still be interesting, 'but one can also decide not to stop to see it'.

Many evaluations were made after discussions lasting for days. There had been considerable difficulty in judging Italian squares; clearly Michelin preferred the symmetry of a Place des Vosges or Place de la Concorde in Paris to the seductive disorder of Italy's public places, like the mélange of styles of the Piazza del Popolo in Rome (accorded only two stars). One could object that in the same city, the dull mass of Santa Maria Maggiore did not deserve three stars, while the Byzantine mausoleum of Santa Costanza deserved more than the one it got. Michelin's response was that the enormous Santa Maria struck the imagination, while diminutive Santa Costanza was too subtle, especially for rank and file tourists, and Michelin was publishing for tourists and not for art historians. If the Sacré Coeur basilica in Paris had three stars, it was 'because 20 million French Catholics have their eyes trained on it'.

The director agreed to let his visitor meet one of the writers, the one who had compiled the green guides to Normandy, Germany and Austria, the Alps and the Pyrenees. It was immediately clear why Michelin insisted on anonymity. For this slight, somewhat donnish gentleman with thick spectacles would hardly have been able to stand up to a landowner who felt that his family castle had been given insufficient attention, not to speak of a lifeguard upset by a derogatory reference to his beach.

For that writer's first assignment, Normandy, when he was still a relative newcomer to Michelin, earlier reference books were of little help, since so many towns and monuments had undergone considerable reconstruction after the war – if they were salvaged at all. To explore what was virtually a newly discovered province, assistants had been assigned to accompany him in an old Citroën along the coast and through the countryside. He remembered that they had scrupulously avoided meeting museum directors and caretakers of monuments, so as not to get into arguments.

And arguments they certainly would have had. Even the present writer, talking to the author of the Normandy green guide, was tempted to ask why the well-preserved old port of Honfleur had been given only two stars while the nearby Deauville beach resort received three? 'Sometimes it's not a matter of intrinsic value,' the Michelin man replied. 'Stars are a compromise between the quality of the site and its attraction for tourists.'

His chief broke in to explain what had happened when they were preparing the Burgundy guide. The head of Michelin's travel services had warned that they were giving out too many stars – thereby depreciating them. There had been plans to award three stars both to the basilica at Vézelay and to the Eglise St-Philibert at Tournus, but he insisted that it be one or the other. Animated discussion followed, until one of the guide-book specialists put in, 'Then it should be St-Philbert because of its greater archaeological value'. 'That settles it,' declared the chief of travel. 'Vézelay wins. We are publishing for tourists!'[2]

Of course, there were users of the green guides who would have preferred a broader view of what tourists might care about. A French lawyer who purchased a new edition of the Brittany guide to replace the one he already possessed but which had been published in 1950, discovered that the earlier volume's brief reference to the execution of 27 hostages by German Occupation troops at Châteaubriant in 1941 had been removed. The suppression could not have been made in order to bring the volume up to date, argued the lawyer, since the entry on Châteaubriant still included a description of a love affair between King François I and a local lady, Françoise de Foix – which seemed to him even less timely.

Michelin replied to this complaint. If the guide-book no longer mentioned the killing of hostages, this was not due to an error or the need for updating. 'But episodes of recent history aren't necessarily the ones most interesting to tourists,' explained the letter from Michelin. 'And there are so many events that call up less emotion as time passes than they did during a troubled moment.' Far from overlooking the Resistance, the letter went on, the green guides often highlight them.

'But the events we describe strike the reader even more because they are selected...'

Publishing the exchange of correspondence, *Le Monde* commented that many readers would not accept the Michelin position, for the executions at Châteaubriant were at least as 'historic' an event as the love life of a king. Indeed, the shooting of the hostages by German troops had drawn protests from Churchill and Roosevelt, while even Marshal Pétain in Vichy expressed the desire to take the place of the next group of hostages the Germans were threatening to kill. At least one historian believed that the events of Châteaubriant marked a turning point in the perception of the German Occupation of France.

The incident moved *Le Monde*'s writer to look at how the green guide treated the town of Vichy: the four years during which it was the seat of the collaborationist government were dismissed in a phrase. 'At best,' concluded the newspaper, 'this way of proceeding indicates a curious disdain of tourists, who are dismissed as frivolous and irresponsible'.[3]

That opened the door to further protests. For a time, it was noted, Anne Frank's house in Amsterdam had disappeared from Michelin's Benelux guide. The president of the French Association of History and Geography Professors called the attention of *Le Monde* to the green guide for Germany, which in the three pages accorded to historical events devoted half a page to Luther and the Reformation, a third to the Thirty Years' War, half a page to Bismarck, but nothing to Kaiser Wilhelm II or to Adolf Hitler. 'From 1890 they skip to 1949 and the German Federal Republic.' The professor thought that Michelin's attitude 'allows a number of suppositions'.[4]

Surely there was nothing political in Michelin's choices or omissions. It was a matter of anticipating what tourists wanted to know. When they wanted it badly enough, they might be given the truth, however grim. A buyer of the later editions of the green guide to Brittany in the French version will find that the reference to the execution of the hostages by the Nazis has been restored, in two slight but meaningful lines: 'At the gates of the city, on the road to Pouancé, at the quarry of the Executions [Carrière des Fusillés], a memorial recalls the 27 hostages killed here by the Nazis on October 22, 1941'.[5] The English-language version even adds a line: 'The recesses at the base [of the memorial] contain soil from the place of execution'.[6] Sadly, the German edition omits the story of the hostage shooting entirely, so that German readers must content themselves with the adultery of François I and Françoise (wife of the Count of Châteaubriant).[7]

*   *   *

It was clear all through the 1970s that what Michelin thought and said, even what Michelin did not say, could matter to people. On painful questions such as war and Resistance of course, but also in the hedonistic travel world. Earlier in the decade, and prior to the visit to green guide headquarters, the present writer decided to see for himself how a chef worked for his Michelin star, and what happened when he got it.

The point was to choose a locality far from well-travelled roads to pleasure towns of north or south, away from chic. Who had heard of Bourth-sur-Iton, how many travellers – even Frenchmen, even Parisians – had so much as driven through it (although Bourth was only 80 miles west of the capital)? Here, in 1970, Michelin men had found a new worthy candidate, one of 41 restaurants which received the coveted star for the first time that year.

The visitor to Bourth is easily convinced that the town leads to no beach or ski resort, no casino. From Paris, one follows the old national highway to Verneuil-sur-Avre, with Bourth some ten kilometres north from the road running between Verneuil and l'Aigle. It is a region of woods and pleasant streams; Parisians who have weekend homes nearby go for the trout and perch or the walking. While the village itself had been losing population over the years, and then scarcely counted a thousand inhabitants, a young chef, Bernard Champion, with his wife Nicole, had migrated there from Paris in the early 1960s, finding an old coach-house on the main square that seemed just the right size for their enterprise (with six upstairs rooms for overnight guests).

Champion had worked alongside his father, a pastry chef and caterer in Neuilly, going on to become a pastry chef in his own right, then cooked in a number of famous Paris kitchens including Maxim's, earning some citations along the way. Soon his new inn was listed in several guide-books, but he knew that it was Michelin that mattered. He also understood that he would have to wait until a number of diners wrote in to express their satisfaction before attracting the attention of the editors of that prestigious reference book.

Apparently there had been some convincing letters, for chef Champion's Auberge Chantecler received a first listing in 1965 – without a star of course. The listing had the not incidental effect of installing that forgotten village in the red guide for the first time.

Now Champion was ready to go out for every chef's dream – a star. Both he and his wife knew what a formidable task that would be, for no guest, at any table, at any time, should have cause for complaint. The needs of his clients would have to be anticipated (for smokers, always a clean ashtray, which meant changing them as soon as ashes appeared, which also meant having enough ashtrays to supply each table at least twice).

They'd never know, of course, when a Michelin inspector might walk in. Perhaps he would stay overnight and sit down to breakfast, which meant serving star-quality breakfasts – and also meant that Champion would have to be present and attentive for all three meals. For the rest of the day, there would have to be some specialities, along-side less fancy dishes for those not wishing to eat particularly rich food. And good wines, but also some adequate and cheaper ones. In a word, the Champions tried to imagine what the inspector's questionnaire would be like, and to have the answers ready.

In 1969 – the present writer learned, and from a good source – several inspectors stopped off at Bourth, and apparently liked what they saw and tasted. They concluded that the chef was a wizard at sauces, using Normandy cream to good advantage. That, after all, was what cooking was all about.

The first word that the Champions had won their bet came from a producer of a well-known champagne, who apparently had seen an early copy of the 1970 guide, and sent off a magnum of champagne to Bourth to congratulate the chef. Dared they believe him? When the star was confirmed they deserted their restaurant to drink champagne at a friend's one-star restaurant at l'Aigle, some nine miles distant. On return they opened more champagne to share with the staff. (Perhaps that would not have been a good day to dine at the Chantecler.)

Villagers were the last to hear the good news; they did not read much, and copies of the Michelin guide would not be flooding the town. But soon everybody who had anything to do with the inn received a windfall (including two butcher shops – since Champion preferred one for its chicken and another for its beef).

And the proliferation of automobiles around the village square was definitely noticeable; now on Sundays one had to park at a distance and walk a bit.

The Michelin star doubled the Champions' business, although there was room for only 60 guests at each meal and, like most reputable chefs of the time, he would not have dreamed of expanding. Most of the new customers had never been to Bourth before, drawn now by a star which was one of only five in the Eure *département*. It was expected that their numbers would grow (many people do not buy a new Michelin each year, and it would take time for the news to reach everyone, even fervent believers in the red book).

The typical Parisian client, Champion found, drove out from Paris expressly for lunch, carrying a copy of the guide and placing it on the table (a gesture Michelin recommends). Usually the guest then ordered the listed specialties (Michelin asks for such a list from each establishment it honours with one or more stars). Champion's were a terrine of duckling with hazelnuts and fillet of veal with a Normandy cream sauce, brill fillets in cider.

Walking about the village, one discovered that local inhabitants were unsurprised that the star had put them on the map. They had all been there to stare as the film star Jean Gabin, who owned a nearby farm, walked into the Champions' place. Another time it was a national political figure who was also the mayor of the regional capital. Some tradesmen who were not suppliers of the restaurant would not admit to having benefited from the star, although they agreed that 'for some reason' they were seeing a lot more people. The antique shop alongside the inn did not try to hide the bounty, nor did the local horticulturist. As for Champion, he was seldom visible, never leaving his kitchen during meal hours.

After the present writer's report on Bourth appeared in the *New York Times*, Champion was smothered by letters from readers, many of them French residents of the United States who congratulated him and promised they would make it a point to dine at Chantecler on their next trip home. A regional newspaper published a report on how the *Times* brought sudden fame to this Norman village. 'A Star is Born ... For the Americans,' read the headline, and an accompanying photograph showed the Champions holding up the article proudly. Chef Champion was quoted expressing astonishment that the New

York paper had dispatched a photographer, who spent two days working in Bourth.[8]

Henceforth, there would never be a time when a major Michelin upgrading, or an unexpected Michelin downgrading, failed to become local, national, even international news. We shall see that this is still true today, when a severe verdict is reached, say, on an institution as sacred as the Tour d'Argent in Paris.

But in March 1978, when the guide for that year was released, there was another tempest. Maxim's, that turn-of-century marvel, the back-drop to so many plays and films, the scene of so many real-life celebrations, had totally disappeared from its pages. A year earlier, Maxim's had been listed with its habitual three stars, and with five sets of spoons and forks (the maximum, signifying great luxury and tradition).

That kind of reversal of fortune deserved an explanation, and Michelin offered one. The previous autumn, the owner of the legendary establishment, Louis Vaudable, had asked the guide-book editor to create a special category for Maxim's that would give it credit for its special atmosphere as well as its food. The editor refused; Vaudable asked to be removed from the book (apparently one had the right to make such a request).

Astute reporters who talked to other sources in the restaurant world came up with a more elaborate explanation. Vaudable had only been looking for a face-saving alternative, they said, because he sensed that he was about to be downgraded to two stars. He had an agreement with designer Pierre Cardin to use the restaurant name on such items as mustard, foie gras, even tea sets and ashtrays; the loss of a star would have hurt the new marketing scheme. Better to be forgotten by Michelin than to be slapped in the face publicly.[9]

37

MICHELIN
INTERNATIONAL

If the 1970s were Michelin's American years, we should not forget that Michelin was still making its money elsewhere. Reporting in 1977 (on the previous business year), the directors reminded shareholders gathered at Clermont-Ferrand that the Manufacture Française des Pneumatiques Michelin – still and forever the corporate name of the flagship tyre-maker – now sold its products in 150 countries and territories. The United States was a significant customer, but so were Germany and Benelux (although Michelin also produced tyres locally in Germany, Belgium and the Netherlands).[1]

In 1977, thanks to a vigorous export market, sales rose 11.7 percent at the Manufacture (exports alone had increased by 17.2 percent). Michelin was doing more hiring, capacity was expanded; business would have been better still had it not been for France's price controls and soaring costs. Michelin's Swiss investment arm, the Compagnie Financière Michelin, had been shovelling money into foreign subsidiaries, notably the American venture, financing these investments through loans. (In the United States, Michelin was building a factory in Alabama to make tyres for commercial vehicles.)

By going international, François Michelin and his aides knew that they were waging war against a narrow concept of nationalism shared by many French conservatives but also by the principal labour unions – the Communist-led CGT for political reasons (the investment was going to enemies of the USSR), all the others in the name of bread-and-butter doctrine (investments should stay at home). In their annual report, the owners chose to meet those objections head on, arguing that 'free international trade is the basis of all stability'.[2]

Thinking international could be risky. Michelin was now the world's number two tyre-maker after America's Goodyear, and was looking over its shoulder at a future challenger in Japan; the point was not only to maintain the technological advance of the new American factories but to improve performances in France as well. And that met with immediate resistance.

When a new work week was announced in the home factories of Clermont-Ferrand in November 1977 – rescheduling shifts to keep machines running from Sunday night to the following Saturday at midday, with compensatory weekday rest for workers robbed of their weekends – the unions called for a limited protest. Their members ignored the 'limited' and shut down the plants.

The proposed scheduling was shelved. But François Michelin intended to teach his workers, and their supporters, just how wrong they were. In a rare public appearance, at a session of the Economic and Social Committee of the Auvergne in January 1978, within weeks of the labour action, he warned that manufacturing would have to adapt to present-day realities. Tyres shipped abroad, and in difficult markets, paid for 40 percent of Michelin salaries in France. And foreign customers were choosing the cheapest tyres available. 'If Michelin abroad didn't exist, Michelin France would be bankrupt.'[3]

Now that he had begun to speak up for himself and his world view, nothing seemed to stop him. Michelin lent himself to a rare interview in a popular French weekly. 'If we continue to be idle all weekend, we risk not being able to work on weekdays either; Michelin will have disappeared,' Michelin declared. 'With the same equipment and the same number of hours weekly, the Americans and the Japanese produce 80 percent more than we. Because their factories operate 330 days each year while ours operate only 260.'

The interviewer mentioned paternalism; Michelin replied that he was not ashamed of the word. If clinics had been built it was because a worker died after being treated in a public hospital. As for education, at the time, there had been no decent schools for the children of Michelin workers. They had not needed unions to accomplish these things. 'Unions aren't at all necessary for the existence of the company. They are only the expression of the inadequacy of company owners.'

The interviewer expressed curiosity about the decor – or lack of it, at the Michelin works: 'These facades crying for cleaning up, these offices with linoleum rugs...' Michelin explained that the reporter had been looking at the old buildings, built at a time when one could not 'build prettily without building expensively'. The new plants were not like that at all.

Of course they tried to save money wherever they could; it was true, as the legend had it, that they turned envelopes inside out so that they could be utilized a second time. 'To save a million envelopes a year is important,' Michelin insisted. Michelin posed a question of his own. How could they ask workers to save a gram of rubber per tyre if office workers weren't also asked to save a gram of paper?[4]

He could at least be satisfied with the intelligence of his managers, for the year 1978 would prove a good one for the group. In its first season equipping racing cars in the Formula 1 competition, Michelin twice crushed its chief rival, Goodyear.[5] 'When tyremen meet these days it is France's Michelin, not Goodyear, that is acknowledged as the world's technological leader,' is the way the American business magazine *Forbes* put it.[6]

At the Manufacture sales soared by 15.7 percent that year, driven in part by American activity, which included sending machine tools from France to equip the South Carolina plants. But François Michelin was not going to overlook an opportunity to hammer home the lesson that domestic success was due to the reform of the work day in Michelin's French factories – those not located in Clermont-Ferrand of course.

They did have a choice, he said. Either Michelin continued to move quickly to build its American plants – inevitably creating losses – or the group could spread investment over a longer period to show better short-term profits. But then the company exposed itself to a greater danger, 'that of missing out on our expansion in the United States...'

Clearly that would be a blow to the future prosperity of the company, and it is to the credit of the cautious man whose neo-feudal lifestyle suggested a permanent rejection of the modern world, that he fully understood that world, and embraced it when that seemed the best thing to do. If Michelin wanted to survive and prosper in the face of its principal rivals, he concluded, 'its policy must be entirely dominated by the fact that there is now only one market for tyres: the world market'.[7]

Not everyone saw it that way, of course. For moderate labour leaders, Michelin was investing abroad while reducing activity at home – it 'thins itself out in Auvergne, by reducing the investments that enabled it to survive, without speaking of progressing'.[8] For the Communists – for their chief Georges Marchais, who came down from Paris at the beginning of December 1979 to address Michelin's party members – Michelin was mocking them.

> While the workers in the Manufacture haven't profited in their pay packets from the formidable development of the company for which they are responsible, the boss is doing everything he can to pump the resources of the French company, to prevent its strengthening, to put it at the mercy of the speculative jolts of the strategy of the multinational group – all that to increase its enormous profits abroad.[9]

There had not actually been any enormous profits that year, certainly not from those new markets overseas; a strong franc and a weak dollar were both responsible for that. It had been the year of the second 'oil shock', following revolution and turmoil in Iran, raising oil prices to new levels, inflating all prices everywhere.

The Manufacture – turning out tyres in France for French and foreign markets both – reported strong sales, up 15 percent to over 10 billion francs – some $2.35 billion (but of course inflation had something to do with these high figures). America's Michelin Tire Corporation was in the red that year.[10]

* * *

Perhaps the risk François was taking makes it a more interesting story. Could one survive with a single product in bad times? 'That is the question,' summed up an analyst in a Paris financial weekly in 1980. ('The response is undoubtedly yes,' he concluded helpfully.)[11]

But aeroplane designer and builder Marcel Dassault, a genius in another certainly more gratifying profession, dismissed tyres as 'a provincial speciality', and François Michelin as unimaginative. 'He began like that, he continued like that, he always made tyres. It's less spectacular all the same than a chap who is born a farmer and who makes automobiles, or a newspaper dealer who becomes Edison.'[12]

There was no improvement in the balance sheet in 1980; America seemed less and less of a good thing. By the end of that year, a New York financial weekly was able to say that despite an investment of more than one billion dollars in the United States, Michelin was simply not selling; the company appeared to be 'stumbling' in its efforts to create a suitable marketing strategy. Michelin possessed one clear advantage in the quality of its radials, but now 'the quality gap has closed'. Henceforth, Michelin would have to place more emphasis on advantageous pricing.[13]

Reporting to shareholders, Michelin confirmed that American business had been unprofitable in 1980, yet the company had performed brilliantly in France, with sales at the Manufacture rising nearly 17 percent. Exports, representing over half of total business, had risen by 17.5 percent. Here, as in the United States, good sales did not mean good profits; soaring production costs resulted in a net loss.[14]

Michelin was hurting, but even a normally sceptical observer, the Committee of Establishment, was ready to believe that the deficits of the early 1980s could be blamed on world recession as well as an overly ambitious development programme. At the same time, it regretted the policy of secrecy which at times hindered rational production and in all cases was bad for labour relations.[15] Labour relations were poor enough as it was, with the erosion of sales calling for a reduction in personnel from the all-time high of 29,982 in Clermont-Ferrand to 25,986 in 1983, and another reduction in force announced in April 1984 that would see the departure of nearly 5000 more workers.[16]

Less charitable than the Committee of Establishment, the Communists singled out Michelin as 'a symbol of capitalism,' in the unoriginal words of Communist Party chief Georges Marchais, who spoke in February 1981 to assembled Michelin workers in Clermont-Ferrand. Marchais was campaigning in the elections which were to bring a Socialist-Communist coalition to power in France on 10 May. To the Communist chief, Michelin was wasting money in the United States and elsewhere that it should be spending in France. Therefore, he concluded, 'we must nationalize Michelin'.[17] After their victory, the party did indeed demand that Michelin be included on the list of companies to be nationalized; it was not included.[18]

François Michelin did what he could. In his talk to shareholders summing up that dismal period (during which the Manufacture had its worst year since its establishment in 1951), he admitted that the company was particularly vulnerable, with its heavy investments in the United States and Brazil – where two new Michelin plants were going into service – and 1982 was unlikely to be any better. To avoid more firings, Michelin was producing tyres in France that could not be sold and so were being stocked – and this in a period of high interest rates.[19]

It was about now that the Chief sat for another portrait in words, although the writers who interviewed him were impressed above all by his silences. 'During the hour and a half he gave us, his expressions occupied nearly as much space as his words,' they reported. 'Confronted with this immense and transparent silhouette, slightly bent, one is taken immediately by those eyes that focus on you, scrutinizing and interrogating.' He wished to convince.

Michelin had not been surprised by the electoral victory of the left in 1981, but of course he continued to reject 'the power of the unions', which he defined as 'irresponsibility in command'. A good union would be one that began by explaining to workers what a patron was for. The state could play no useful part in the economy; the educational system was designed so that on finishing school one automatically considered all factory owners 'scoundrels'. Did he spend more time in Paris or in Clermont? 'In Clermont, thank God. In Paris you go mad. Madness, by definition, signifying being cut off from reality.'[20]

*   *   *

He had much of the business world on his side, and this despite his clear contempt for the leaders of industry represented by the manufacturers association (the Conseil National du Patronat Français, which for him was also 'irresponsible').[21] In a sympathetic analysis of Michelin's problems in the context of global crisis – 'Bibendum also suffers' – a French financial weekly blamed Bibendum's woes on the recession, while pointing out that Michelin was a victim of its own genius, since radial tyres lasted longer and longer – thereby reducing the need for replacements.[22]

These first years of the 1980s were bad for everybody; sales at the Manufacture actually declined in 1982 (dragged down by the drop in exports – which now accounted for over half the business).[23] But had Michelin been hit harder than others? Even the prudent business editor of Le Monde wondered about that: 'The details of its operations are unknown'. Which of course invited speculation. How much was being held back as reserves against future troubles?[24]

'The group is paying for its American strategy,' so the Communist Party's official daily explained it, stressing the elimination of nearly 10,000 jobs in 1982, 3000 of them in France.

> In effect, to establish itself elsewhere in the world and principally in the United States, the French group had let its Clermont factory become obsolete...For Michelin as for many other French groups that had bet on America, the morning after is painful.[25]

38

THE ROAD
BACK

Before 1983 was over, Dunlop-France – a landmark of Montluçon, just 55 miles distant from Michelin-Ville – had filed for liquidation. The British owner was selling off its continental affiliates to the Japanese rubber group Sumitomo, but the French Dunlop company had not been part of the package.[1] Then, after drawn-out discussions, Dunlop-France was saved after all – Sumitomo took it on. The French government had sought a 'European solution', with Michelin and other companies joining to purchase the British subsidiary, but the European candidates insisted on considerable job-cutting, while the Japanese promised to spare most of the existing workforce.[2]

The news from Clermont-Ferrand was somewhat better. First signs of improvement in the world economy had come from North America, while Europe was 'still hesitant' – but of course Michelin was now also a North American company, and to a certain extent shared that continent's fate or good fortune. Turnover at the Manufacture in 1983 had risen by 6.3 percent, thanks chiefly to exports, which increased by 10 percent and now accounted for 51.6 percent of total French sales. But if business in foreign export markets including the United States was generally better now, Michelin's American plants reported disappointing results, notably because of insufficient use of plant capacity.

At least morale was high. 'The reversal of the situation...that we expected did indeed take place and is confirmed daily,' François Michelin assured his flock at the annual meeting in June 1984.

Restructuring – reduction in personnel, in other words – had been handled with delicacy; it would bear its fruits in that year.[3]

A Paris daily was able to reveal that Michelin was negotiating with major banks for a low-interest loan of four billion francs (then some $460 million) to reconstitute a reserve. Indeed, President Mitterrand's Socialist cabinet had been drawn in to help, and never mind François Michelin's proverbial hostility to government meddling. He had actually talked to Mitterrand during a visit of the chief of state to Clermont-Ferrand early in July 1984, and of course the banks involved in the discussions would be government-controlled banks.[4]

Eight months later, a French news weekly underscored the turnabout. 'In having recourse to the government to get out of a tight corner François Michelin did serious violence to his doctrine,' the report concluded. 'But could he have done otherwise?'[5]

Skilled managers and rationalized production could do only so much. For a single-product company like Michelin, especially when the product happened to be tyres, depending on the health of the market for passenger and commercial vehicles – this market itself tributary of the state of the economy, French and foreign – genuine recovery had to wait for general recovery. And something like that was happening now.

Michelin's directors announced the good news at their general assembly in June 1985. There had been a reprise in the world economy, and the United States appeared to be leading the pack, with a 4.75 percent rise in GNP (against 2.2 percent for Europe, a modest 2 percent for France alone). But if sales of cars and tyres were down in France, the Manufacture nevertheless saw turnover climb by 7.4 percent, while exports (now representing 53 percent of total sales) were up by 10 percent.

Some of the rosiness of the results fades when inflation is taken into account. In 1983 the cost of living had risen by 9.3 percent; the inflation rate was only 6.7 percent in 1984, but it still signified that an increase of 4 percent in turnover actually represented a fall, however slight, in sales volume.[6] 'Less bad' all the same, a business reporter commented, and in any case much of the deficit was due to expenditures connected with a reduction in personnel.[7]

Michelin's plight was described in colourful terms by an American periodical. 'For 25 years, thousands of technicians have been secretly working under the paternal gaze of François Michelin, trying to devise a virtually indestructible tire to succeed the radial,' it reported – undoubtedly with some exaggeration. 'But hard times are forcing his company to think more about survival than technical revolutions.' 'Tomorrow the great new tyre might well change things,' a Michelin banker is quoted. 'But today they realize that only better management can save the company.'[8]

Once again, chief managing partner François sat down to a 'rare' interview, this one with the influential London daily *Financial Times*; it was described as Michelin's first talk with reporters in six years, held in a hotel meeting room since 'there was no question' of letting the British newsmen into the factory grounds. 'Even so, the secrecy-conscious manager sheepishly checked the next room, apparently to make sure no one was eavesdropping.'

The surroundings were unostentatious; setting the tone, the Chief had driven his own small car to the hotel. He was 'a tall, gaunt man who cuts a figure reminiscent of Jacques Tati...' He took time to think, then spoke 'clearly and to the point... often... with a mischievous grin on his cherubic face'. The report on the encounter appeared on François Michelin's fifty-ninth birthday.

Times had changed; both the British interrogators and their subject knew that. Clermont-Ferrand had ruled the roost for nearly 30 years because of the radial, but now the Americans and Japanese were catching up. Michelin denied that he had received a loan at subsidized interest rates from the French government, adding mischievously: 'But we would like to be treated like the Soviet Union'. Asked where he most expected improvement, in product development or manufacturing processes, he replied with a question of his own: 'Which of your legs do you think is most important?'

Describing Michelin's American adventure, the writers recalled Michelin's initial success with radials – when the American giants had avoided producing tyres that would last so long, and then found radials difficult to make. By the time they had caught up, the market had collapsed and Michelin found itself with excess capacity, while a higher dollar made Michelin's debt payments more expensive. Some of its factories had been closed in Britain, Italy and Belgium, and the global payroll had been reduced from 137,000 to 110,000. The group continued to place its hopes on the American market. 'If we had not gone to the US,' François Michelin said, 'we would be dying'.

Despite the investment in research and development, Michelin was judged to be slow in following customer demands, notably for an all-weather tyre for North American winters. At the same time, its new radials for aircraft allowed increased payloads while reducing the risk of tyre failure, and the United States Air Force was buying them for the new F-15 fighter. Michelin was confident about the future: 'You will always need a spring between your bottom and the road, and air will always be the cheapest spring'.[9]

Soon after that, one of the interviewers was able to report that after four years of losses Michelin had returned to the black in the first half of 1985.[10] And when the full year's results were ready, François himself told the 'Ladies, gentlemen, dear shareholders' at the annual meeting that they could contemplate one billion francs ($111 million) in profit this year. For the first time in a long time, earnings exceeded investment needs, and the firm had begun to reimburse debts 'which are, as you know, considerable'. If the year 1985 had gone better than expected, considering the state of the global economy, the early months of the current year contained still more promise.[11]

Fulfilling that promise would take strong nerves. There was some help in the decline of oil prices, but for the most part the Michelin triumvirate would have to make its own alterations – closing an unprofitable factory in Belgium, for example (which employed over a thousand workers), initiating a gradual 'restructuring' in France affecting another 2200 employees. Most jobs targeted (1650) were in Clermont-Ferrand, but workers willing to move could hope to fill similar positions in Michelin units elsewhere in France.[12]

The company's energetic attempt to purge its books, washing away red ink and reducing debt, was described favourably in a Paris weekly newspaper at the end of 1986, by which time analysts agreed that Michelin was on 'the right track'. 'If all goes well we'll be out of trouble in two or three years,' an anonymous Michelin man confided.[13]

In 1986, the results showed that the optimism had been justified. 'For the fourth consecutive year,' management informed shareholders, 'global economic activity has gone in a positive direction'. Domestic sales still had not reached their level of half a dozen years back, and exports had only begun to equal those of that happier time, yet cautious management had kept the old family firm on that right track.[14] Then, in June 1987, just 10 days before the annual shareholders meeting,

Michelin 'opened its doors to the public,' as the premier British business daily headlined it. 'For the first time in its secretive history', François Michelin played host to a group of European financial analysts at a buffet lunch under a huge tent alongside a testing track a few miles north of the city.

The invitation was not a foolhardy gesture; the point at this and similar briefings was to prepare the public, and the market, for a stock issue representing 10 percent of the equity of the Swiss holding company, the Compagnie Financière Michelin – this to reduce debt accrued in the course of mounting foreign operations.[15]

François Michelin himself admitted that for a long time he had been 'worried stiff' about his American investment. Now, in the words of Michelin's financial director Behrouz Chadid-Nourai, Michelin plants in the United States and elsewhere were the most up to date in the industry. Michelin owed its American success to 'the mistakes of our competitors', who had delayed the move into radial tyres 'because of quarterly earnings preoccupations'.

And then it was time for the annual meeting. 'An annual event which is one of the rare opportunities to see the only great French company owner who never gives interviews,' the left-wing Paris daily *Libération* explained. 'Discreet little ceremony open only to those inscribed on the list of shareholders.' There were two checkpoints at the entrance door, and stock certificates were registered in the name of the bearer.

That was not going to stop an obstinate journalist. He simply had to remember, some months in advance of the June meeting, to buy the minimum 10 shares that guaranteed entry. That got him into a gloomy hall, as one of some 200 persons seated in squeaky chairs that had been 'modern' some 30 years earlier, facing 'thirteen passive and largely bald heads', who in turn 'stare intently at the audience'.

After a dull reading of the annual report by a subordinate in a monotonous tone, it was the turn of 'Monsieur François', visibly content to be able to announce the year's good news. 'The true capitalist is an ecologist,' he was heard to say, 'who looks far into the future'. French workers and engineers were exceptional, while most politicians of the past 60 years were 'Marxists'.

The shareholding reporter thought of the downsizing which in six years had reduced the total payroll of Michelin from 137,000 to

102,500. Would there be more firings, a financial analyst asked from the floor. 'I prefer not to reply, considering the social consequences,' Michelin replied frankly. 'I don't feel like sawing off the branch on which we are seated.' 'But who cares about that question?' a complacent stockholder in the back of the room was heard to comment.[16]

Michelin workers, certainly. It took them some time to react – they had not done so in years – and when they did, the issue (as almost always) was higher wages for those in place, not pity or regret for those no longer employed. The strike which began in the second half of April was the first at the mother plant in 10 years. Strikers were articulate as they explained to the press that it was not only the amount of the hourly increase in wages that was at issue, but the arbitrary way in which a portion of each hourly salary was now determined, based on the foreman's evaluation of individual performance.[17]

*   *   *

Michelin would win, of course – it always did; fortunately, it did not ask for public support of its position, for such support was unlikely. *Le Monde*, while not a business newspaper, thanks to its circulation in political as well as business circles, had more influence than all the financial press combined, and its judgment was severe. The headline, 'Archaisms', told part of the story. Michelin was a multinational 'which doesn't hesitate to play a major role on the international scene...while at home practising an outmoded paternalism reinforced by a long tradition of secrecy'. Michelin men, the correspondent asserted, were convinced that their very special approach to labour-management relations worked in practice; to change their method would mean to recognize the role of trade unions. On the contrary, Michelin's new system of individualization of salaries tied to perceived productivity virtually made collective action impossible.[18]

Yet, collective action there would be. When it was time for the mid-year reunion of shareholders in 1988, participants were confronted by several hundred demonstrators – Michelin workers mobilized by their respective unions. There was some pushing and shoving, but the marchers never got close to François Michelin and his guests, nor were their delegates received as they apparently hoped they would be.[19]

Shareholders got a briefing on these 'social movements'. 'It's classic,' François Michelin told them. 'A train that arrives late interests the public more than hundreds of trains that arrive on time. A few hundred strikers on the street make people forget the tens of thousands of people who at the same moment are doing their jobs.'

Michelin's wage policy, he added, was long term, not improvised from day to day, which is how the firm had been able to maintain the standard of living of its personnel during the years when the Manufacture suffered considerable losses, and had even raised that standard slightly. 'Today's events tend to make us regret this, for if wage earners had received fewer raises during years when we reported losses, something everybody would have understood, we'd begin today at a lower level of pay...'

An oddity, all the same, this Michelin. One imagines a financial analyst scratching his head as he contemplates this ancient firm with its archaic structure, its arcane practices rare indeed for a company traded on the stock exchange, for if a raider acquired the majority of shares he would still have no say in a change of management. Michelin was a multi-national, yet run like a small business, counting 80,000 shareholders and yet as stingy with information as an Auvergnat with his money...[20]

The chief had warned his shareholders about being overly optimistic, and he had been right: a recovery does not last forever. On the sales side, 1988 was a good year in France and the United States, although competition weighed on prices, and profits were down.[21] Then in September 1989, three short months after this complaint about profits, Michelin took another decision that only he could have made, buying America's number two tyre company and the world's fifth largest, Uniroyal Goodrich, which surpassed Michelin's North American operations in sales and workforce. 'The chubby Michelin tyre man didn't get fat by devouring rivals,' an American financial weekly reminded its readers. But now it had issued a convincing challenge to the world's market leader, Goodyear, even if some analysts felt that Michelin had paid too much for a company that had been in serious trouble only recently.[22]

Later, François would reveal the reason for this surprising development: 'It was our duty to block the Japs'. (This was after the takeover of Dunlop by Sumitomo and soon after Japan's Bridgestone had absorbed America's Firestone.)[23]

Michelin and Uniroyal Goodrich...on one hand a French company that took pride in its superior products, on the other a downscale

American manufacturer which marketed almost a third of its output under other labels (although Uniroyal and Goodrich were two of the oldest names in American tyres). Michelin now had a better chance of winning customers who looked for cheaper labels, while acquiring a truly colossal client in General Motors, which bought 35 percent of its original equipment tyres from Uniroyal.[24]

Not everybody was prepared to applaud. Michelin's stock fell on the announcement of the acquisition, rose when it was thought that the United States government might oppose the sale, and slid lower again when the United States approved. But, as the principal owner told his annual meeting the following June, globalization required growth in America. To buy Goodrich or to expand through investment cost the same, but by choosing the former path Michelin bought time.[25]

39

GLOBAL
GUIDE

All along these years, the good and the bad, it occurred to no-one to link the fate or the fortune of those venerated, impatiently waited-for red-covered guide-books to the tyre company that sponsored them. If those who followed the stock market rather than the food market could at times feel that the expansive Michelin manufacturing group was taking immoderate risks, nobody in their right mind would have said that about the *Guide Michelin* for France, whose judgments were solid, if sometimes too conservative for the adventurous.

Michelin tyre companies in France and abroad were tightly compartmented, as if so many intelligence agencies; the Michelin travel department was as autonomous (and secretive) as any other unit in the group. In each new red guide, a jolly Bibendum all but leaped from its pages to reassure and encourage winers and diners, even in those unhappy times when the Manufacture and its overseas affiliates were reporting losses.

Where Michelin products and Michelin tourist guides most resembled each other was in quality. No one doubted that Michelin tyres were reliable (and this even before the whole world embraced radial tyres), or that Michelin red guides could be trusted. The radial tyre changed driving in America; no small achievement in what had long since been the world capital of the automobile. The red guide to the United Kingdom got the British excited about good food served in their own restaurants – which at the time many would have thought an impossible feat.

The latter exploit has been given a date, 1982, the year that a dining establishment in London, Le Gavroche, became the first in Britain to be awarded three Michelin stars; it just happened that the restaurant had a French chef (Albert Roux). It took another 13 years for a British-born chef to rise to three-star status in London. He was Marco Pierre White, born in Yorkshire despite his exotic given names; the restaurant so honoured was called, simply, The Restaurant, lodged in the Hyde Park Hotel.[1] Between those two events the atmosphere as well as the kitchens of London changed, as a population well-versed in the delicate cuisine of other nations found that they could try it, if only they looked hard enough, in their own capital.

By now, of course, the Michelin travel department in Paris, still modestly called Tourism Services of Michelin Tyres, had become a multinational as pervasive as its parent company down in Clermont-Ferrand. While it could hardly have taken on the American continent, probably not even New York City's food world (at least not in the 1970s and 1980s), it did noble service to Western Europe with its hotel and restaurant guides in the familiar format: over the years 1954–78 guides for Italy, Germany, Spain and Portugal, Great Britain and Ireland, and Benelux were published.

By the end of the 1980s, the green guides had spread out from France to cover the sights and monuments of Spain, Canada and New England, Greece, London and Mexico. In all, with French regions and Paris, there were 40 titles in print in French, 38 more in foreign languages.[2] At the same time the Manufacture, which had been drafting its own advertising and promotional material ever since André Michelin's day, at last took on a world-class advertising agency (BDDP), which devised an all-European strategy to spread Bibendum's message.[3]

*   *   *

If the style and sobriety of Michelin guides changed little, many of the most prominent restaurants described in them did, and very often because of Michelin. What began to happen in the 1980s was that a restaurant owner who had earned a Michelin star would begin to 'prettify'. A chef-owner with two Michelin stars might undertake extensive redecoration. The assumption was that the face-lifting would not only please customers already drawn to the restaurant for its reputed kitchen, but was likely to convince Michelin inspectors that this establishment with, say, one star, was worthy of two – or, if it already had been honoured with two stars, was deserving of the supreme honour. A most unfortunate assumption, as shall become apparent.

The 1991 *Guide Michelin* for France, released at the beginning of March of that year, contained one promotion to three-star status – the Côte d'Or in Saulieu, bringing that small hotel-cum-restaurant back into the news. This, of course, was the establishment which had earlier won three stars under legendary chef Alexandre Dumaine. Now the Côte d'Or belonged to 40-year-old Bernard Loiseau, who made no attempt to hide his ambition to bring his inn back to the top. 'I knew I could do it,' he said in a telephone interview with the *New York Times*. 'I've worked hard and some said I was crazy. I started with nothing but my toothbrush, and now it's all mine.' The authoritative newspaper reported that the owner-chef had taken 'considerable' risks, investing more than $5 million over the years in decorating the restaurant and making over the hotel's 26 rooms. A meal here could come to what was then an expensive $100 – or higher, depending on the wine.

There was more to say, of course – notably about the simplicity of Loiseau's cuisine, which deliberately eschewed butter and cream.[4] The previous year's guide had listed the Côte d'Or with two stars and a three-gabled house (signifying 'very comfortable'). Furthermore, the little house was coloured red, meaning that the hotel was 'pleasant', and a boxed 'M' indicated modern amenities. The listing also noted the dishes that its chef chose to feature: snails cooked with nettles, frogs cooked with a garlic mash and parsley juice, and the famous chicken named in tribute to Saulieu's late master chef Alexandre Dumaine.

And then – an exceptional occurrence – the prestigious New York daily chose to return to Saulieu some months later for a further look at this chef who had deliberately set out to capture his stars (the reason he was so bald, he told the *New York Times* half in jest, was because he had pushed himself so mercilessly to earn the third). Confirming the $5 million investment of borrowed funds, Loiseau admitted that 'it's not easy to live this way' (meaning to work 365 days a year, without a holiday in the past 16 years).

Loiseau's strategy was part of a trend, the reporter noted, 'in which promising chefs become builder-entrepreneurs because they have learned that good cooking alone is not enough to merit a third star'.

And so he had designed a 'resplendent' dining space, an oversized kitchen, and luxurious hotel accommodations to impress his guests 'and Michelin's inspectors'.

The third star had come none too soon, for Loiseau 'was spiralling deeper into debt'; now he hoped to increase his income by 50 percent and to save himself from drowning under the $40,000 per month he owed to the banks. Early signs were encouraging, as faxes arrived from as far off as New York and Tokyo, requesting reservations two months in advance, while Parisians came down for lunch via the rapid express TGV. Loiseau became a familiar face on television, received offers to write cookbooks, and confidently expected a 'hefty' contract to serve as consultant to a food company.

The journalist – actually a financial rather than a gourmet specialist – got further details from this entrepreneur-chef. The son of a travelling clothing salesman, Loiseau had won a first star at the Côte d'Or when he worked for its previous owner, then purchased the establishment and invested $330,000 in renovations before winning a second star in 1983, borrowed still another $300,000 to purchase the hotel of which the restaurant was a part. In 1985 he invested $1.1 million in luxury suites, in 1990, $2 million more to purchase a next-door hotel-restaurant. He expected revenues to reach $4.3 million in 1991, after the $2.9 million earned the previous year.

The reporter cited other stories of business success, such as that of Le Crocodile in Strasbourg, which saw its revenues rise by 35 percent with its third star (won in 1989). He mentioned such by-products of three-star status as the wristwatches sold with the portrait of Lyons chef Paul Bocuse, or Senderens-brand food products in Japan named after the chef of Lucas Carton in Paris. He pointed out that Michelin seemed to encourage 'building binges' such as Loiseau's, by letting it be known that the food in three-star kitchens was not necessarily better than in some holding only two stars, while service, friendliness, and decor were expected to be better. (Tired of hearing that stars were being given for architecture, Michelin was believed to be discouraging owners from engaging in conspicuous expenditure.)[5]

Bernard Loiseau's saga was spelled out in considerable detail in *Burgundy Stars*, a full-length book – a treatment more often reserved for poets and generals – written by another American journalist (he too a financial specialist). It was a seemingly reverent account of the final year of Loiseau's dogged campaign to convince Michelin that he deserved a third star.

There was never any doubt about what this chef was after, or what he thought Michelin would be watching for. Concerning his investment in building new dining rooms and a garden, he explained: 'All the great chefs are doing the same. The client asks for it and Michelin asks for it.' Clearly, he was living for the star; already he was listed with 19.5 points out of a possible 20 in another guide-book. His clients included the president of France, a Rothschild baron and celebrities of the entertainment world. He was fully aware of how business improved for owner-chefs when at last they had pinned down their third star. His models included Georges Blanc, who had transformed a simple inn at Vonnas, en route to Lyon, into a millionaire's paradise (complete with helicopter pad); after winning his third star, the same chef had opened a Georges Blanc boutique to sell food and kitchenware. (Eventually Blanc would control three restaurants, as well as a vineyard with its cellar and retail wine shop.)[6]

Surely not everybody would have wished for Loiseau's life, even as described by this admiring chronicler. As described in this biography, Loiseau seemed to be ruining his own life as well as everybody else's in his pursuit.

President Mitterrand was a regular client of the Côte d'Or, but when the Legion of Honour list was published and the owner-chef did not find his name on it his 'ego was bruised'. Loiseau seemed jealous of more famous colleagues. As the time approached for the new edition of Michelin, he sought (without success) to obtain advance information about his fate. A week before official publication, the director of the guide, Bernard Naegellen, telephoned to inform Loiseau that he had won his third star, but insisting that the renovations had nothing to do with the decision. Loiseau did not believe that. In his own replies to questioners, Loiseau 'revised history,' as his 'Boswell' put it charitably, by saying that he would have made the investment even if Michelin had not existed. (For his part, Naegellen was quoted to the effect that no simple bistro with paper napkins and aluminum tableware could win three stars today.)

The Loiseau quest may seem distressing to romantics, but one can see how getting a third star would be an exhilarating moment for him and for his admirers, as the classy limousines pulled up at the newly crowned Côte d'Or (and were entitled to a free car wash). While the new customers seemed not to care how much they spent, the restaurant, with its steep overheads earned little profit, even with every table occupied and every room reserved.

The real money would come from endorsements, in the manner of a Paul Bocuse. Loiseau made a pot of gold – more money than he had earned in 16 years at Côte d'Or – by putting his name on packaged soups for Unilever.[7]

Every supermarket customer could now participate in the feast. 'The secrets of Bernard Loiseau,' the Royco soup prospectus reads, introducing the Côte d'Or's fabulous menus. 'I am convinced,' Loiseau wrote in his introduction, 'that the great chefs can also bring their expertise to bear on products that you consume every day'.

The brochure contained an order form, to be posted with the appropriate payment to La Côte d'Or in Saulieu, for such boutique items as a burgundy wine glass and a carafe with Loiseau's monogram, or gingerbread, jam and other gourmet specialities marketed under his name, not to forget three cookbooks bearing his signature. One could enter a drawing, 50 winners entitled to dinner for two at Loiseau's restaurant.[8]

As *Burgundy Stars* takes leave of Bernard Loiseau, the author hears him ask a friend, quite seriously, 'Don't you think Michelin should create a fourth star?'[9]

The Loiseau saga did not end with the publication of *Burgundy Stars*. The triple-starred chef behaved as if in a race against time, borrowing, building – opening not one but three theme restaurants in Paris, for example (Tante Louise, Tante Marguerite, Tante Jeanne), selling his prepared foods – and then going public. Indeed, in 1998 the 'Groupe Bernard Loiseau' joined the Paris Stock Exchange – apparently the first time a chef had ever become a floated stock. The story went around that this public appeal for funds was the only way he could handle what had become 'mountains of debt'.

On 4 February 2003, Loiseau, by then 52 years old, was found dead in his home in Saulieu, apparently after shooting himself with a hunting rifle. It was immediately said that he had been depressed by his demotion, in the annual Gault-Millau guide, from 19 to 17 points (out of 20). An unlikely motive for killing oneself, for 17 points were still a considerable number. 'On paper as well as in life, Loiseau was both a huge winner and shamelessly ambitious,' food critic Patricia Wells wrote. 'In death, his lesson may be to somehow learn to control one's appetite for fame and success. Or at least not to make it count for more than it is.'[10]

It was time for a respite. A 'return to order,' as a Paris newspaper called it. There would be no new promotions to three-star status in 1992.[11] And perhaps the true adventure, the enjoyable experience, had shifted ground. Walking into an elegant restaurant with its show-cases and souvenir displays, one could suddenly become very bored. There was as much anxiety as pleasure in ordering from a *maître d'hôtel* so sure of himself; non-celebrities could feel that, as they were granted admission to the dining room, permitted to look at a menu and to order, they were being granted a favour.

Anxiety replaced pleasure. In earlier years, foreigners might find themselves – to their annoyance – placed alongside other non-Frenchmen in a far corner of the dining room, sometimes in a less-fashionable room adjoining the main one, so that regular clients would not be disturbed by strange tongues in what seemed like raised voices, or by unconscionably odd dress. In more recent times, at three-star restaurants that can be filled every noon and night and require advance reservations, foreigners might not be given a table at all, no matter how long in advance they attempt to reserve. 'Unfortunately, we shall not be able to welcome you at this period of the year; our restaurant is very small and our dining room is already overcrowded,' was the way that famous restaurant replied to a distinguished foreign publisher and printer (an honorary French consul in his own country). 'Unfortunately', he was not welcome when he tried at another 'period of the year' (autumn) either. Nor in a third period – winter. He finally decided to send all the letters back to the restaurant to ask what would be the ideal period; by that time the owner had retired.[12]

Happily, these unlucky foreign gourmets could try a more interesting experience. Ever since 1954 the guide had been calling attention to restaurants serving good food at moderate prices. Chefs in these restaurants would try very hard to hold on to such a listing, for it too attracted customers, and obviously required little investment except in imagination.

*   *   *

Travelling around the European continent with a pile of red Michelins in hand, one American gourmet writer had only bad things to say about the thrice-starred. All of them were overpriced, for one thing – which he attributed to their owners' belief (a belief shared by that writer) that Michelin 'demands prodigious improvements and refinements before it will upgrade a restaurant'.

The stars had made these restaurants 'rigid, stuffy, and formulaic', performing for Michelin and not for their clients. That might be acceptable in France, where food served in these 'cathedrals of consumption' could still be interesting, but elsewhere they were promoting what he dismissed as high European cuisine. 'When you're eating Michelin three-star food outside France, it matters little where you are, because it's all going to look and taste pretty much the same.'

He cited a three-star Italian restaurant (which by the time his article had appeared was listed with only two stars) – which had taken on the manners (bad) of a French restaurant. Or another, outside Milan, a fine place if one likes 'Italian ingredients transformed into quasi-French food'. (The establishment has since lost one of its three stars.) Or, in France itself, a restaurant in Strasbourg, whose food was 'prissy and atypical of France's Alsace region'.[13]

Indeed, a gourmet journalist for the Wall *Street Journal*, who was also tasting his way around Europe, was not quite certain that Michelin's men in Britain had mastered their trade – that is, that they were giving three stars to the right chefs. That year there had been a change to Michelin's credit, he said, when Le Gavroche in London lost one of its three stars (because of a change in chefs), and La Tante Claire was raised to three. Critics were contesting the retention of a third star by the Waterside Inn at Bray-on-Thames, as well as the failure to give third stars to such restaurants as Nico Ladenis's Nico at Ninety in London.[14] (Ladenis got that third star the very next year – one of only 36 chefs 'in the whole of Europe' to have that honour, as he would boast.)[15]

Commenting – with gentle causticity – on a third star just then bestowed on a restaurant in Belgian Flanders, De Karmeliet in an ancient patrician residence in Bruges, the restaurant critic of *Le Monde* noted that the chef in question, Geert van Hecke, had trained in France (*chez* three-star chef Alain Chapel at Mionnay) before returning to his country of origin – and Michelin had followed him there.

For the [*Guide Michelin*] has caught the habit [argued the critic] of enlarging its zones of influence and mixing itself without shame in strictly domestic matters, playing the role of international policeman with an all-powerful veto; soon it will be the judge of the proper way to cook Bantu millet and to slice the Eskimo seal...[16]

In truth, someone or something had to set standards, and Michelin was the first to be bold enough to try to do it beyond the borders of its home country. Italians in Italy, Germans in Germany, Britons in Britain, Spaniards and Belgians and Dutchmen were lucky that Michelin wanted to sell tyres to them and subsequently also offered them assistance in locating their own best hotels and dining places, and (above all) make sure that the chosen establishments maintained their standards.

In France itself, the plight of three-star chefs obliged to spend more than they should – or believing that they had to – began to make the morning news for readers who otherwise might never have heard of these lucky restaurant owners who had suddenly become unlucky. One was the brilliant Pierre Gagnaire, whose first establishment in St-Etienne had been honoured in the 1992 *Guide Michelin* with three sets of spoons and forks (for the decor), and two stars (for his excellent cooking, deserving a detour to a town that would not otherwise find a place on a tourist's itinerary). There was also an ominous note: the restaurant would move to another location, probably that May.

Sure enough, in the 1993 guide, Gagnaire's restaurant was described as a '1930s villa decorated with elegance and originality' – the description enclosed in red quotation marks, another signal that the surroundings were agreeable. Not surprisingly, Pierre Gagnaire had been upgraded to four sets of spoons and forks; happily – or so it then seemed – he had also won the supreme honour for a chef, the luckiest attribute for an owner-chef – three Michelin stars.

But even the best food in France could not make money for its chef in St-Etienne, a long 320 miles from Paris, and not on the main road leading from the capital to the Riviera. The town itself was not inviting to outsiders, while insiders were busy coping with the business slump. Before the deadline for printing the 1996 *Guide Michelin*, Gagnaire was obliged to ask Michelin to withhold his stars, as he filed a petition for bankruptcy, requesting the French equivalent of Chapter 11, allowing him two further months to try to make do with less.

But it was not to happen; the gap was too wide. Press reports of heavy debts to the banks – 12 to 15 million francs' worth, and an immediate deficit of 400,000 francs – could well have been accurate.[17]

An American food writer happened to be present at the final hour; unwittingly, he dined *chez* Gagnaire on the very last day. The restaurant seemed 'like a mansion that Marie Antoinette might have built, the urban equivalent of the quaint farmhouse…she fabricated at Versailles'. A young doorman 'stooped under the weight of an epauletted grenadier's greatcoat'. Most of the women at the tables wore 'enough perfume to overwhelm the bouquet of the ripest cheese' (and their escorts seemed to admire them for it). In the lavatory he used one of the liquid soaps and found it was a cologne reminiscent of the perfumes in the dining room.

'Our table was generous in size and lavishly set with lush white damask and warm, polished silver, the mandatory accoutrements of three-star establishments.' Yet the visitor found the service perfunctory – for which he forgave Gagnaire when he learned that this was the end of the road. The food, however, was remarkable – only it was too expensive; he would not look forward to another such meal at such prices (nearly $60 a course). 'I say leave to the French the worship of food that even they cannot afford.' His conclusion was that three stars encourage pomp, and are hard to live up to, not to speak of what they do to pricing (due to the high cost of fine ingredients and bank interest on loans). Two Michelin stars represent purgatory. Only the one-star establishments, for this earnest food traveller, are really worth the visit – and then in the French countryside, not in Paris.[18]

There was a happy ending – or a safe landing – for Pierre Gagnaire, thanks to a generous and (one imagines) food-loving benefactor who helped to set him up in a proper Parisian environment.[19] In 1997, the *Guide Michelin* accorded him the same four sets of spoons and forks, but only two stars. He found a haven in the Hôtel Balzac (rue Balzac), a fine (but not luxury-class) hotel; his prices had risen significantly since St-Etienne, with a 450-franc all-in lunch menu, regular fixed-price menus ranging from 480 to 1200 francs, and an à la carte menu which ran from 540 to 750 francs without wine – menus that won him back his third star in the 1998 red guide.

　　　　*　　　　　　　　　　*　　　　　　　　　　*

Back in September 1996, another three-star palace had announced that the end was near. Even television and radio news reported that Marc Veyrat, owner and chef of the Auberge de l'Eridan at Veyrier-du-Lac, near Annecy, could not meet interest payments on his bank loans although he was earning as much as was possible, with every one of his tables booked in the evening for the next six weeks. He owed 43 million francs for work undertaken on his establishment, which included an 11-room hotel. Here the cheapest rooms went for 1500 francs a night, the most expensive 4850. His dining room had been awarded five sets of spoons and forks (in red) from Michelin, as well as three stars; there was even a special symbol for tranquil surroundings.

Veyrat had tried without success to renegotiate his loans; the banks had been putting him off for well over a year. He planned to close for a month's vacation in October, and during that time would try to make an agreement with his creditors. Otherwise, he was in trouble.

Veyrat's cry for help drew sympathy. How could it be otherwise in France? It was noted that, after his first significant recognition in Michelin and other guide-books in 1992, he had undertaken the stunning transformation of a villa overlooking the lake of Annecy. He had done everything right, and the state of the nation's economy was blamed for his straits, with companies as well as individuals reducing expenses. Undoubtedly, the owner-chef had committed some mistakes in management too, since cooking well did not necessarily mean that one could run a business.

Moreover, explained the successful chef Pierre Troisgros, proprietor of a three-star restaurant and luxury hotel in Roanne, young chefs like Veyrat had invested in their enterprises after 1990, by which time conditions had become difficult. The older chefs had done their renovating in the 1980s. Had he invested after 1990, admitted Troisgros, he would have been in the same mess.

It was also true that while Pierre Gagnaire failed because of a lack of clientele, Veyrat had been doing better than ever when he made his announcement, with annual turnover of $5.9 million, up 12 percent over the previous year. But even that had not permitted him to handle his overheads and also meet his bank payments, which alone amounted to more than $3500 a day.

Here, too, there would be a happy ending. By appealing to the national conscience (and stomach), Marc Veyrat also won over his bankers, and his debt was renegotiated at last, the daily payment reduced (reportedly to half), the time period doubled.[20]

*   *   *

To be recognized by Michelin was to become a media star, and not only in France. From then on, one's bad deeds as well as good ones became food for everybody's table. There were shockwaves at the beginning of 1996 when two of Paris's most famous chefs, those in charge of the kitchens of the Tour d'Argent (still a three-star restaurant) and the Hôtel Crillon (two stars), were indicted on charges of accepting payments from a fish merchant. The lawyer for one of the accused explained that what was being called corruption was in fact 'gratification', said to be a regular custom among suppliers and chefs, 'the money then being distributed by the chef to kitchen staff'.[21]

Two months later – surely there was no connection between the two events – when the new Michelin appeared, it was discovered that the Tour d'Argent in Paris had lost one of its three stars. With its famous pressed duck – the blood still squeezed from the lightly cooked bird in a massive silver press alongside the diner's table – the establishment was virtually a national institution (and definitely an international one, judging by its heterogenous clientele). Its degrading also had to be a national event (if not an international one).

The venerable quayside restaurant had worn its three stars proudly ever since the Michelin people began awarding them to dining places in Paris (in 1933); only once, in 1952, had there been a temporary demotion, but as soon as the owner carried out some necessary improvements, the Tour d'Argent had returned to its three-star status.

The disgrace merited the attention of the *New York Times*, where it was noted that gourmets now found the famous restaurant's cuisine less impressive than the ceremony. Other critics attributed the debacle to the inability of the owner and his kitchen to renew their style, joined to the difficulty of making the great old dishes today (if only because one is no longer allowed to keep stock from one day to the next).

Later that year, the Tour's chef and most of his staff were replaced – a consequence of Michelin's decision, it was said, and not the corruption charge. In the next (1997) guide, the Tour d'Argent appeared with all its trappings – the five sets of red spoons and forks – but still with a little less glory, since the third star had not been restored.[22]

For those who had grown up with Michelin, for whom the quest for stars – the motor trip across France, the telephoning to first one and then another Paris establishment until at last there was a favourable response – still brought excitement, the bad press of recent times is not easily overcome. 'The Michelin Plague' was the cruel term used in a prestigious American newspaper to sum up the situation of the guide, and its admirers, in the middle of the 1990s decade. It focused on the experience of wonder-chef Joël Robuchon, whose restaurant of that name in a ravishing art nouveau townhouse on avenue Raymond Poincaré then bore three Michelin stars.

Robuchon had announced his intention to retire on his fiftieth birthday (which would be on 7 April 1995), but for a long time could not find a successor, since his debt meant that he had nothing to sell but his name – and of course his name would disappear on his retirement. 'The third Michelin star is not given for the quality and quantity of food alone,' the correspondent reported what so many in France were saying, 'but for the quality and quantity of marble in the bathrooms and other emblems of luxury'.[23]

Perhaps it was a cruel fate, all the same, for a Robuchon, whose father had been a mason, and who had learned cooking when lending a hand in the kitchen of a *petit seinaire* in the town of his birth, Poitiers. He became an apprentice at a local restaurant, the Relais de Poitiers, at the time it was earning its Michelin star, worked in some of Paris's toughest kitchen brigades, becoming chef in two successive first-class Paris hotels before opening his own restaurant in 1981.[24]

Now a successor had been found, and a credible one, in another three-star chef, Alain Ducasse of the Louis XV restaurant in the Hôtel de Paris in Monte Carlo. (In fact, Ducasse would simply change the restaurant's name from the famous Joël Robuchon to the almost as famous Alain Ducasse.)[25]

But all this came at a price, as the *Wall Street Journal* man remarked. He had gone to the Tour d'Argent after it lost a star, found it better than ever (but this was after a new chef had been engaged). He had also visited the Arpège on rue de Varenne, which had won a third star in 1996 when the Tour d'Argent lost one; he found it excellent, although he feared that the owner had taken the third star as a licence to print money, since the bill for two persons came to nearly $500 – and Joël Robuchon's restaurant had been even more expensive.

'Perhaps, for the common good,' concluded the reporter, 'Michelin might consider a moratorium on awarding three stars – or even abolishing the category and reducing, at a stroke, the cost of eating out'.[26]

40

MICHELIN IN OUR TIME

T he 1990s should have begun with a dose of adrenaline, thanks to the triumphal acquisition of a venerable American tyre-maker (with not one but two famous brand names). But something was going very wrong at Michelin, in the back office where the accounts were drawn up, and inevitably in the hearts and minds of workers on the factory floor. The morosity clearly had an effect on Michelin stock, which had never fully recovered from the market crash of October 1987. At best, as an analyst observed, Michelin's was not an equity one acquired lightheartedly, due to both the treatment of minority shareholders (who got little information and fewer dividends) and the inconvenient rule that shares were issued to bearers by name (discouraging foreign investors – those, at least).[1]

Although the scaling down of Michelin activity in Clermont-Ferrand would inevitably be blamed – and not only by militant trade unionists – on the diversion of investment to the United States, restructuring came first. In March 1990, the Manufacture made it known that there would be 'serious' cuts in personnel in Clermont-Ferrand because of a decline in tyre sales, and an expected continuation of that decline – in addition to which modernization would call for fewer hands at the machines. As it was, Michelin's total payroll in the Auvergne capital was 20,500, compared to 29,969 a decade earlier; in all of France, the roster had fallen from 52,953 to 36,898 in the same period.[2]

At the end of April, American authorities at last cleared the way for the takeover of Uniroyal-Goodrich, which represented half of Michelin's world production of tyres for passenger cars, its factories in the United States, Canada and Mexico earning most of its $2 billion turnover in North America.[3] Defending his strategy at the annual shareholders meeting in late June, François Michelin asserted:

> Our activity is in the middle of a phase of restructuring, which requires that we move quickly to set up new ways to come out of it as winners. At first we shall be confronting three or four difficult years because of an increasingly competitive market, but we shall also be making investments that must be understood to be long term.[4]

By then, everybody should have been prepared, but the news deserved unusually big headlines in September when Michelin announced the results of the first half-year. 'Michelin plunges into the red,' so *Le Figaro* phrased it.[5] Apparently determined to tell all, and quickly, François Michelin followed the bad news with more, predicting a deficit of 2.3 billion francs for the full year. 'Steering Through Hard Times,' was the pun Britain's *Financial Times* permitted itself.[6]

After listening to chief François Michelin's own explanation – during a meeting with the press in Clermont-Ferrand which was said to be the first such face-to-face encounter in four years – the correspondent of the *Financial Times* concluded that Michelin seemed 'to have taken all the wrong turns at the worst moment', the turns including the Uniroyal purchase, and borrowing at a time when interest rates were rising and the dollar was falling. 'It is easy to be beguiled by the provincial charm of 64-year-old Mr Michelin [the FT envoy observed] ... A tall, slightly frail-looking figure, Mr Michelin's imp-like face is inclined earnestly as he makes a point in his typically simple but vivid style.'[7]

Henceforth, much of Michelin's time would be devoted to explaining himself, and in public – an uncustomary role for him. He assured a meeting of the Clermont-Ferrand Municipal Council that he was attached to his city. 'It's true that we are obliged to take difficult steps. But why should we get rid of people who have done such a good job?' Personnel would be reduced, all the same, in the United States as well as in Europe, for a total of 16,000 employees, representing 15 percent of Michelin's global workforce.[8]

The chief explained what seemed to be the abruptness of his decision in a rare dialogue with a business correspondent early in June 1991. 'We've known for three or four years that our payroll is too large, but in this country it is difficult to take preventive measures... In Germany, in Italy, such measures can be taken, but here we're in a yoke...'

The journalist did not hesitate to ask all the embarrassing questions. About the company's partnership structure which gave François Michelin absolute power, for example. He replied: 'It allows us to gain a considerable amount of time, to make decisions without submitting to outside pressures...' On the firm's proverbial secrecy: 'Any leak would be suicide. It takes us years to bring out a new tyre or to develop new machinery. But in five minutes a competitor can get an idea of the technological innovation and copy it.'

He no longer rode around in a dinky 2CV, the journalist observed, but now used a not very classy Citroën BX, in which he drove the interviewer to the airport, explaining with a smile, 'that will save a taxi'.[9]

In his more formal role as managing partner François had another opportunity to explain the situation to shareholders in the same month of June. The slowdown in the automobile industry had at last caught up with tyres, reducing demand for original equipment, while competition had stiffened. It was a global phenomenon, influenced more than was usual by non-economic events such as the Gulf crisis (Iraq had invaded Kuwait in August 1990 and the allied reprisal offensive began in mid-January 1991).[10]

*   *   *

He had spoken to the man from *Le Monde* about his son Edouard, chosen to succeed him. Like François, Edouard had worked his way through the company, 'and it's because he did this that he was chosen. He is exceptional; in the name of what should we appoint someone who is incapable?'[11]

François's characterization of his son was in itself '*exceptionnel*'; surely no-one outside the family circle had ever heard so strong a word in the mouth of a Michelin (and no matter that he was describing another Michelin). 'We therefore believe that the time has come to bring into our management a person who after years of observation we believe to be fully qualified to take over responsibility for this company' was the way management put it to shareholders, who (immediately following their regular June meeting) were called into session as an extraordinary assembly to hear of the forthcoming retirement of a managing partner and his replacement by a member of the next generation. 'This person is Edouard Michelin, fifth child and fourth son of François Michelin,' his elders continued. 'Born in 1963, he is about the same age as most of his predecessors when each of them became a managing partner.'

Edouard – born more precisely on 13 August 1963, he was not yet 28 years old at the time of his nomination – was a graduate of the Ecole Centrale in Paris, which of course was his great-great-uncle André's engineering school. He had done his compulsory military service as an officer of the watch on a nuclear submarine. His first formal contact with the family plant had been as an apprentice while still a student at Centrale, after which he was assigned to a succession of factory departments – the Michelin way. Now he was to run Michelin's North American companies, reporting to their former director, who was moving up a notch to take charge of both Michelin and Uniroyal-Goodrich on that continent.

And should anyone think the contrary, the surviving managers, François Michelin and René Zingraff (now 54), made it clear that they still had many years ahead of them, while Edouard applied himself to field operations, learning on the job before being summoned to join his seniors on the board.[12] Had any programme for a young man's perfecting been laid out in such detail since Rousseau's Emile?

Note that François Michelin had three older sons. So why Edouard? One can't help remembering what François had said of his own appointment to the management – the 'factory' had chosen him, and the 'factory' would choose his successor.[13] In fact Edouard's oldest brother Etienne had joined the priesthood. The next sons in line, Damien and Benoît, had both done well in school, and Benoît was then an engineer at the Ladoux research centre, but neither seemed to possess the leadership qualities demanded by their father. 'From the choice of his name to his stupefying resemblance to his father,' a business writer summed it up, 'Edouard seemed predestined to be a synthesis of the two greats of the dynasty, Edouard the founder and François the conqueror'.[14] 'He's an iconoclast, it's wonderful,' so François described his son, shortly after his appointment to the management board was ratified.[15] It remained to be seen whether his iconoclasm would survive daily encounters with his father – and 'the factory'.

41

BIBENDUM'S
BIG BUSINESS

It was during the 1990s that touring became another serious Michelin money-making operation, and never mind that every book and all the bric-a-brac carried Michelin's name, often Bibendum's image too – thereby promoting tyres. In the first half of the decade, the travel department could report that 130 green guides were on sale in the familiar four-and-three-quarter by ten-and-a-quarter inch format, and in eight languages.

Some three million green guides were sold in 1994; 1995 saw three new titles in French (*Florence et la Toscane, Ecosse, Californie*), five more in English (*Atlantic Coast, Auvergne-The Rhone Valley, Burgundy-Jura, Belgium, California*), three in German, Dutch and Italian, two in Japanese and Spanish, one in Portuguese. By now, the austere format had all but blossomed into colour, and that was only the beginning.[1]

In 1997 the first green guide of a new type was put on the market (*Guadeloupe-Martinique-Petites Antilles*), with 200 photographs and drawings in colour, and a separate section for a listing of hotels and restaurants, with practical tips for travellers.[2] And then to meet the competition of a new generation which tends to favour 'rough guides' and hitchhikers' guides, Michelin has recently come out with a small-format, easy-to-read, easy-to-flip-through series called 'In Your Pocket', covering individual towns (Amsterdam, Budapest, London), regions (the Loire Valley castles, Florida) and whole countries (Morocco, Thailand); the English versions add the Greek Islands, the south of France and southern Spain.

So of course – the era called for it – they were soon making films of the green guides, in the form of 50-minute videos co-produced with a French television channel. Michelin created the scenarios, which in fact followed the format of the printed green guides.[3]

As early as 1989, the Avenue de Breteuil began disseminating its travel advice – that favourite activity of the guide's patron saint André Michelin – via Minitel, the French electronic telephone service directory, dispensing the good word on hotels and restaurants for paying customers, above all calculating travel itineraries through most of Europe (70,000 localities covered). For those wishing to have their route on paper, fax delivery was introduced.[4] And when the Internet gave clear signs that it was going to surpass Minitel, opening the way to global dissemination of a service that until then had been limited to France, Michelin went online, transmitting itineraries and maps tailored to individual requests, coupling them with the resources of the red guides on hotels and restaurants, allowing a print-out – all for a nominal fee.[5]

For the future? It is moving in fast. Michelin has made its contribution to onboard computer navigation, an electronic computerized directional system developed in partnership with Sony. By means of a dashboard computer connected to a network of GPS satellites placed in orbit by the United States Defense Department, motorists can pinpoint their location and then call up the appropriate Michelin town maps, read green guide travel tips, red guide hotel and restaurant data (stored on CD-ROMs).[6]

Less lofty, but inevitable in an age that makes commerce of everything, is the Boutique Michelin. The first shops were opened in 1994 on Paris's Avenue de l'Opéra and rue Montlosier in Clermont-Ferrand (a brief stroll from the old Carmes factory site). They sell current Michelin maps and guides, videos and other travel aids, and offer access to Minitel travel information and demonstrations of new techniques such as onboard navigation.

But each shop is also stocked with souvenir posters, postcards and knick-knacks in all shapes and sizes (having in common the Michelin name and Bibendum image). One imagines the spirit of old André Michelin poised over the counters, dipping down now and then to examine some of the nearly 300 gadgets, articles of dress or decoration bearing the beloved image of Bibendum: keyrings, as a starter, T-shirts, sweat shirts, umbrellas, a windscreen scraper, a Bibendum pen attached by cord to a Bibendum statuette, fireplace decorations in crystal, a mantelpiece clock, a snow globe, a Bibendum who walks when you wind him up, a Bibendum bottle opener, a Bibendum beer mug, Bibendum ties, tie clips, scarf, Bibendum ashtray, piggy-bank, pen holder, pencil holder, coffee cup, cigarette-lighter holder (and of course cigarette lighter); for the kids, Bibendum toys (planes, cars, tops), skipping rope, dominoes and other games; for Madame, Bibendum earrings, bracelet, necklace, brooch; for quiet evenings at home, Bibendum playing cards ... [7]

But if Bibendum could seem frivolous, he had also become big business, at least in the minds and hearts of others.[8] For we have begun to understand what the star system has done to the bank balances and even the behaviour of some otherwise worthy soul's craving. 'Whom to accuse?' demanded the restaurant critic of *Le Monde*, in an resumé of the plight of the famous three-star restaurants. 'The Michelin guide, with its regrettable way of judging the velvet of curtains as much as the velvety texture of the soup, or simply those young lords of the table, who are skilful, temperamental, and have expensive tastes?'[9]

*   *   *

One big question for culinary journalists (and presumably for a great many gourmets, French and foreign) was how Naegellen and his knights of the round table would resolve the conundrum posed by wonder-chef Alain Ducasse, who while holding on to his responsibilities at Monte Carlo's three-star Le Louis XV restaurant (in the famous Hôtel de Paris alongside the casino), had taken over retiring Joël Robuchon's three-star restaurant in Paris in July 1996.[10]

Could 40-year-old Ducasse, who had earned his three Monte Carlo stars in 33 months, apparently setting a record, hold on to these stars as well as the three that Robuchon had earned for his eponymous Paris restaurant (since rechristened Alain Ducasse)? Apparently he could not. In the new guide, the establishment on avenue Raymond-Poincaré was listed with three stars (surely merited), while the Louis XV in Monte Carlo was reduced to two.

Total injustice, Ducasse exclaimed – but he still sat atop an unprecedented total of five stars, 953 kilometres apart. Later he would be quoted: 'I want the French to admit that a chef doesn't necessarily have to be in his kitchen'. Apparently this was a response to Michelin's

Solomon-like judgment, but also to restaurant critics and simple customers who expect a prestigious chef to be cooking on the day they enter a restaurant, and not flying around the world advising here, speech-making there, endorsing everywhere.[11] Who was right?

Apparently Michelin decided that the matter deserved further reflection, for when the next *Guide Michelin* appeared at the beginning of March 1998, readers discovered that Ducasse had recovered the star lost in Monte Carlo while keeping his three Paris stars, becoming a redoubtable six-star chef, albeit a commuting one.

Speaking to a correspondent of the *New York Times*, the Michelin guide director Bernard Naegellen explained that his people had been engaged in a manhunt for new three-star chefs, but none had been found. He also took the opportunity to reiterate that, contrary to popular belief, three-star restaurants need not be fancy nor fantastically expensive (although in fact most of them are both).[12]

For its part, the new Michelin made a contribution to deflation, obviously concerned by the economic realities of recessionary France and its slow-growth neighbours. This concern took the form of a new symbol, a dot-sized caricature of a smiling Bibendum – baptized Bib' Gourmand – placed alongside the names of restaurants judged to have interesting, often typically regional food – in simple surroundings, and at reasonable

17. François (left) and Edouard Michelin at the Paris Motor Show, 29 September 2000. Reuters/Jack Dabaghian.

prices (100–130 francs on average, now some $17–22). There were 410 such establishments in this first (1997) listing, spread over the map (although none was in Paris, and few were even close to the capital).[13]

Pressed by an inquisitive reporter, Naegellen admitted that the total printing of the Michelin had fallen off, from an average of 600,000–650,000 copies, of which 480,000 were distributed in France. But the budget was balanced.[14] As soon as the new edition appeared in the shops, it climbed to the top of the French bestseller list of practical books. It was still number one at the end of June; it was number three late in August, number fifteen late in September, climbing back to the eighth position in mid-October, slipping to twelfth in early November, up to ninth position again at the end of November – and back up to seventh place again in December![15]

It is not clear what all those purchasers of the *Guide Michelin* are looking for. Do they still reach for the stars, despite soaring menu prices, thereby extending already long waiting lists for reservations at the most popular of the two and three-star restaurants (and often it is a matter of months and not weeks)? Have they succumbed to the universal admiration of celebrities which has put the faces of three-star chefs on jars and boxes in supermarkets?[16]

It had started, it was said, with the wonder-chef Alain Senderens of three-star Lucas Carton in Paris, who had given his name to the French supermarket chain Carrefour to be used on house products. Lyons' Paul Bocuse confessed that he had waited until 10 other famous chefs had signed contracts with food processors before lending his own name to William Saurin, an inexpensive brand of canned goods. And we have seen how quickly Bernard Loiseau signed his name to packaged soups after winning his third star.

In 1997, the prestigious chef Joël Robuchon yielded to a similar temptation by agreeing to sponsor a line of inexpensive albeit well-conceived dishes which the food packager Fleury-Michon produced for supermarkets.

Will readers of the inimitable *Guide Michelin* go, instead, for the unstarred but not undeserving? Michelin has always made that easy, most recently by putting its own label of quality on those provincial inns which might otherwise escape the notice of the hurried traveller. It is just possible that this reshuffling of the cards represents Michelin's future, certainly its best chance of renewal.

42

THE NEXT
TURN IN
THE ROAD

A tremor of euphoria ran through the conference room when François Michelin stood before shareholders at the Clermont-Ferrand airport conference hall in June 1995. Their group had returned to profit, the global economy was showing signs of new vitality, promising still better years ahead. Automobile sales had risen in most places, and tyres followed obediently. In their flagship company, Manufacture Française des Pneumatiques Michelin, sales reached new heights, helped along by the new lower-priced 'classic' tyres, as well as an upscale 'pilot' line – but also by the excitement built around the fuel-saving 'green' tyres.[1]

In this atmosphere of wellbeing, few in the audience would have seen the irony represented by the triumphal announcement of the agreement concluded with the hereditary enemy, Germany's Continental, Europe's number two tyre-maker. But now there was a European community, and in a context of aggressive global competition it seemed to make sense for neighbours to make and sell tyres together (at least, it made sense at the lower end of the market). The point was to keep out cheap tyres produced in other markets (meaning Japan and North America).[2]

In July 1995, *Le Figaro* achieved a coup by bringing together François, then 69, and his 32-year-old son Edouard for an interview. Edouard explained Michelin's new European strategy which, by assigning every plant a specialization – rather than running a chain of multiproduct factories – allowed considerable gains in productivity. The hope was to apply American methods, such as keeping plants operating longer hours to reduce fixed costs.[3]

The strategy of the Michelins, father and son, seemed justified. When all returns were in for 1995, Michelin had doubled net profits.[4] By the second half of the 1990s, the battle of the tyre giants – Michelin was then number one, followed closely by Japan's Bridgestone, with America's Goodyear trailing – was a regular concern of business analysts. Yet, in actual tyre sales, the United States remained at the top, Japan second with about half as many units sold, and France was third with less than half of that.

Clearly Michelin, 'large, energetic and secretive,' to quote the headline in the *Financial Times*, had succeeded better than anyone else in other people's markets.[5]

Now, in an attempt to attack the marketing problem from the inside, François Michelin's son showed himself to be an organizer in the best tradition of American management schools. Henceforth, the directional centre would be split into separate units, of which nine would be product lines – such as wheels and tyres for passenger vehicles, for trucks, farm equipment, aviation, bicycles – another eleven would be group services (including purchasing, accounting, communication, personnel and, of course, security), and a new technology centre would be with based in three strategic regions. Michelin's world was divided into geographic zones, whose managers would co-ordinate all activities in their regions.[6]

'Reorganization, American style,' the unionized workers of Michelin's Committee of Establishment called it – a phrase not intended to flatter. 'The monarchy will remain constitutional and the legitimists will remain in the key jobs.'[7]

*   *   *

Before the year 1996 was over, two Michelin factories – one of them in Clermont-Ferrand, the other at Saint-Priest in the Rhône district – had quietly been equipped with a new and secret wonder-machine, tantalizingly called the C3M, whose development was said to have marshalled the brainpower of 2500 persons over a 10-year span. Henceforth, Michelin could turn out a tyre in one-eighth of the usual time. 'Each machine is a factory in itself, which can fit into my dining room of 375 square feet,' was all that François would say about it.[8]

At the other end of the spectrum, Michelin continued to manufacture – with the loving care they demanded – a wide variety of
tyres for vintage and classic cars, pre-1914 models, post-1918, the
automobiles of the 1920s and 1930s – conventional passenger and
racing cars both.[9] It equipped world champions in the Formula One
automobile race, 'a business as serious – if not quite as big – as the oil
and auto industries that support it,' so an American weekly described
this contest held every two weeks from March to October at 17 circuits
around the world, and which drew nearly as many television viewers
as the Olympics or the football World Cup.[10] So it should come as no
surprise that in a poll commissioned by a business magazine in the
summer of 1996, Michelin was voted one of the brand-names most
admired by average French men and women (the other high-rankers were
Chanel, Mercedes, Philips and Nestlé).[11] Consumer advocates agreed
that Michelin tyres were the best.[12]

Did those who voted for Michelin realize that the Michelin they
admired was changing, and rapidly? That it no longer had both feet
planted in the Auvergne, for instance, but was making a constantly
increasing share of its famous tyres beyond France's borders? That of
its global payroll of 114,000 persons, only 30,000 were based in
France, and only half of them in the Auvergne capital?

And then, in the second half of the 1990s, Michelin was found to
be losing market share to Bridgestone, which, with 19 percent of global
sales to Michelin's 18 percent, became the world's number one in tyres.[13]
Founded in 1931 by a Japanese engineer who adopted the trademark
Bridgestone – a translation of his own name into English – for sound
marketing reasons, it had been expanding rapidly in recent times,
buying out America's venerable Firestone in 1988, now making tyres
in factories in France, Italy and Spain that came to it with the Firestone
acquisition. Bridgestone had chosen both the high and the low ends
of the market, equipping the likes of Porsche and Ferrari as well as
Ford and Volkswagen, and also making tyres for sale under the names
of some of France's biggest supermarket chains.[14]

As for Michelin, and thanks to France's stock-exchange control
commission, it was telling the world more about itself these days. In
a document filed with the Commission des Opérations de Bourse
(COB) in December 1996, much that was guessed about the group
was confirmed, much new information revealed, the whole attested

to by Monsieur François Michelin, identified humbly as 'one of the managers'.

The company remained what an American publication once described as 'a kind of unlimited liability joint-stock company'. The senior Michelin was believed to hold less than 1 percent of the stock, yet was personally liable for all the company's debts. As he himself explained this odd arrangement: 'You wouldn't get into an airplane piloted by a remote control. If a pilot has to save his own skin, he'll save his passengers as well.'[15] Not only were the partners responsible 'jointly and indefinitely for corporate debt', but the managers – like the partners chosen by an extraordinary general assembly – 'have total authority to act in the name of the company in all circumstances'. At that time the managing partners were the Michelins, father and son, with non-family executive René Zingraff.

The partners – the three managers and a syndicate of family share-holders – received a first distribution of 12 percent of net profit. The balance was attributed to stock shares (after withholding of a capital reserve and a priority dividend to holders of 'A' stock). There were 143,803 shareholders, none holding or controlling 5 percent or more shares or voting rights.

The group was now making and selling 13,500 different products, utilizing, in addition to the flagship trademark Michelin, brand-names such as Kléber, BF Goodrich and Uniroyal. In 1995, Michelin sold 12.6 percent of its tyres in France, 27.5 percent elsewhere in Europe and 21.4 percent in America. It purchased raw materials on the world market, as well as importing them from its own plantations in Nigeria and Brazil. Synthetic rubber was manufactured in the United States as well as France (the present mix was half natural, half synthetic).[16]

But in 1997 Michelin was still number two. Bridgestone, seemingly unstoppable, continued to hold world-market leadership.[17]

So, what now?

*   *   *

No doubt was possible. Even looking at Michelin from a distance – a distance rendered obligatory by the continued existence of its nineteenth-century management structure – one felt that one was privy to the thinking of its directors. The future of Michelin was in advanced technology. But that future was not necessarily centred on Clermont-Ferrand.

One more time, then, the fat had to be excised at headquarters. In February 1997, despite clear signs that Michelin's fortunes were on the rise, a new payroll reduction scheme was announced for France, eliminating 1445 jobs – 852 of them in Auvergne's and Michelin's capital. (And this, local officials observed bitterly, despite Michelin's pledge four years earlier to maintain 18,000 jobs in Clermont-Ferrand; they were now down to 14,850, and each job lost left the city the poorer.)[18] As for technology: unveiled at the Geneva Automobile Show in the spring of 1997, a so-called 'run-flat' tyre was to allow drivers to keep a car on the road for over a hundred miles after a puncture. The architecture of the tyre allowed it to adhere to the wheel despite loss of air pressure; an insert connected to the rim assured stability at a speed below 50 mph, even in curves or when braking.

Heavier, more of a 'gas-guzzler,' so sceptics would say. And then run-flat tyres would cost some 25 percent more than regular replacements. They also required the installation of a sensor to alert drivers to the loss of air pressure, since the tyres themselves, however wondrous, were unlikely to draw attention to punctures. Here was a rich man's product, perhaps, conceived for people ready to pay for the privilege of not having to make repairs on the side of the road (or not to have make repairs, personally, at all).[19]

'The American space shuttle is soled by Michelin,' the company reminded potential customers at the Paris air show at Le Bourget.

> As are... fighting aircraft with names like Rafale and EFA-2000, Mirage and F-22... Even the biggest competitors on the market, Airbus and Boeing, have both put their trust in Michelin tyres...
>
> The first Boeing 777 delivered to United Airlines on May 17, 1995, was fitted with Michelin Air X tyres as original equipment. The whole United Airlines Boeing 777 fleet of thirty-four aircraft is scheduled to be fitted out by 1999.[20]

There would be increased automation, thanks to what was still being called 'the top-secret C3M'. At the beginning of spring 1997, the output of this miracle machine reportedly accounted for no more than 1 percent of Michelin production.[21] But that would soon change, with the inauguration in May of a 200,000-square-foot plant in Greenville, South Carolina – alongside the existing radial tyre facility – in which the C3M would reign supreme. The new factory, together with those already outfitted with the mystery machines in France and Sweden, would be responsible for 30–40 percent of the company's passenger tyres by the end of the century. Naturally, Michelin did not reveal production figures.[22]

In a consumer-satisfaction study that spring, American motorists voted Michelin the best overall replacement tyre for passenger cars, compact vans and light trucks. (Dunlop was number two in the first two categories, Uniroyal number two for light trucks.)[23] Meanwhile, the old family partnership in Clermont-Ferrand, however antique and arcane, had edged out Japan's Bridgestone to become the world's number one tyre-maker again. A decline in the value of Japanese currency was partly to blame, but Michelin's improved tyre sales had clearly much to do with the new ranking. Goodyear actually produced more tyres than either of the top two – but they were sold more cheaply in the highly competitive North American market.[24]

* * *

Despite the apparent health of his empire, Edouard Michelin – Edouard the Second – who was called 'the American' because of his New World experience – was coming to power at a difficult time. He knew, but could not say, that the future of Michelin was elsewhere. He had taken his father's place at the head of the table in June 1999; by September he discovered what plain talking might do to his company.

It was time for the proclamation of Michelin's half-year results; profits were up 20 percent and the world had to know that. At the same time, frankness called for an announcement of the business plan, focused on a tightening up of European operations to improve competition, including restructuring of as many as 7500 Michelin workers in France and elsewhere in Europe over a three-year period. The almost simultaneous announcements – increased earnings, a reduction in personnel – produced a shockwave. Even the French prime minister, chief of a government grouping Socialists and Communists, felt that he had to make a statement. The Socialists' first secretary found the firings unacceptable.

In Europe, France had become the problem child, thanks to a new labour law calling for a 35-hour week, and this at a time when pro-ductivity was a problem everywhere on the continent.[25]

And recession. All things considered, Edouard Michelin's tactics – anticipating a slowdown – served him well in his early months in power. For before it was over, the decline in growth affected the United States market as well (which represented 40 percent of Michelin activity); production had to be reduced accordingly.

Despite these setbacks, at the end of February 2002 Michelin management was able to announce a slight rise in sales for the previous year, which, despite a decline in profits, represented a better performance than Michelin's principal global competitors, Goodyear and Bridgestone. Edouard Michelin's secret seemed to be his focus on upmarket products, such as the run-flat tyres (now called the Pax System),[26] and a willingness to overturn traditional ways: in the spring of 2002 he announced an opening of Michelin capital to Michelin workers.[27]

*   *   *

As for the *Guide Michelin* and its derivatives, no innovation was excluded in future. The volume for France shed its sobriety and became verbose, adding thumbnail descriptions of all the thousands of hotels and restaurants it listed – chatter that some readers felt was a betrayal of André Michelin's genial plan. And Michelin went online, of course, allowing its users to click instead of turning pages. Naturally, travellers were invited to contribute their input via email.

But perhaps the most convincing sign of Michelin's reaching out to the world came in the year 2000, with the appointment of a British subject, Derek Brown, as the successor to the *Guide Michelin*'s director Bernard Naegellen; he had joined the Michelin team as a young man, serving as an inspector for the Great Britain and Ireland edition.[28]

Notes on text

Notes on Chapter 1

1   'A propos de notre guide', Paris, June 1900 (circular from Messieurs Michelin & Cie).
2   Jean-Pierre Dauliac, Jean Menu and Pierre Saka, *Histoire de l'Automobile en France* (Paris, Nathan, 1982), p. 28. In 1900, French workshops produced some 4800 vehicles against 4000 in the United States, at a time when technology and even sales expertise began in France and moved outward, even toward the United States (Americans would take the lead only in 1904–5). James M. Laux, 'Genèse d'une révolution', in Jean-Pierre Bardou et al., *La Révolution Automobile* (Paris, Albin Michel, 1977).

Notes on Chapter 2

1   The principal source for this chapter is René Miquel, *Dynastie Michelin* (Paris, Table Ronde, 1962), a *tour de force* of research supplemented with conjecture to bridge the gaps – conjecture that is always reasonable and usually credible. Miquel makes it clear that Michelin refused to open its archives for him, a disappointment which (he adds) freed him to go his own way. Miquel's account has been used alongside Michelin's own material, especially a succinct history – call it the official version – first published in 1908: 'L'Industrie dans le département du Puy-de-Dôme', a paper presented by Maximilien Gerber to a congress of l'Association Française pour l'Avancement des Sciences devoted to Clermont-Ferrand et le Puy-de-Dôme (Paris, 1908), pp. 609–26. Gerber was a chemical engineer at the Michelin company, and his paper was subsequently republished under the signature of André Michelin in the *Revue Générale du Caoutchouc* (Paris), April 1924, pp. 53–56, May, pp. 45–46.
2   (André Michelin), 'Comment Clermont-Ferrand devint la Cité du caoutchouc', *L'Illustration* (Paris), 21 February 1920.
3   So the story appears in the memorial booklet published by the Michelin company on the death of Edouard: *Edouard Michelin (1859–1940)* (Clermont-Ferrand, Michelin, 1940), unnumbered pages.
4   Gerber, 'L'Industrie dans le département', p. 619. The Dunlop case will be described in its place.
5   Gerber, 'L'Industrie dans le département', pp. 610–13; Miquel, *Dynastie*, pp. 298–302.
6   Christian Lamy and Jean-Pierre Fornaro, *Michelin-Ville: Le Logement ouvrier de l'entreprise Michelin (1911–1987)* (Nonette, France, Créer, 1990), pp. 10–11.

Notes on Chapter 3

1   But even a factory could be a town's pride, as evidenced in a local tourist guide-book which draws the attention of visitors to 'the handsome Daubrée establishment': *Le Vrai Guide de Clermont-Ferrand et du département du Puy-de-Dôme* (Clermont-Ferrand, Duchier, 1865), p. 20.

2   In addition to the sober account by Maximilien Gerber – surely written with André Michelin – 'L'industrie dans le département du Puy-de-Dôme', and the imaginative work of René Miquel, *Dynastie Michelin* (Paris, Table Ronde, 1962), we have drawn on a more prudent account of the rise of Clermont-Ferrand as rubber capital in the thesis of Lionel Dumond, *Etude d'une main d'oeuvre: les ouvriers Michelin à Clermont-Ferrand (1889–1916)* (Clermont-Ferrand, Université Blaise Pascal II, 1989).

3   This advertisement is dated 23 July 1863. Reprinted in *Michelin Magazine* 583 (Clermont-Ferrand), April–May 1989 ('Rubrique d'un siècle' no 1). The village of Blanzat is only a few kilometres north of the original factory site.

4   For an account of these years see Dumond, *Etude d'une main d'oeuvre*, pp. 15–16. Dumond, who had partial access to company archives, attributes the decline to neglect by Ernest Daubrée. Miquel holds the contrary view that Ernest was overenthusiastic and encouraged by senior manager Bideau, which led to unplanned and unjustified growth. I have also drawn upon Georges Ribeill, 'Du pneumatique à la logistique routière', in *Culture Technique* (Neuilly s/Seine, Centre de Recherche sur la Culture Technique, 19 March 1989), pp. 191–204 (and Ribeill in turn had drawn upon Michelin archives).

5   Dumond, *Etude d'une main d'oeuvre*, p. 15.

6   *Le Temps*, 18 June 1870. This would be the Musée Adrien-Dubouché, named for its benefactor, who became mayor of Limoges in the year of Jules Michelin's death. (Today's *Guide Michelin* gives this museum two stars.)

7   Alain Jemain, *Michelin: Un siècle de secrets* (Paris, Calmann-Lévy, 1982), p. 30.

8   Ribeill, 'Du pneumatique', p. 192.

Notes on Chapter 4

1   Adolphe Joanne, *France: Auvergne-Morvan* (Paris, Hachette, 1880), p. 167. The population of Clermont-Ferrand is given in this volume as 41,772.

2   Apparently 'The Silent' was the invention of a Michelin employee at Clermont-Ferrand: Edouard Michelin, *Quelques Notes d'Edouard Michelin recueillies de 1919 à 1939* (Clermont-Ferrand, 1940), conférence no 12; Dumond, 'L'Arrière-Plan Technique et Commercial', in André Gueslin et al., *Michelin, les hommes du pneu* (Paris, Editions de l'Atelier, 1993), p. 13. André Michelin would have liked consumers to believe that his brake shoe came from Britain. See the wording of one of his advertisements for 'the new brake shoe "The Silent" (…), already well known in England', *Michelin Magazine* 583, April–May 1989 ('Rubrique d'un siècle' no 1).

Another advertisement stresses that the brake shoe was protected by patent in the United States as well as Britain, Italy, Spain, Austria, Switzerland...

3   Dumond, 'L'Arrière-Plan technique', p. 13.

4   Edouard Michelin, *Quelques Notes*, conférence no 12, 6 April 1928. See also *Edouard Michelin (1859–1940)* (Clermont-Ferrand, Michelin, 1940), unnumbered pages.

5   *Michelin Magazine* 583, April–May 1989 ('Rubrique d'un siècle' no 2).

6   'Le 60e Samedi de Michelin', *L'Illustration*, 26 June 1920.

7   From René Miquel's version in *Dynastie Michelin*, pp. 41, 366–67.

8   'Le 60e Samedi de Michelin: La genèse du pneu', *L'Illustration*, 26 June 1920.

9   All such equivalents must be considered broad approximations; economists agree that there is no reliable conversion table.

10 From Jemain, *Michelin*, p. 31 (quoting Edouard Michelin's grandson François, born in 1940).

11 Edouard Michelin, *Quelques Notes,* conférence no 6, 18 September 1925. Cf. *Edouard Michelin (1859–1940)*, 'L'Apprentissage du métier de patron'.

Notes on Chapter 5

1   In *Edouard Michelin (1859–1940),* (Clermont-Ferrand, Michelin, 1940).

2   Jemain, *Michelin*, p. 32.

3   *Michelin Magazine* 583, April–May 1989 ('Rubrique d'un siècle' no 1).

4   James M. Laux, *The European Automobile Industry* (New York, Twayne, 1992), pp. 8–9.

5   This is the version published only three decades after the event, most probably in the words of Edouard's brother André, responsible for publicity (and inventor of the best Michelin promotional material of his lifetime): 'Le 61e Samedi de Michelin: Le Grand Pierre et le Petit Père des démontables', *L'Illustration*, 3 July 1920.

6   *Edouard Michelin (1859–1940)*, 'Invention du pneu démontable'.

7   'Une invention d'avenir', *Michelin Magazine* 584 ('Rubrique d'un siècle' no 2).

8   'Le 62e Samedi de Michelin: Une course historique', *L'Illustration*, 10 July 1920.

9   *Edouard Michelin (1859–1940)*, 'Le Course Paris-Brest et Retour'; *Revue du Sport Vélocipédique* 419, 18 September 1891, from *Michelin Magazine* 584, June–July 1989.

10 Reproduced in *Edouard Michelin (1859–1940)*, unnumbered pages. See also Ribeill, *'Du pneumatique'*, pp. 192–93.

11 *Edouard Michelin (1859–1940)*, ibid.; 'Le Lundi de Michelin', *L'Auto-Vélo* (Paris), 18 March 1901; Dumond, 'L'Arrière-Plan Technique', in Gueslin et al., *Michelin*, p. 14.

12 Ribeill, *'Du pneumatique'*, p. 193.

13 *Mémoires de la Société des ingénieurs civils de France*, 1893, quoted in Ribeill, *'Du pneumatique'*, p. 193; 'Le Lundi de Michelin: La Fortune d'un mot', *Le*

Journal, 24 January 1910. Cf. 'Le 57e Samedi de Michelin: Un mot historique', *L'Illustration*, 5 June 1920.

14 'Lundi de Michelin: Par Bonds et par Vaux!', *Le Journal* (Paris), 16 December 1907.

Notes on Chapter 6

1   *Rubber and Plastics News* (Akron, Ohio) 22 August 1988, pp. 13–14, 16; Jemain, *Michelin*, pp. 34–35, 53–54.

2   'Le Lundi de Michelin: Histoire du pneu', *Le Journal* (Paris) 30 March 1908. Fifty-five years later Michelin was still singing the praises of the English pioneer: 'Thomson avait tout prévu', *Bib-Revue: Bulletin intérieur Michelin* (Clermont-Ferrand) 349, 6 December 1963.

3   'Le Lundi de Michelin', *Le Journal*, 22 November 1909.

4   Dumont, 'L'Arrière-plan Technique', pp. 11, 19, 23; 'Progression des Ventes des Pneus Michelin', *Michelin Magazine* 584, June–July 1989 ('Rubrique d'un siècle' no 2).

5   *Le Cycle* (Paris), December 31, 1892, quoted in Dumond, '*L'Arrière-plan Technique*', p. 17.

6   Dumont, '*L'Arrière-plan Technique*', pp. 17–19.

7   Revue du Sport Vélocipedique (Paris) 457, 458, June 10 and 17, 1892, reprinted in *Michelin Magazine* 584, June–July 1989 ('Rubrique d'un siècle' no 2).

8   Jemain, *Michelin*, pp. 39–40.

9   *Revue du Sport Vélocipedique*, ibid.

10 The source is the official company history: Michelin Informations Presse, *Historique* (Paris, 1989).

11 'Le Lundi de Michelin: Le Pneu a Sauvé le Fiacre', *Le Journal*, 4 May 1908.

12 *Le Petit Journal* (Paris), 11 February 1896.

13 Paper presented by André Michelin to Congrès international d'automobilisme, 1903, p. 352, cited in Dumond, *L'Arrière-plan Technique*, p. 22; Dumond, *Étude d'une main-d'oeuvre*, p. 26.

14 Michelin, *Historique*.

15 Jemain, *Michelin*, p. 42. In this version, Edouard Michelin is the doubter, André all in favour of investing in tyres for automobiles. Ibid., p. 47. In fact, as Maximilien Gerber reported in 1908, the doubters were the manufacturers of automobiles themselves.

16 James M. Laux, 'Genése d'une révolution', in Jean-Pierre Bardou et al, *La Révolution automobile* (Paris, Albin Michel, 1977), pp. 18–23, 28–29. Cf. Jacques Wolgensinger, *André Citroën* (Paris, Flammarion, 1991), pp. 61–63.

17 'Le Lundi de Michelin', *Le Journal*, 22 November 1910.

Notes on Chapter 7

1 Pierre Dumont, *Peugeot d'hier et d'avant-hier* (Paris, Edifree, 1983), p.24; Alain Jemain, *Les Peugeot* (Paris, Lattès, 1987), p.29.
2 Paris-Bordeaux, which took place on 11 June 1895, was the second recorded race in the annals of the automobile. *Rubber and Plastic News*, 22 August 1988, p.48.
3 'Le Lundi de Michelin', *L'Auto-Vélo*, 18 March 1901.
4 Flier, in *Michelin Magazine* 584, June–July 1989.
5 Ribeill, *Du pneumatique*, pp.193–94.
6 'Le Lundi de Michelin', *Le Journal*, 22 November 1910.
7 Dumond, *L'Arrière-plan technique*, pp.23, 30–33, 50; Dumond, *Etude d'une main-d'oeuvre*, p.119.
8 Miquel, *Dynastie Michelin*, p.378.

Notes on Chapter 8

1 Dumond, *L'Arrière-Plan Technique*, p.22.
2 Capt. Antoine Champeaux, 'Michelin et l'aviation', *Revue Historique des Armées* (Paris) 196, March 1995, p.33.
3 Dumond, *L'Arrière-Plan Technique*, pp.22–23.
4 Dumond, *L'Arrière-Plan Technique*, p.50.
5 Gueslin, *The Système Social Michelin*, pp.93–95. Gueslin notes that the original plan withheld retirement fund pay-outs for five years, reduced to three years in 1901. Michelin's labour contracts, as will be seen, maintained the five-year pledge not to work for competitors in rubber (or even to operate one's own rubber business).
6 *La France Automobile* (Paris), 3 December 1898, p.412.
7 Miquel, *Dynastie Michelin*, p.46.
8 Ribeill, *Du pneumatique*, p.194; *L'Illustration*, 5 June 1920, 'Le 57e Samedi de Michelin: Un mot historique'. Cf. Jemain, *Michelin*, p.57.
9 P. Datz, *Histoire de la Publicité* (Paris, J. Rothschild, 1894). For a useful overview, see the chronologie in Philippe Schuwer, *Histoire de la Publicité* (Genève, Rencontre, 1965). Cf. Stephen Fox, *The Mirror Makers: A History of American Advertising and its Creators* (New York, Morrow, 1984), pp.38–39.
10 From the history of Coca-Cola on the company's own web site. Coca-Cola's slogans became more pungent in the 1920s ('Thirst Knows No Season', 'The Pause that Refreshes').

Notes on Chapter 9

1 'Les Guides et les Cartes Michelin', *Bulletin Intérieur Michelin* (Clermont-Ferrand), 20 June 1946, reproduced in Antoine Champeaux, *Les Guides illustrés Michelin des Champs de Bataille (1914–1918)*, Thesis, Université de Paris IV-Sorbonne, 1984, p.132.

2   *L'Auto-Vélo*, 8 July 1901.

3   *L'Auto-Vélo*, 22 July 1901.

4   *L'Auto-Vélo*, 27 May, 3 June, 1901. Sometime later a Michelin 'Monday' quoted the president of Dunlop in the affirmation that Michelin made the best tyres money could buy. 'Le Lundi de Michelin: Suum Cuique', *Le Journal* (Paris), 22 November 1909. For more on the tyre wars: Jemain, *Michelin*, p. 56; Martin, *Trois siècles de publicité*, p. 184.

5   *L'Auto-Vélo*, 17 March 1902.

6   *L'Auto-Vélo*, 21 July 1902.

7   Ibid. [*L'Auto-Vélo*, 17 February 1902]. As Paris dailies went, the circulation of *L'Auto-Vélo* was still modest; only after the first Tour de France in June–July 1903 would it reach 50,000 copies (it would take some years before it sold 100,000). *Histoire Générale de la Presse Française*, III, pp. 383–84.

8   *L'Auto-Velo*, 8 December 1902. In a subsequent Monday, Michelin nevertheless praised the exhibition, claimed first place in automobiles for French industry, and observed that even if Michelin lacked a stand, 95 out of 127 exhibitors put Michelin tyres on their vehicles; 51 of them showed no other brand. *L'Auto-Vélo*, 22 December 1902.

9   The court's judgment, delivered in April 1914, is discussed in chapter 17.

Notes on Chapter 10

1   See Chapter 9.

2   *L'Illustration*, 3 January 1903.

3   *Encyclopaedia Britannica*, 11th edition, (Cambridge, Cambridge University Press, 1910–11), III, article 'Motor Vehicles'. 'France is the centre of the motor-car industry in Europe, and up to the year 1906 it undoubtedly led in the production of motor vehicles, but in that year the United States of America... took the lead.'

4   Dumond, *L'Arrière-Plan Technique*, pp. 23, 49–50. In 1905 Michelin was the largest consumer of rubber in France. Ibid., p. 26.

5   Dumond, *Etude d'une main-d'oeuvre*, 122–23. See also Gueslin, *Le Système Social Michelin*, p. 83.

6   Miquel, *Dynastie Michelin*, pp. 19–20.

7   Gueslin, *Le Système Social Michelin*, p. 84.

8   Miquel, *Dynastie Michelin*, p. 18.

9   *L'Illustration*, 23 and 30 May 1903.

10   *L'Auto-Vélo*, 1 June 1903.

11   *L'Auto-Vélo*, 28 December 1903.

12   *L'Auto*, 19 September 1904.

13   *L'Auto*, 12 December 1904.

14   *L'Auto-Vélo*, 17 August 1903.

15   *L'Auto-Vélo*, 6 June 1904.

16   *L'Auto*, 18 July 1904.

17   *L'Auto*, 9 October 1905.

Notes on Chapter 11

1   Dumond, *Etude d'une main-d'oeuvre*, pp. 264–65.
2   *L'Ami du Peuple* (Clermont-Ferrand), 27 November 1904.
3   *L'Ami du Peuple*, 4 December 1904.
4   *L'Ami du Peuple*, 11 December 1904.
5   *L'Ami du Peuple*, 1 January 1905.

Notes on Chapter 12

1   Dumond, *L'Arrière-Plan Technique*, p. 31. Michelin's headquarters were on Sussex Place in South Kensington, London; *Encyclopaedia Britannica*, op. cit., p. 919.
2   Urbain Vedel, 'Michelin, premier géant de la publicité', *La Montagne* (Clermont-Ferrand), 22 March 1991. In 'Sir Galahad' by Alfred, Lord Tennyson, the original phrase is 'Because my heart is pure'.
3   Pierre-Gabriel Gonzalez, *Bibendum: Publicité et Objets Michelin* (Paris, Editions du Collectionneur, 1995), p. 8; Vedel, in *La Montagne*, 21 March 1991.
4   From a Michelin advertisement in *L'Auto*, 9 October 1905. But the un-polished text suggests that this may have been a project rather than a poster actually used in the Michelin overseas sales effort.
5   *L'Auto*, 6 February, 22 May 1905; advertisement for *Guide Michelin* 1905 in *Lectures pour Tous* reproduced in Martin, *Trois Siècles de Publicité en France*, 184.
6   *Guide Michelin Belgique, Hollande* 1908, p. 11; *Michelin Guide to France 1908*, which bore a 2/- (two shilling) price, and the addresses of the Michelin Tyre Co. Ltd in London and the Michelin Tire Company in Milltown, New Jersey, in the United States.
7   Information on dates of the first editions of foreign guide-books from Goulven Guilcher.
8   *Michelin Magazine* 585, August–September 1989 ('Rubrique d'un siècle' no 3).
9   *L'Auto*, 1 May 1905.
10 Reproduced in Marc Martin, *Trois siècles de publicité en France* (Paris, Odile Jacob, 1992), p. 185.
11 *L'Auto*, 10 July 1905.
12 *Michelin Magazine* 585, August–September 1989 ('Rubrique d'un siècle' no 3).
13 'Une Nouveauté Automobile', *L'Illustration*, 7 July 1906.
14 Louis Baudry de Saunier, 'Le Salon de l'Automobile', *L'Illustration*, 15 December 1906.
15 *L'Illustration*, 5 June 1920.
16 Clermont-Ferrand, 1906.
17 *Guide Michelin* 1909, pp. 648–49.
18 *Le Caoutchouc et la Gutta-Percha* (Paris) 46, 15 December 1907, pp. 1570, 1575.

19 Laux, *Genèse d'une révolution*, p.38. France remained the leading motorcar maker and exporter in Europe, producing 25,000 vehicles in 1907, twice as many as the runner-up, the United Kingdom. Jemain, *Michelin*, pp.55–56.

20 *Le Caoutchouc et la Gutta-Percha* (Paris) 45, 15 November 1907, p.1498. The Michelin Tire Co. was incorporated by L. Semple, J.E. Hopkins and J.P. Murray. *India Rubber Review* (Akron OH), 15 April 1907, p.171.

21 Murray, *India Rubber Review* (Akron OH), 15 April 1907, p.140.

22 *The Rubber Age and Tire News* (New York), 25 August 1917, p.447.

23 H. Rodney Luery, *The Story of Milltown* (Cranbury NJ, A.S. Barnes, 1971), pp.98–100; This work was brought to our attention by Christine F. Reed, director of the Milltown Public Library. See also Jerry Cheslow, 'A Factory Blue Collar Town is Fading', *The New York Times*, 14 September 1997. Cheslow says that Michelin in the best years employed nearly 3000.

24 *Rubber Age and Tire News*, 25 August 1917, p.447.

25 Luery, *Story of Milltown*, ibid.; *Rubber Age and Tire News*, ibid.

26 Luery, *Story of Milltown*, ibid.

Notes on Chapter 13

1   Apparently the world's first pneumatic tyre for aircraft was made in 1908 by the United States Rubber Company, later to become Uniroyal, a company later acquired by Michelin. *Rubber and Plastic News*, 22 August 1988, p.28.

2   Gilbert Hatry, 'L'Exploit d'Eugène Renaux', *Bulletin de la Section d'Histoire des usines Renault* (Boulogne-Billancourt) 7 December 1973, pp.254–55.

3   *L'Aurore* (Paris), 8 March 1908.

4   Jules Mercier, 'Les Prix d'aviation (1908–1914)', *Icare, Cahiers de l'Aviation* (Paris-Orly) 28 December 1963, pp.69–70.

5   André and Edouard Michelin, *Notre Sécurité est dans l'Air* (Paris, Michelin, 1919), pp.4–5.

6   *Le Journal*, 9 March 1908. The prizes were justified in more or less the same terms in another Michelin 'Monday' on 17 August in the same newspaper.

7   Mercier, 'Les Prix d'aviation', p.70.

8   *Les Sports* (Paris) 1 January 1909. See also *L'Illustration*, 5 August and 26 September 1908.

9   Mercier, *Les Prix Michelin*, p.70. Farman won the Coupe Michelin 1909 with 234 kilometres flown in 4 hours 17 minutes.

10 *Le Journal*, 24 February 1908.

11 *Le Journal*, 20 April 1908. A subsequent Monday column pointed out that Michelin no longer solicited advertising from repair shops either. *Le Journal*, 27 April 1908.

12 *Le Journal*, 6 July 1908.

13 *Le Journal*, 10 August 1908. The certification indicates a total printing of 60,900 copies.

14 *Le Journal*, 14 March 1910.

15 *Le Journal*, 10 May 1909.

16 *Le Journal*, 28 June 1909.

17 Champeaux, *Michelin et l'aviation*, p. 34.
18 *Le Journal*, 18 October 1909. Michelin returned to the offensive in the same newspaper on 14 February 1910.
19 *Le Journal*, 4 October 1909.

Notes on Chapter 14

1   Gueslin, *Le Système Social Michelin*, p. 98.
2   *Edouard Michelin (1859–1940)*, 'Les Cités', (Clermont-Ferrand, Michelin, 1940).
3   Christian Lamy and Jean-Pierre Fornaro, Michelin-Ville: *Le Logement ouvrier dans l'entreprise (1911–1987)* (Nonette, Créer, 1990), pp. 183–84.
4   Lamy et Fornaro, *Michelin-Ville*, p. 184; Gueslin, *Le Système Social Michelin*, pp. 101–102.
5   *Oeuvres sociales de Michelin et Cie* (Clermont-Ferrand, Michelin, 1927), p. 13.
6   Lamy and Fornaro, *Michelin-Ville*, p. 22.
7   Lamy and Fornaro, *Michelin-Ville*, pp. 45–46, 67–70, 125–27.
8   André Gueslin, 'Introduction', in Gueslin et al., *Michelin*, pp. 7–8.
9   Lamy-Fornaro, *Michelin-Ville*, p. 175.
10 Gueslin, *Le Système Social Michelin*, pp. 96–97.
11 *Les Advantages dont vous pourrez profiter chez Michelin* (Clermont-Ferrand, Michelin, 1948), pp. 2–3.
12 *L'Ami du Peuple*, 20 May, 1909; *Bulletin de la Bourse du Travail de Clermont-Ferrand*, 20 June 1909, both quoted from Dumond, *Etude d'une main-d'oeuvre*, pp. 266–68.
13 Gueslin, *Le Système Social Michelin*, pp. 100–101.
14 *Le Journal*, 28 March 1910.
15 *Guide Michelin* 1910, pp. 649–51.
16 *Le Journal*, 10 January 1910, 31 July 1911. The same map printed on canvas sold at 2 francs. In 'Michelin et la Route', op. cit., pp. 47–48, Alain Arnaud observes that the description of the actual condition of roads – their real width and type of surfacing – was unique, while many of the conventional symbols introduced then are still in use today.
    It was also in 1910 that Michelin began donating signs to be placed at town entrances, e.g., 'Please slow down – AUTUN. Watch for children.' Each bore the identification 'Gift of Michelin', and by the end of 1911 10,000 French towns were utilizing them. *Le Journal*, 25 December 1911.

Notes on Chapter 15

1   Hatry, 'L'Exploit d'Eugène Renaux', 255, *L'Illustration*, 8 October 1910.
2   H. Bergeron, 'Chronique Aéronautique', *Le Monde illustré* (Paris), 11 March 1911, pp. 156–57.
3   Marcel Viollette, 'Le Vainqueur du Puy de Dôme', *La Vie au Grand Air* (Paris), 18 March 1911, p. 166. Rather than a rotary engine of the kind

utilized in most races, Renaux's Farman biplane used a Renault eight-cylinder air-cooled motor.

4   *L'Illustration*, 11 March 1911.
5   8 March 1911.
6   Mercier, 'Les Prix Michelin d'aviation', p.71.
7   Champeaux, 'Michelin et l'aviation', pp.33–34; Mercier, 'Les Prix Michelin d'aviation', p.73.
8   Miquel, *Dynastie Michelin*, p.383.
9   [André Michelin,] *Notre Avenir est dans l'Air* [Paris, Michelin, 1912], p.2.
10 [André] Michelin, *Notre Securité est dans l'Air* [Paris, Michelin, 1919], p.5. Michelin explains that the experience that day confirmed what the brothers already knew about German industrial potential – thanks to their Frankfurt subsidiary.
11 Champeaux, 'Michelin et l'aviation', p.34. Commenting on the Michelin bombing prize, the *Revue d'Artillerie* had conceded that information was then lacking on the practical effects of a projectile launched from an aeroplane – with or without an explosive charge. *Prix de l'Aéro-Cible Michelin*, Paris: Librairie Militaire Berger-Levrault: 1913, pp.3–4.
12 As a finale, André prints a letter of congratulations said to be from the wife of a Michelin worker. 'They do sing silly things on payday, but they are patriots all the same. They'd all like to go up in aeroplanes': *Le Journal*, 28 August 1911.
13 'Bibendum en Bombe', *Le Journal*, 18 December 1911.
14 *Le Matin*, 6 December 1911, quoted in Champeaux, 'Michelin et l'Aviation', p.36.
15 Doug Nye, 'Mr. Michelin's Remarkable Building', *Road and Track* (New York), April 1978, pp.142–44.
16 *Le Journal*, 23 January 1911.
17 *Le Journal*, 13 March 1911.
18 *Le Journal*, 31 July 1911.
19 Gueslin, 'Le Système Social Michelin', p.107; *Michelin Magazine* 586, October–November 1989 ('Rubrique d'un siècle' no4).
20 Bulletin de la Bourse du Travail (Clermont-Ferrand), March 20, 1911, quoted in Dumond, 'Etude d'une main-d'oeuvre', p.266.
21 *Le Journal*, 18 September 1911. In a Monday column promoting twin tyres Michelin reported that 20 ten- to 12-passenger buses in Italy used Michelin twins for intercity transport, as did a hundred trucks or delivery vehicles in the United States, Mexico, and Brazil (among them the *New York Herald* delivery trucks). But they also equipped the limousines of both the queen mother of Italy and the Russian czar. *Le Journal*, 11 December 1911.

Notes on Chapter 16

1 Michelin, *Notre Avenir est dans l'air*, pp. 1–2, 40.
2 Champeaux, 'Michelin et l'aviation', pp. 36–37.
3 'Gare dessous!', *Le Journal*, 19 August 1912; Mercier, 'Les Prix Michelin de l'aviation', p. 73.
4 *Le Journal*, 7 July 1913; *Michelin Magazine* 586, October–November 1989.
5 *Le Journal*, 22 April 1912.
6 *Le Journal*, 27 May 1912.
7 *Le Journal*, 17 June 1912.
8 *Le Journal*, 29 April 1912. By then 30,000 place name signs had been distributed: *Le Journal*, 13 May 1912.
9 *Circular*, 10 August 1912. The court concluded that the French Continental Company had been founded solely to import German tyres and to efface indications of their origin.
10 F. Honoré, *L'Illustration*, 8 June 1912.
11 *Le Journal*, 2 September, 14 October 1912.
12 Ribeill, 'Du pneumatique', p. 198.
13 *Le Journal*, 28 October 1912.
14 *Le Journal*, 16 December 1912.
15 *Le Journal*, 28 April, 5 May, and 14 July 1913; Arnaud, 'Michelin et la route', p. 48.
16 *Le Journal*, 23 December 1912; *Michelin Magazine* 586, October–November 1989.

Notes on Chapter 17

1 Yves Essarovitch, 'François Michelin: L'Obsession du secret', *Le Figaro* (Paris), 1 August 1994.
2 Gueslin, 'Le Système Social Michelin', p. 112.
3 'Les scandales de l'Usine Michelin', *L'Ami du Peuple*, 17 November 1912, quoted in Dumond, 'Etude d'une main d'oeuvre', p. 265.
4 Dumond, 'Etude d'une main-d'oeuvre', pp. 268–69.
5 Aimée Moutet, 'Les origines du système de Taylor en France: Le point de vue patronal (1907–1914)', *Le Mouvement Social* (Paris) 93, October–December 1975, pp. 15–49. Taylor's work had been introduced to France by an engineering professor, Henri Le Chatelier, who founded *La Revue de Metallurgie* at the beginning of the century and published some of Taylor's essential papers in translation: Frederick Winslow Taylor, *A Memorial Volume* (New York, Taylor Society, 1920), pp. 16–21.
6 Dumond, 'L'Arrière Plan Technique', pp. 49–51.
7 Dumond, 'L'Arrière Plan Technique', p. 51 n. 206, quoting P. Fridenson, *Histoire des Usines Renault* I (Paris, 1972), p. 65, who gives Renault's turnover for that year as 57 million francs.
8 *Le Journal*, 31 March 1913; Mercier, 'Les Prix Michelin d'aviation', p. 72. With a very visible presence in the United Kingdom. Michelin now

sponsored British cups as well; one, a distance prize, was taken by a pilot flying 315 miles on a given course; another was a prize for maximum speed – not won in 1913.

9 *Le Journal*, 14 April 1913.

10 *Le Journal*, 16 June 1913, 20 April 1914.

11 Curnonsky [Maurice-Edmond Sailland], *Souvenirs littéraires et gastronomiques* (Paris, Albin Michel, 1958), p.53. The style of the one available Monday column signed 'Curnonsky' is quite unlike those signed Michelin or Bibendum in this period.

12 *Le Journal*, 22 December 1913.

13 *Le Journal*, 20 April 1914. On 9 July the judgment of the tribunal was confirmed on Continental's appeal: *Le Journal*, 13 July 1914.

14 Michelin et Cie, 'Le *Guide Michelin* est une oeuvre originale et ne peut être impunément plagié', courtesy of Goulven Guilcher.

Notes on Chapter 18

1 In fact the distribution was done in 1916. Champeaux, 'Michelin et l'aviation', p.37.

2 Michelin, *Notre Sécurité est dans l'Air* ([Paris], Michelin, 1919), p.9. A historian was to amend the figures given by André Michelin: in August 1914 the French had 162 planes of 11 types, divided into 27 flights. Champeaux, 'Michelin et l'aviation', p.36 n.18.

3 Champeaux, 'Michelin et l'aviation', pp.37–38.

4 Michelin, *Notre Sécurité est dans l'air*, pp.10–12.

5 Champeaux, 'Michelin et l'aviation', pp.36–39. Captain Champeaux dismisses allegations made at the time that the Breguets were unreliable or dangerous to fly. Criticism of the plane actually appeared in the press during the war – which was especially prejudicial to pilot morale.

6 Michelin, *Michelin pendant la guerre (1914–1917)* (Paris, Michelin, 1917); Dumond, 'Etude d'une main-d'oeuvre', pp.302–4; Champeaux, 'Les Guides illustrés Michelin des champs de bataille', pp.61–62; Gueslin, 'Le Système Social Michelin', pp.110–12. Gueslin cites a Michelin brochure of 1926 whose title is explicit: *A Birth-Rate Experiment: Can we have more children in France? Results obtained at Michelin permit the reply: Yes!*

7 Dumond, 'L'Arrière-Plan Technique', p.52.

8 Miquel, *Dynastie Michelin*, p.385.

9 The author is grateful to Captain Antoine Champeaux for making this brochure available.

10 Antoine Champeaux, 'Michelin et l'Aviation de Bombardement (1911–1916)', in *L'Emergence des armes nouvelles* (Actes du Colloque organisé pour le 80e anniversaire de Verdun), 25 October 1996 (Paris, Economica), pp.89–110

11 Michelin, *Notre Sécurité est dans l'air*, pp.12–27; Champeaux, 'Michelin et l'aviation', pp.37–44.

12 Dumond, 'Etude d'une main d'oeuvre', p.302.

13 Collection of the author.

14 Dumond, 'Etude d'une main-d'oeuvre', pp. 300–1; Dumond, 'L'Arrière-plan technique', p. 53.

Notes on Chapter 19

1   For the opportunity to examine these guide-books, and useful discussion of their purpose, the author is grateful to Jacques Salles and Goulven Guilcher. Note that the German volume contains a conversion table of marks into francs – and the francs are Swiss francs; an introduction to the table indicates that 'at the end of April 1915' the mark had dropped 12 percent – presumably from the values given in the Michelin table – at the Swiss post office. (p. 529)

2   There is simply a notice to the effect that the information contained in the book was obtained from German public sources.

3   In his thesis, Antoine Champeaux says that he found no supporting evidence of this, although he discovered that André Michelin's tourist information specialist, Fernand Gillet, served in an official propaganda action centre beginning immediately after the Armistice (which does not tell us what Gillet was doing at the time André was planning the new guide-books in 1916). Antoine Champeaux, 'Les Guides illustrés Michelin des champs de bataille (1914–1918)' (Paris, Université de Paris IV [Sorbonne], 1984), p. 22.

4   Michelin, *L'Ourcq*, p. 16.

5   Michelin, *Champs de Bataille de la Marne*, II, *Les Marais de Saint-Gond* (Paris: Berger-Levrault, 1917; reprinted 1920).

6   Michelin, *Rheims and the Battles for its Possession* (London, Michelin, 1919).

7   Michelin, *Nos Champs de Bataille* (Paris, Berger-Levrault, 1917), pp. 8–10, 15–19, reprinted in Champeaux, 'Les Guides illustrés Michelin des champs de bataille', pp. 173–82. Champeaux also cites (p. 60) a draft brochure in which André Michelin identifies the alleged German rival as Baedeker, publisher of multilingual guide-books since 1836. At the end of the war André Michelin considered writing a flyer in English to discourage purchase of Baedeker guides and to promote the Michelin (Champeaux, p. 53).

8   Champeaux, 'Les Guides illustrés Michelin des champs de bataille', pp. 165–72.

9   Clermont-Ferrand, *Michelin*, October 1918.

10 The copy seen by the writer in the New York Public Library bears the name of an American sergeant, who obviously took it home with him from France.

Notes on Chapter 20

1   Jemain, *Michelin*, p. 104.

2   Ribeill, 'Du pneumatique', p. 200.

3   Dumond, 'L'Arrière-Plan Technique', pp. 36–43, 53–54.

4   Edouard Michelin, *Quelques Notes*, no 1.

5   *Edouard Michelin (1859–1940)*, 'Les Allocations Familiales'.

6 Michelin, *Notre Sécurité est dans l'air*, pp. 35–38.
7 *L'Illustration*, 19 April 1919, advertising section, p. 12. The magazine was then selling 110,000 copies over the counter of each issue and another 90,000 by subscription.
8 *L'Illustration*, 3 May 1919, advertising section, p. 8.
9 'Le Quatrième samedi touriste de Michelin: En éclaireur', *L'Illustration*, 10 May 1919, advertising section, p. 9.
10 Michelin, *Notre Sécurité est dans l'air*, pp. 38–44.

Notes on Chapter 21

1 Information from Goulven Guilcher. Cf. *Guide Michelin* 1920.
2 Ribeill, 'Du pneumatique', pp. 200–1.
3 Dumond, 'L'Arrière-plan technique', pp. 54–55; Gueslin, 'Le Système Social Michelin', pp. 102, 127–34. Gueslin, no apologist for Michelin, offers evidence that Michelin wages were higher than the provincial average in 1920. Ibid., p. 99.
4 Dumond, 'L'Arrière-plan technique', pp. 55–56.
5 *L'Illustration*, 19 March 1921, inside back cover advertisement. In the same article Michelin announces distribution of a brochure on 'the case of the European vs. the American rim'.
6 Dumond, 'L'Arrière-plan technique', pp. 43–44.
7 *Michelin Magazine* 587, December 1989–January 1990.
8 Edmond Petit, *La Vie quotidienne dans l'aviation* (Paris, Hachette, 1977), pp. 146–47.

Notes on Chapter 22

1 Charles Faroux, 'Le Salon français de 1921', *L'Illustration*, 8 October 1921.
2 Jacques Wolgensinger, *André Citroën* (Paris, Flammarion, 1991), esp. pp. 17–23, 67–68, 93–95, 129, 266–67, 272.
3 Wolgensinger, *André Citroën*, pp. 205–8; Jean-Louis Loubet, 'Les trois France de l'automobile', *Enjeu* (Paris) October 1996, p. 146.
4 Wolgensinger, *André Citroën*, pp. 273.
5 Jacques Wolgensinger, *La 2CV: Nous nous sommes tant aimés* (Paris, Gallimard-Découvertes, 1995), pp. 13–15.
6 The police report is dated March 1923: Gueslin, 'Le Système social Michelin', p. 99.
7 *Rubber and Plastics News*, 2 August 1988, p. 28.
8 Reproduced in *Journal des anciens, publication destinée aux retraités et préretraitees Michelin* (Clermont-Ferrand), March 1995, p. 4.
9 *Michelin Magazine* 587, December 1989–January 1990.
10 Ibid.
11 *L'Echo de Paris, Le Danger Aérien allemand, Discours prononcés à la Sorbonne le 31 Octobre 1923* (Paris: L'Echo de Paris, 1923), pp. 36–48.

Notes on Chapter 23

1 The year is given as 1926 in 'Une Histoire passionante', a chronology published by Michelin's own travel department, presumably because this was the year that recommended hotel restaurants received a star.

2 *Guide Michelin* France 1925, p. 9. Another misconception is that restaurants (outside Paris) first received two and three stars for good food in 1931. Their food had of course been judged under a five-tier star system since 1925. In 1930 the five-tier star system for good restaurants was given up, and recommended restaurants were graded only by comfort, while hotel restaurants were graded with one, two or three stars for their kitchens. Only in 1932 was the three-star system as we know it inaugurated in the provinces, broadened to include Paris the following year.

3 Julian Street, *Where Paris Dines* (New York, Doubleday, Doran, 1929), pp. 28, 30, 41.

4 *Guide Michelin* France 1925, 8, 10.

5 *Guide Michelin* France 1925, 276.

6 *Guide Michelin* France 1938, p. 11. In the most recent Michelin guide-books the formulations 'Excellent cooking, worth a detour' and 'Exceptional cuisine, worth a special journey' are still utilized.

7 This in the second edition of *Guides Michelin Régionaux: Auvergne*, dated 1932–33, thus after the introduction of the simplified star system – for hotels only – in the 1931 *Guide Michelin* for France.

8 From Services de Tourisme Michelin.

9 *Bulletin Intérieur Michelin*, 20 June 1946, reproduced in Champeaux, *Les Guides illustrés Michelin*, p. 133. See also Services de Tourisme Michelin, 'Une Histoire passionnante'.

Notes on Chapter 24

1 *Ce que l'auto coûte réellement – Les benéfices qu'elle procure* (Clermont-Ferrand, Michelin, 1924).

2 Dumond, 'L'Arrière-plan technique', pp. 55–56; *Rubber and Plastics News*, 2 August 1988, p. 75.

3 Edouard Michelin, 'Oeuvres sociales', in *Le Livre d'Or de l'Industrie de Caoutchouc* (Paris: Revue Générale de Caoutchouc, January 1927), pp. 59–63.

4 *Oeuvres Sociales de Michelin et Cie* (Clermont-Ferrand, Michelin, 1927).

5 Clermont-Ferrand, Michelin, 1927.

6 Edouard Michelin, *Quelques Notes*, no 15, 'Suggestions' (31 July 1928); *Michelin Magazine* 587, December 1989–January 1990.

7 Edouard Michelin, *Quelques Notes*, no 12 (April 6, 1928).

8 Edouard Michelin, *Quelques Notes*, no 13 (May 7, 1928).

Notes on Chapter 25

1   From table in Dumond, 'L'Arrière-plan Technique', p.62. See also p.59.
2   Dumond, 'L'Arrière-plan Technique', p.61.
3   Comité National d'Etudes Sociales et Politiques (Ministère de l'Air, Paris, 1929), *Séance du 21 Janvier 1929*. Communication d'André Michelin, pp.44–50.
4   Edouard Michelin, *Quelques Notes*, no18 (2 July 1929).
5   See also messages 19, 20 and 21 (9 August, 15 and 23 October 1929) in *Quelques Notes*.
6   *Micheline Magazine* 587, December 1989–January 1990; Jan P. Norbye, *The Michelin Magic* (Blue Ridge Summit PA, Tab Books, 1982), pp.19–24.
7   *Guide Michelin* 1929, opposite p.1023.
8   Clermont-Ferrand, Michelin, 1930. It was put on sale at 50 francs, and contained explanatory notes in English and German.
9   *Guide Michelin* France 1930.
10 Jean-Gabriel Fredet and Denis Pingaud, *Les Patrons face...la gauche* (Paris: Ramsay, 1982), 205.
11 In 1932 Michelin shareholders formerly put an end to the Michelin Tire Co. Dumond, 'L'Arrière-plan technique', 70.
12 Luery, Story of Milltown, 99–101. In our day, a real estate journalist tells us, 'many of the 200 sturdy company bungalows are still in use', most of them on Riva Avenue; they are now in the cheapest price category in the area. Cheslow, 'A Factory Town's Blue Collar is Fading'.
13 Figures from Chamber of Commerce and police reports in Panthou; L'Année 1936, 146–147.
14 Panthou, L'Année 1936, 148.
15 For example, in Gueslin, 'Le Système social Michelin', 135.
16 Edouard Michelin, *Quelques Notes*, no29 (3 October 1930).
17 Edouard Michelin, *Quelques Notes*, no31 (5 January 1931).
18 Edouard Michelin, *Quelques Notes*, no32 (7 May 1931).
19 See chapter XXVIII.
20 *Michelin Magazine* 588, February–March 1990.
21 *Michelin Magazine* 588 February–March 1990.
22 Michelin & Cie, *La Micheline 100 Places* (Clermont-Ferrand, 1936); Norbye, *Michelin Magic*, pp.21–22.

Notes on Chapter 26

1   G. de Lafrete, 'La mort de M. André Michelin', *L'Echo de Paris* (Paris), 5 April 1931.
2   *Guide Michelin* 1932 (opp. title page).
3   Miquel, *Dynastie Michelin*, p.49.
4   As published, for example, in a very authorized source, the Michelin company's *Edouard Michelin (1859–1940)*, '25 Août 1940'.
5   'La vraie figure de Michelin', *Le Cri du Peuple*, 20 August 1932.

6   The Michelin family's unofficial chronicler René Miquel calls him 'the heir apparent': *Dynastie Michelin*, p. 22.

7   *Le Temps* (Paris), 29 August, 1932. Another version of the accident is given by Jemain, *Michelin*, 81, who says that Etienne had obtained his pilot's licence in secret, and intended to enter the competition for the Prix Michelin; he was killed when a violent wind caught his Farman plane just after he touched down on the summit of the Puy-de-Dôme (some two-and-a-half miles from where *Le Temps* seems to place the crash). According to Jemain, Edouard Michelin then halted all encouragement to aviation; France would be even less prepared for air combat at the beginning of World War II than it was in August 1914.

8   Vernol, 'Etienne Michelin est mort: 'A genoux devant le Veau d'Or', *Le Cri du Peuple*, 3 September 1932.

9   *Edouard Michelin (1859–1940)*, '25 Août 1940'. In our day, only two descendants of André hold positions of significance in the family firm, grandchildren Bruno and Xavier Jeanson (André's daughter had married a Marcel Jeanson and they had nine children). All the other Michelins and their in-laws in top management descend from Edouard's line.

10 That is, the year when the gross national product was the lowest in that decade: see Henri Dubief, *Le Déclin de la IIIe République (1929–1938)* (Paris, Seuil, 1976), p. 20.

11 2 April 1932. Although Edouard Michelin had long resisted pay cuts as a means of dealing with the economic crisis (see the previous chapter), wages were indeed reduced at the height of the slump.

12 Donald Moffat, 'Le Tourisme and the "Guide Michelin"', *New Yorker*, 30 March 1935, pp. 44–50.

Notes on Chapter 27

1   Quoted in Wolgensinger, *André Citroën*, p. 234. See also James M. Laux, *The European Automobile Industry* (New York, Twayne, 1992), pp. 121–22.

2   Jacques Wolgensinger, *Citroën: Une vie à quitte ou double*, Paris, Arthaud, 1996, p. 146.

3   Wolgensinger, *André Citroën*, 243–44. Another source affirms that the parts supplier that took Citroën to court and thereby initiated the liquidation process had ties to Michelin, which suggested that Michelin saw liquidation and a new start as the best solution. Laux, *The European Automobile Industry*, p. 123.

4   Wolgensinger, *André Citroën*, pp. 245–47. Cf. Jemain, *Michelin*, pp. 83–89; Miquel, *Dynastie Michelin*, pp. 387–90.

5   Jemain, *Michelin*, p. 117.

6   Eric Panthou, *'L'Année 1936* dans le Puy-de-Dôme' (memoir, Université Blaise Pascal), in *Cahiers du Centre fédéral* (Paris, Fédération de l'Education Nationale, 1995), pp. 54–56, 75–77, 145–47, 272–73, 316.

7   Dubief, *Le Déclin*, p. 180.

8   Pol Echevin, *Echec au roi: Charles Tissier, 40 ans de combats*, Paris, Editions Ouvrières, 1985, pp. 22–23; *L'Humanité* (Paris, organ of the French Communist Party), 8 June 1936.

9   Panthou, *L'Année 1936*, p.173.
10 *La Montagne*, 16, 17, 18, 19, 20, 21 and 22 June 1936. See also Panthou, *L'Année 1936*, pp.192–93. The non-strikers were called 'foxes', and real foxes were burned in front of their houses. Panthou, *L'Année 1936*, p.179.
11 Echevin, *Echec au roi*, p.25.
12 Philippe Bourdrel, *La Cagoule* (Paris, Albin Michel, 1970), pp.181–85; Eugen Weber, *L'Action Française* (Paris, Stock, 1964), pp.437–39; translation by Michel Chrestien of Action Française (Stanford CA, Stanford University Press, 1962).
13 Bourdrel, *La Cagoule*, pp.184–85. See also the new revised and enlarged edition (Paris, Albin Michel, 1992), p.92. Cf. Henry Coston, *Partis, Journaux, et Hommes politiques* (Paris, Lectures Françaises, 1960), pp.133–37.
14 *L'Humanité* (Paris), 11 January 1938. *Le Temps*, 12 January, described Locuty as 'a bewildered young man'.
15 *L'Humanité*, 14 January 1938. The story names Marcel, but the context – an automobile accident – suggests that Pierre is meant. One of the arrested men, Gustave Vauclard, was according to another source in charge of 'special services' at the factory, a job not otherwise explained. *Le Temps*, 13 January 1938.
16 *L'Humanité*, 15, 16 and 20 January 1938.
17 *L'Humanité*, 21 January 1938.
18 *Le Temps*, 1 January 1938.
19 Wolgensinger, *La 2CV*, p.19. The arrests in the Cagoule plot would, as already indicated, take place within the fortnight. Later that year a book published by the Communists repeated rumours that documents found in the automobile of the dead Pierre Michelin had led to the arrests of the Michelin men involved in the Cagoule bombings. Fernand Fontenay, *La Cagoule contre la France* (Paris, Editions Sociales Internationales, 1938), p.72.
20 Miquel, *Dynastie Michelin*, pp.22–23.
21 *Edouard Michelin (1859–1940)*, '25 Août 1940'.

Notes on Chapter 28

1   Wolgensinger, *La 2CV*, second printing (edition no76767), pp.18–19. When the first edition of this book was published in November 1995 its author received a telephone call from François Michelin, who regretted that Pierre Michelin's role in developing the *deux chevaux* had been overlooked (actually the author, like other writers, had not been authorized to use Michelin archives). A second printing of *La 2CV* found room for this information. Talk with Jacques Wolgensinger. On the national survey for a people's car, see chapter 22 above.
2   Wolgensinger, *La 2CV*, pp.20–21.
3   *Bulletin Intérieur Michelin* 29, 20 June 1946, p.2.
4   Note de June 30, 1940 from Boulanger to Weygand, archives of Service Historique de l'Armée de Terre, quoted in Claude Paillat, *Dossiers secrets de*

la France contemporain, VI, L'Occupation: Le Pillage de la France (Paris, Laffont, 1987), pp. 81–82.

5 Antoine Barrière, *Michelin vu de l'intérieur* (63340 Nonette, Créer, 1983), p. 42. Pétain, who was to be responsible for the fate of France in confrontation with Adolf Hitler, was already 84 years old.

6 Robert Aron, *Histoire de Vichy* (Paris, Fayard, 1954), pp. 95–96.

7 John F. Sweets, *Choices in Vichy France: The French under Nazi Occupation* (New York, Oxford University Press, 1986), pp. 4–5.

8 Edouard Michelin, *Quelques Notes*, no 37, 1 February 1939.

9 Jemain, *Michelin*, p. 103; Miquel, *Dynastie Michelin*, p. 53; Pascal Galinier, 'Les Héritiers: Edouard Michelin', *Le Nouvel Economiste* (Paris) 1005, 13 July 1995, p. 36.

10 *Bulletin Intérieur Michelin*, June 1945; Miquel, *Dynastie Michelin*, pp. 50–55.

11 Jemain, *Michelin*, p. 129, who adds that Pierre Boulanger's name was found on a Gestapo list of individuals considered dangerous to the Reich, while his deputy Pierre Bercot was actually arrested and jailed by the Gestapo after objecting to the transfer of giant presses to Germany.

12 Wolgensinger, *La 2 CV*, pp. 22–26.

13 'Le pneu Michelin radial', *Michelin Magazine*, June 1966, pp. 2–9; Norbye, *Michelin Magic*, pp. 34–40; Informations Presse (Michelin), Mondial de l'Auto (Paris, October 1996).

Notes on Chapter 29

1 From letters sent by Michelin & Co. to the Ministry of National Defence, 5 and 10 July 1940, archives of the Service Historique de l'Armée de Terre, published in Paillat, *Dossiers secrets*, pp. 100–1. Robert Puiseux told Paillat of an exchange of Michelin rubber for Italian cotton. After being contacted by the Italian emissary, Puiseux went to Vichy to talk to Pierre Laval, who encouraged the exchange so as to renew his contact with Mussolini. Ibid., pp. 101–2.

2 Jemain, *Michelin*, p. 124.

3 Correspondence with Prof. John F. Sweets.

4 Miquel, *Dynastie Michelin*, p. 391. Automobile historian James Laux, who repeats the story that 'the Michelin family had some Jewish ancestry' in *The European Automobile Industry* (New York, Twayne, 1992), p. 166, told the author he had no source of his own, but relied on what had already been published (by Miquel).

5 Miquel, *Dynastie Michelin*, pp. 74–75.

6 Henry Coston, *Dictionnaire des dynasties bourgeoises et du monde des affaires* (Paris, Alain Moreau, 1975), pp. 383–90.

7 Renaud de Rochebrune and Jean-Claude Hazera, *Les Patrons sous l'Occupation* (Paris, Odile Jacob, 1995), p. 393; Miquel, *Dynastie Michelin*, pp. 392–93. Miquel wrote that Jean-Pierre Michelin, wishing to avenge the arrest and deportation of his father Marcel, had left a hospital bed to join a submarine en route to Corsica. In battle with the Germans he was surrounded and told

to surrender; instead he threw his last grenades at the enemy and died under enemy fire. Another Michelin hero was Jean-Luc, son of André Michelin's oldest son Jean. Deported to work in a German factory, he set up a clandestine radio transmitter in Munich to guide Allied bombers in their raids. Arrested and sentenced to death, he was saved by the collapse of the German armies. Cf. Jemain, *Michelin*, pp. 124–25.

8 Sweets, *Choices in Vichy France*, pp. 8, 195.

9 Lamy and Fornaro, *Michelin-Ville*, p. 14.

10 Commissariat Général à l'Education générale et aux sports, *Le Métier et le Sportif* (Vichy, 1942), pp. 4–8.

11 Sweets, *Choices in Vichy France*, pp. 100, 201, 207, 211. On the life of Michelin workers during the Occupation, and their resistance to forced labour in Germany, see ibid., pp. 5–7, 17–20.

12 Jemain, *Michelin*, pp. 121–22. At the time this event supposedly took place Michelin had already been manufacturing for Germany for at least a year and probably two, which necessarily involved many visits to Michelin by the Germans. Cf. Sweets, *Choices in Vichy France*, p. 12.

13 Quoted in Sweets, *Choices in Vichy France*, p. 12. Sweets says that Michelin management refused to allow Vichy labour officials to enter the plant to try to convince workers to go to Germany. Ibid., p. 76.

14 *The New York Times*, 18 March 1944.

15 Henry Ingrand, *Liberation de l'Auvergne* (Paris, Hachette Littérature, 1974), pp. 84–85.

16 US Strategic Bombing Survey, *Michelin Tire Factory* (Washington DC: Physical Damage Division, 1947), pp. 1–12, 57, 65, 69, 71.

Notes on Chapter 30

1 *BIB-Revue – Bulletin intérieur Michelin* 357, 22 July 1964.

2 Sweets, *Choices in Vichy France*, pp. 94, 193–94.

3 Nineteen other lower-ranking supervisors and engineers were investigated by the purge committee and acquitted. Archives Départementales du Puy-de-Dôme, Comité interprofessionnel d'épuration, côte 253 W 199. Correspondence of the author with Archives Départementales du Puy-de-Dôme. Ingrand, *Liberation de l'Auvergne*, p. 194, says that the district purge committee examined 116 cases, nine of them involving factory heads or managers; in this group there were four acquittals, two reprimands, one suspension, two dismissals. The largest number of sanctions were in mining and the rubber industry, he adds – naming no names.

4 Echevin, *Echec au roi*, p. 36.

5 Jemain, *Michelin*, p. 125. See another version of the story, which also keeps de Gaulle out of the factory, in 'Michelin Goes American', *Business Week* (New York), 26 July 1976, p. 59.

6 *Bulletin Intérieur Michelin*, August–September 1945. The fact that this description of the visit appeared in a publication distributed to Michelin personnel within weeks of the event suggests strongly that it is a faithful account.

7 *Bulletin Intérieur Michelin*, April 1946. Another destroyed factory, in Karlsruhe, was not to be rebuilt, and Michelin stayed out of Germany for the time being, while a factory in south Holland at heavily damaged S Hertogenbosch, whose construction had been suspended during the war, was at last completed in 1947 – making it the twelfth Michelin plant then in operation. The Indochinese plantations were found intact, although installations had been stripped or destroyed, and had to be replaced. Jemain, *Michelin*, p.127; *Michelin Magazine* 589, April–May 1990.

8 *Bulletin Intérieur Michelin*, March 1945.

9 Compagnie Générale des Etablissements Michelin, 'Allocution de M. François Michelin', *Assemblée Générale Ordinaire, Exercice 1990*, p.32. This was a homage to Puiseux, who had died on 23 February 1991.

10 *Michelin Magazine* 589, April–May 1990.

11 *Guide Michelin* 1950, p.864; *Michelin Magazine* 589, April–May 1990.

Notes on Chapter 31

1 *Guide Michelin* 1946, p.9.
2 *Guide Michelin* 1947, p.20.
3 *Guide Michelin* 1947, p.535.

Notes on Chapter 32

1 *Le Monde*, 5, 12 and 14 October 1948.
2 Bourdrel, *La Cagoule*, p.27.
3 *Le Monde*, 19 October 1948.
4 *Le Monde*, 28–29 November 1948.
5 Wolgensinger, *La 2CV*, pp.26–27, 30–31.
6 Wolgensinger, *La 2CV*, pp.30–36, 84.
7 Norbye, *Michelin Magic*, p.40; Jemain, *Michelin*, p.127; *Michelin Magazine* 590, June–July 1990.
8 Jemain, *Michelin*, p.131.
9 *Michelin Magazine* 589, April–May 1990.
10 *Bulletin Intérieur Michelin*, reprinted in *Michelin Magazine* 589, April–May 1990.
11 *Michelin Magazine* 589, April–May 1990.
12 Wolgensinger, *La 2CV*, p.40; Echevin, *Echec au roi*, p.58.
13 Personal experience of Martha and Willy Zuber.
14 Wolgensinger, *La 2CV*, pp.40–41.
15 Jemain, *Michelin*, p.210.

Notes on Chapter 33

1   *Le Monde*, 29 March 1950.
2   *Time* (New York) 28 April 1952, pp. 90–92.
3   Cf. Herbert R. Lottman, 'A Skeptical Guide to Michelin', *Harper's Magazine* (New York), June 1966, pp. 82–85.
4   Wertenbaker, Charles, 'The Testing of M. Thuilier', *New Yorker*, 6 May 1954, pp. 81–86.
5   Michelin Informations Presse, Guide Rouge Michelin *Europe 1997* (March 1997).
6   P.E. Schneider, 'La Plus Belle France', *The New York Times Magazine*, 4 May 1958, pp. 28, 30.

Notes on Chapter 34

1   Barrière, *Michelin vu de l'intérieur*, pp. 34–35.
2   Jemain, *Michelin*, pp. 145–46.
3   Antoine Barrière, *Michelin vu de l'intérieur* (Nonette, Créer, 1983), p. 94.
4   *Combat* (Paris), 10 February 1953.
5   *La Croix* (Paris), 10 December 1952.
6   *Bulletin intérieur Michelin*, 10 June 1955, reprinted in *Michelin Magazine* 590, June–July 1990.
7   Jean Brigouleix, in *Le Populaire de Paris*, 15 November 1951, reprinted in *Michelin Magazine* 590, June–July 1990.
8   Ibid.
9   Michelin, *Assemblée Générale Extraordinaire*, 30 October 1959, pp. 21–24.
10 Jean Lacouture, *Pierre Mendès France* (Paris, Seuil, 1981), pp. 445–47; Echevin, *Echec au roi*, p. 93. Cf. Miquel, *Dynastie Michelin*, pp. 21–22, who notes that François' older sister Marthe was married to still another Montagne, Rémy's brother Marien.
11 Echevin, *Echec au roi*, pp. 93–94.
12 Jemain, *Michelin*, pp. 150–53.
13 Michelin, *Assemblée Générale Annuelle du 17 Juin 1960* (*Exercice 1959*), pp. 3–7.
14 Daniel Cohen, *Richesse du monde, pauvreté des nations* (Paris, Flammarion, 1997), p. 102.

Notes on Chapter 35

1   *La Vie Française*, 19 June 1970. See also *Le Figaro*, 12 September 1970.
2   Michelin, *Assemblée Générale Annuelle du 29 Juin 1971* (*Exercice 1970*), pp. 4–7, 13–14; *La Vie Française*, 2 July 1971.
3   Pierre Péan, 'L'Empire Michelin', *L'Express*, 8 March 1971, pp. 95–96.
4   *Financial Times* (London), 14 July 1971.
5   Adrian Dicks, 'Company Keeps to Itself', *Financial Times*, 3 August 1971.
6   Jemain, *Michelin*, pp. 183–84, 210–11.

7   Vivian Lewis, 'The Enigmatic Monsieur Michelin', *Dun's Review* (New York), November 1969, pp. 97–100. The first green guide to New York City was issued simultaneously in French (in Paris) and in English in 1968 (by the Michelin Tire Corp. in Lake Success, New York).

8   *Business Week*, 14 August 1971, pp. 40–41. See the previous chapter on the counterattack of Akron tyre-makers on the French invader.

9   *Le Monde*, 7 December 1972.

10 *Forbes*, 15 April 1973, p. 58.

11 *Exercice 1972*, p. 7.

12 'Michelin Go Home', *The New Republic* (New York), 19 May 1973, p. 8.

13 E.S. Browning, 'Michelin is Setting Out on the Road to Transformation', *Wall Street Journal*, 2 September 1994. These examples are given in an article on changing methods at Michelin, which include a relaxation of traditional secrecy.

14 Comité d'Etablissement Michelin, *Le Groupe Michelin: Situation et Stratégies*, I (Paris, ADEC, 1984), pp. 7–8.

15 *Business Week*, 26 July 1976, pp. 56–60. Cf. *L'Express* (Paris), 6 September 1976, pp. 60–61.

16 Michelin, *Assemblée Générale Annuelle du 22 Juin 1979, Exercice 1978*, pp. 7, 9, 24, 27.

Notes on Chapter 36

1   *New York City* (Lake Success, New York, Michelin, 1976).

2   Herbert R. Lottman, '*** for the Green Guides of Michelin', *New York Times*, 16 February 1975.

3   'Les Guides et l'Histoire', *Le Monde*, 4 July 1967.

4   'Hitler, connais pas', *Le Monde*, 25 July 1967.

5   Michelin, *Bretagne* (Paris, Pneu Michelin, 1997).

6   Michelin, *Brittany* (London, Michelin Tyre PLC, 1997).

7   Michelin, *Bretagne* (Karlsruhe, Germany, 1996).

8   Herbert R. Lottman, 'A * is Born in Guide Michelin', *New York Times*, 10 January 1971; see also ibid., 14 March 1971.

9   *Newsweek*, 20 March 1978, p. 76. The same edition promoted a small Left Bank restaurant, L'Archestrate, owned by unorthodox chef Alain Senderens, from two stars to three.

Notes on Chapter 37

1   Michelin, *Assemblée Générale Annuelle du 24 Juin 1977, Exercice 1976*, pp. 6, 10–14.

2   Michelin, *Assemblée Générale Annuelle du 23 Juin 1978, Exercice 1977*, pp. 6–7, 14.

3   *Le Monde*, 21 January 1978; *La Croix*, 21 January 1978.

4   Interview by Georges Menant, *Paris-Match*, 3 February 1978, pp. 74–78.

5   *La Montagne*, 7 April 1978, reprinted in *Michelin Magazine* 592, October–November 1990.

6   Paul Gibson, 'Goodyear vs. Michelin', *Forbes* (New York), 7 August 1978, p.62.

7   *Exercice 1978*, pp.6, 15–16, 24–25.

8   Gilbert Declercq, 'Quand Bibendum domine l'Auvergne', *CFDT Aujourd'hui* (Paris) 30, March–April 1978, p.28.

9   *L'Humanité*, 3 December 1979.

10 Michelin, *Assemblée Générale Annuelle du 20 Juin 1980, Exercice 1979*, pp.3–7.

11 'Michelin s-r d'avoir raison', *La Vie Française*, 21 July 1980.

12 Jean-Gabriel Fredet and Denis Pingaud, *Les Patrons face… la gauche* (Paris, Ramsay, 1982), p.202.

13 *Business Week*, 1 December 1980.

14 Michelin, *Assemblée Générale Ordinaire du 19 Juin 1981, Exercice 1980*, pp.3–11.

15 *Le Groupe Michelin*, I, pp.34–35; III: *Les Tendences Récentes* (31 October 1984), pp.1–2.

16 Echevin, *Echec au roi*, p.150.

17 *L'Humanité*, 14 February 1981.

18 Jemain, *Michelin*, p.257.

19 Michelin, *Assemblée Générale Annuelle du 25 Juin 1982, Exercice 1981*, pp.8, 27.

20 Fredet and Pingaud, *Les Patrons face… la gauche*, pp.203–9.

21 Fredet and Pingaud, *Les Patrons face… la gauche*, p.204.

22 *La Vie Française*, 27 December 1982.

23 Michelin, *Assemblée Générale Annuelle du 28 Avril 1983, Exercice 1982*, pp.8–9, 54.

24 *Le Monde*, 27 April 1982. See also *Financial Times*, 26 April 1983.

25 *L'Humanité*, 27 April 1983.

Notes on Chapter 38

1   *Le Monde*, 7 October 1983.

2   *International Herald Tribune* (Paris), 20 April 1984.

3   *Exercice 1983*, pp.3, 7–8, 11, 29.

4   *Le Monde*, 19–20August 1984.

5   *L'Express*, 26 April 1985.

6   Michelin, *Assemblée Générale Ordinaire du 21 Juin 1985, Exercice 1984*, pp.3–7.

7   *Le Monde*, 19–20May 1985.

8   *Business Week*, 28 January 1985.

9   Paul Betts and Ian Rodger, 'A rare interview with the Michelin Man…', *Financial Times*, 3 July 1985.

10 *Financial Times*, 28 August 1985. The same information appears in *Le Monde*, 29 August 1985.

11 Michelin, *Assemblée Générale Ordinaire du 20 Juin 1986, Exercice 1985*, p.32. The annual meeting also introduced a third managing partner (alongside Michelin and 69-year-old Rollier), 49-year-old René Zingraff – who had joined the firm in May 1963 as an chemical engineer and who was not a family member. *Exercice 1985*, p.65; *Financial Times*, 28 April 1986.

12 *Le Monde*, 24–25 August, 30 October 1986; *Financial Times*, 15 September 1986.

13 *L'Express*, 7–13 November 1986.

14 Michelin, *Assemblée Générale Ordinaire du 19 Juin 1987, Exercice 1986*, pp.4, 9.

15 Paul Betts, 'Michelin Opens its Doors to the Public', *Financial Times*, 15 June 1987.

16 *Libération* (Paris), 22 June 1987.

17 *Le Monde*, 22 April 1988.

18 Alain Lebaube, 'Le Paternalisme high tech', *Le Monde*, 7 May 1988.

19 *Le Monde*, 28 June 1988.

20 Yves de Kerdrel, 'Les paradoxes de François Michelin', *Journal des Finances*, 2 July 1988.

21 Michelin, *Assemblée Générale Ordinaire du 23 Juin 1989, Exercice 1988*, pp.3, 8, 30.

22 *Business Week*, 9 October 1989; Michelin, *Assemblée Générale Annuelle du 22 Juin 1990, Exercice 1989*, p.11.

23 Philippe Genet, 'Michelin gonflé à bloc', *Capital* (Paris), November 1996.

24 *Business Week*, 9 October 1989.

25 *Exercice 1989*, pp.23, 31–32.

Notes on Chapter 39

1 Barry Hillenbrand, 'Food, Glorious Food', *Time* (Atlantic edition, Amsterdam), 18 December 1995, pp.44–45.

2 'Une histoire passionnante', pp.3–4.

3 Genet, 'Michelin gonflé à bloc', pp.40–42.

4 'Michelin Finds a New Constellation', *New York Times*, 6 March 1991.

5 Steven Greenhouse, 'So Much More than Food to a Chef's Dream', *New York Times*, 8 July 1991.

6 Harvey Steiman, 'A Chef's Duchy', *Wine Spectator* (New York) 15 December 1994. Still later, Loiseau joined Blanc and other crowned chefs in a low-priced offer designed to fill their dining rooms in slow periods; the organizer was a discount travel agency called Dégriftour. *Le Monde*, 18 December 1996. If we believe the report of a 'test' in a consumer's magazine, the meal Loiseau offered to cut-rate tourists was less than inspired. *Que Choisir* (Paris, Union Fédérale des Consommateurs), December 1997, pp.42–43.

7 William Echikson, *Burgundy Stars: A Year in the Life of a Great French Restaurant* (Boston, Little, Brown, 1995), pp.xii, 5–6, 24–25, 57, 96, 105, 151–54, 217, 223, 227–34.

8 Author, *Les Secrets de Bernard Loiseau* (Nanterre: Royco [1997]).

9 Echikson, *Burgundy Stars*, p. 306.
10 Patricia Wells, 'A chef dies: how many stars are enough? – Loiseau may have succumbed to the pressure of French success', *International Herald Tribune* (Paris), 26 February 2003, 1, 6. See also Le Monde (Paris), 26 February 2003, 25.
11 *Le Monde*, 4 March1992.
12 From Pekka Salojärvi, Helsinki.
13 Alan Richman, 'Catching a Falling Star', *Gentlemen's Quarterly* (New York), August 1995, pp. 79–80.
14 Paul Levy, 'Road Food: New Michelin Three-Stars', *Wall Street Journal*, 19 May 1993.
15 *The Bookseller* (London), 6 September 1996, p. 34.
16 Jean-Pierre Quélin, 'La nouvelle école flamande', *Le Monde*, 20 March 1996.
17 *Le Figaro*, 1 February 1996 (by François Simon).
18 Richman, 'Misguided Michelin', *Gentleman's Quarterly*, September 1996, pp. 273–76.
19 *Le Monde*, 1 January 1997.
20 *Le Monde*, 4 September 1996; *Le Figaro*, 19 October 1996.
21 *Le Monde*, 6 January 1996.
22 Craig R. Whitney, 'Michelin Lops Off a Star', *New York Times*, 6 March 1996. The Tour d'Argent appeared in the *Guide Michelin* 2002 with two stars.
23 Paul Levy, 'The Michelin Plague', *Wall Street Journal*, 15 May 1996.
24 Joël Robuchon, *Ma Cuisine pour vous* (Paris, Laffont, 1986), pp. 11–16.
25 *Guide Michelin* 1996, 1997.
26 Levy, 'The Michelin Plague'.

Notes on Chapter 40

1 *La Vie Française*, 10 February 1990.
2 *Le Monde*, 30 March 1990.
3 Michelin, *Assemblée Générale Ordinaire du 28 Juin 1991, Exercice 1990*, p. 11.
4 *La Tribune de l'Expansion*, 25 June 1990.
5 22–23 September 1990.
6 20 October 1990.
7 William Dawkins, 'Steering Through Hard Times', *Financial Times*, 20 October 1990.
8 *Le Monde*, 11, 13 and 19 April 1991; *Financial Times*, 18 April 1991.
9 François Renard, in *Le Monde*, 7 June 1991.
10 *Exercice 1990*, pp. 15–16, 33.
11 *Le Monde*, 7 June 1991.
12 *Exercice 1990*, p. 39.
13 *Paris-Match*, 3 February 1978, p. 77.
14 Pascal Galinier, 'Les Héritiers Michelin', *Le Nouvel Economiste*, 13 July 1995, p. 36. Galinier notes that Edouard's first contact with the family firm

was as a simple worker at Carmes, at the age of 16, but although he used a pseudonym he was quickly recognized because of his resemblance to his father. In 1987, when he was 24, Edouard had apprenticed at Michelin's research centre in Greenville, South Carolina, which was then run by his uncle Jean Montagne (later director of Kléber).

15 *La Tribune de l'Expansion*, 1 July 1991.

Notes on Chapter 41

1   *Michelin Magazine* 616, June 1995, p.31.
2   *Livres-Hebdo* (Paris), 17 October 1997, p.53.
3   Michelin, 'Partez en images avec les Vidéo Découvertes Michelin' (brochure); *Le Monde*, TV/Radio supplement, 2–3June 1996, p.25.
4   France Telecom, *La Lettre de Télétel et Audiotel* 38, November–December 1995; Michelin, *3615 Michelin: Votre Itinéraire Etudié… l'avance* (1995).
5   Michelin Informations Presse, 'Bienvenue sur Internet' (1 October 1996); *Le Monde*, 11 July 1997, which indicates that itineraries were henceforth available for all of Europe, against payment by secure electronic means, at http://www.michelin.com or http://www.michelin.fr (.) A forum is also available for exchanging comments between users and Michelin. Michelin, Catalogue, *Cartes et Guides Michelin 1997* (Michelin, Paris).
6   *NVX-F160 Système de Navigation Mobile* (Sony, 1996); Michelin Informations Presse, 'Michelin, éditeur international', 1 October 1996. In the first stage France, Belgium, Switzerland and Germany are covered.
7   Catalogue, *Bibendum by Michelin*.
8   Actual revenues from the travel sector alone are not given, although in reporting its results for 1996 Michelin indicated that 1.5 percent of its turnover came from maps and guides, together with manufactured rubber and plastic goods. The year's consolidated sales came to 71.2 billion francs (US$14 billion). Michelin, *Rapport annuel, Exercice 1996*, pp.7, 62.
9   Jean-Pierre Quélin, 'L'année de tous les doutes', *Le Monde*, 1 January 1997.
10 See chapter 49.
11 Jean-Pierre Quélin, 'Tonnerre de chefs', *Le Monde*, 12 November 1997.
12 Craig R. Whitney, 'Michelin Gives and Takes, and Adds a Symbol', *New York Times*, 5 March 1997. See also Jean-Pierre Quélin, 'Le cas Ducasse', *Le Monde*, 2 April 1997.
13 *Le Guide Rouge Michelin* 1997; *Guide Michelin France* 1997.
14 Vincent Noce, 'Notre véritable juge, c'est le lecteur", *Libération* (Paris), 4 March 1997.
15 *Livres Hebdo*, 28 March, 18 April, 27 June, 22 August, 26 September, 17 October, 7 and 28 November, 5 December 1997. In all, Michelin claimed 395,000 copies sold, making the French guide the number two bestseller in practical and reference books that year. *Livres Hebdo*, 2 January 1998.
16 Guillaume Crouzet, 'Les chefs au supermarché', *Le Monde*, 28 May 1997.

Notes on Chapter 42

1   Michelin, *Assemblée Générales Ordinaire et Extraordinaire du 30 Juin 1995, Exercice 1994*, pp. 9, 16–17, 20–21.
2   *Exercice 1994*, pp. 10–11; *Wall Street Journal*, 1 February 1995.
3   Yves Messarovitch, 'François et Edouard Michelin: "Le vrai patron, c'est le client!"' *Le Figaro-Economie*, 11 July 1995. Another father and son interview was to be published later that year in the *Financial Times*, 5 October 1995.
4   Michelin, *Assemblée générale ordinaire du 14 Juin 1996, Exercice 1995*, pp. 12, 16–17, 29.
5   'Survey: World Tyre Industry', *Financial Times*, 29 January 1996.
6   *Le Figaro-Economie*, 6 February 1996; *The Economist* (London), 17 February 1996, pp. 61–62; *Michelin Magazine* 619, April 1996; *Capital*, November 1996, p. 42. Capital estimated the Michelin family's share of the group's stock as '10 à 25%'. Ibid., p. 37.
7   *Spot C.E. Magazine* (Clermont-Ferrand, Comité d'Etablissement Michelin) 110, February 1996, p. 6.
8   *Capital*, November 1996, p. 38; *Le Monde*, 10 October 1995; *Chemical Business NewsBase*, 6 May 1997 (London, Royal Society of Chemistry).
9   Catalogue, *Les Pneus pour véhicules anciens* (Clermont-Ferrand [1996]).
10 *Time*, Atlantic Edition (Amsterdam), 10 November 1997, p. 72.
11 *L'Expansion*, 26 August 1996, reported in *Le Monde*, 30 August 1996.
12 *Que Choisir* (Paris, organ of the Union Fédérale des Consommateurs), October 1997, pp. 46–52.
13 *La Tribune Desfosses*, 18 September 1996; *Le Monde*, 9 October 1996.
14 *Capital*, September 1996, pp. 76–81.
15 *Business Week*, 26 July 1976, p. 59.
16 *Document de Référence* (December 1996), pp. 2, 4–5, 10–12, 35.
17 *La Tribune*, 18 March 1997; *Exercice 1996*, pp. 20, 50.
18 *Les Echos*, 6 March 1997.
19 *Le Monde*, 1 April 1997; *Wall Street Journal*, 3 July 1997.
20 Advertisement, *Valeurs Actuelles* (Paris), 14 June 1997.
21 *Le Monde*, 19 March 1997.
22 *Rubber and Plastics News*, 5 May 1997.
23 *Rubber and Plastics News*, 12 May 1997.
24 *Financial Times*, 27 August 1997.
25 *Le Monde*, 11 September 1999, 7 and 11 November 2000. Interview with Edouard Michelin, *Investir* (Paris), 13 November 2000.
26 *Le Monde*, 27 April 2001, 27 February 2002; cf. *Le Monde*, 3–4 December 2000.
27 *Les Echos* (Paris), 9 April 2002.
28 *Le Monde*, 8–9 October 2000.

Index